Henry Noble Day

Elements of logic: Comprising the doctrine of the laws and products of thought

Together with a logical praxis

Henry Noble Day

Elements of logic: Comprising the doctrine of the laws and products of thought
Together with a logical praxis

ISBN/EAN: 9783337233815

Printed in Europe, USA, Canada, Australia, Japan

Cover: Foto ©Paul-Georg Meister /pixelio.de

More available books at **www.hansebooks.com**

ELEMENTS OF LOGIC.

COMPRISING

THE DOCTRINE OF THE LAWS AND PRODUCTS OF THOUGHT, AND THE DOCTRINE OF METHOD, TOGETHER WITH A LOGICAL PRAXIS.

DESIGNED FOR CLASSES AND FOR PRIVATE STUDY.

BY

HENRY N. DAY,

AUTHOR OF "ART OF RHETORIC," "RHETORICAL PRAXIS," ETC.

Nam neque decipitur ratio, nec decipit unquam.
The mixture of those things by speech, which by nature are divided, is the mother of all error.

NEW YORK:
CHARLES SCRIBNER AND COMPANY.
1867.

Entered according to Act of Congress, in the year 1867, by
HENRY N. DAY,
in the Clerk's Office of the District Court for the District of Connecticut.

RIVERSIDE, CAMBRIDGE:
STEREOTYPED AND PRINTED BY
H. O. HOUGHTON AND COMPANY.

PREFACE.

THE present work is designed for learners. As a branch of science, the study of Logic commends itself by very special, not to say preëminent claims to all lovers of learning and liberal culture. But a leading motive in the preparation of this volume has been to furnish a needed help to the training of thought for effective communication in discourse. The first requisite for good speaking and good writing is the power to think well; and to a good thinker, the study of Logic as the science of Thought bears the same relation as the study of mathematics to a good civil engineer.

The plan of the work has been determined by this governing design. The aim has been to develop the science in strict method. From the determination of the single radical principle of Thought, its Laws and the forms of its Products have been methodically evolved; and the Doctrine of Method with the Exercises is but the end and result toward which the unfolding of the Doctrine of the Elements of Thought has steadily tended. The barbarous terminology of the Scholastic Logic, shown by Sir William Hamilton to be as erroneous as useless, is discarded, except so far as seemed necessary for understanding the forms in which it has entered and modified general literature. The Exercises are prepared for the help of the teacher, rather than to be used just as they are presented, except, perhaps, in small classes, where free conversational discussion and criticism are practicable, and in private study. For large classes there may be found necessary special adaptations of the material here furnished, which may be used to suggest other exercises or to furnish opportunity of ready selection.

The hope that this object of training for effective thinking, and especially with reference to the construction of Discourse, may be better accomplished than through other published treatises on Logic, has been one principal inducement to prepare the present work. But some new things will be found to characterize it, which, if approved and accepted as valuable contributions to the advancement of the science, may, of themselves, justify this address to the public.

These contributions are in part to be found in the following particulars, to which the attention of the cultivators of the science is particularly solicited.

1. The rigid reduction of Thought to its one essential principle — that of Identity.

2. The unfolding of the Laws and of the forms of the Products of Thought under this principle, and the validating of each of them by it.

3. The formal derivation of the Concept and of the Reasoning from the primitive product of Thought — the Judgment — under the principle regulative of all Thought — that of Identity.

4. The determination of the reciprocal relations and distinguishing characteristics of Concepts in respect of their peculiar Quantities, and of the relations of Concepts to Language.

5. The more exact discrimination of the Thought-process itself from its object-matter or *datum*.

6. The determination of the different kinds of Wholes in which Thought may proceed, and the discrimination of those founded in the matter or *datum* to Thought from those which are the pure product of Thought itself.

7. The full development of the relationship of Part to Complementary Part as one of the two relationships in which all Thought proceeds, equally primitive and necessary with that of Whole to Part; this last being the only one recognized hitherto by logicians, who have, by unavoidable consequence, been obliged to give a one-sided and therefore essentially imperfect and unsatisfactory development of the whole science, and either to exclude the consideration of Inductive Reasoning altogether or to give an entirely erroneous and pernicious presentation of it.

8. The formal grounding of all Induction, so far as a process of Thought, on this relationship of Part to Complementary Part, with a full unfolding of its laws, its forms, and its uses.

9. The more exact exposition of Logical Disjunction, of the grounds of distinction between Contradictory and Contrary Oppositions, of Modality and its distinctions, and of Necessary and Contingent Truth.

10. A new classification of Reasonings, — the logical consequence of modifications of logical doctrine already indicated.

11. A new system of Logical Methodology, more precisely defined as the Doctrine of the Conditions of Thought in order to perfect science.

12. A Logical Praxis, comprising copious exercises sep-

arately arranged for each of the forms of the various products of Thought.

A free use has been made of the elaborations of Sir William Hamilton, who, however defective and imperfect his system appears in his posthumous lectures, has done more for the science, it may perhaps be said without extravagance, than all that has been done for it since the times of Aristotle. In some cases, where his language has been used, it has been modified and changed to make his teachings correspond to those that are peculiar to the present work. These borrowings are indicated by the usual quotation marks without more special reference, and without any discrimination of Hamilton's free borrowings from German writers, or of the changes made in his statements. The intended uses of the book as a text-book seemed to forbid the incumbering of the text with such special references, while this general acknowledgment will enable any critical reader to ascertain the extent to which these borrowings have been carried.

NEW HAVEN, Conn., *November*, 1866.

CONTENTS.

INTRODUCTION.

	PAGE
§ 1. Definition of Logic	1
§ 2. Its Utility: — *a.* Objective; *b.* Subjective	3–12
§ 3–6. Its Divisions	12–16

PART I.

THE ELEMENTS OF THOUGHT.

CHAPTER I.

THE NATURE OF THOUGHT.

§ 7. Elements of Thought: — 1. Laws; 2. Products	17
§ 8. Thought a relative Cognition	17–19
§ 9. Nomenclature of Attributes	19, 20

CHAPTER II.

THE LAWS OF THOUGHT.

§ 10–14. The Four Laws of Thought: — 1. Of Identity; 2. Of Contradiction; 3. Of Disjunction; 4. Of Exclusion	21–25
§ 15. Quantity in all Thought	25, 26

CHAPTER III.

THE WHOLES IN THOUGHT. LOGICAL POSTULATE.

§ 16, 17. Kinds of Wholes	27–29
§ 18. Hamilton's Postulate	29, 30

CHAPTER IV.

THE PRODUCTS OF THOUGHT. — I. JUDGMENTS.

	PAGE
§ 19, 20. Judgment defined and explained	31–35
§ 21, 22. Terms: — Subject; Predicate	35–38
§ 23. The Copula	38, 39
§ 24. Division of Judgments	39–47
§ 25, 26. — 1. As to Quality: — Affirmative; Negative; Disjunctive	48–51
§ 27. — 2. As to Modality: — Assertory; Problematic; Apodictic	51, 52
§ 28. — 3. As to Degree of Identity: — Identical; Partial; Tautological	52, 53
§ 29, 30. — 4. As to Character of Terms: — Categorical; Hypothetical; Hypothetico-Disjunctive	53–56
§ 31. — 5. As to Logical Quantity: — Extensive; Intensive	56, 57
§ 32. — 6. As to Kind of Whole: — Integrate; Substantial; Causal	57, 58
§ 33. Judgments in relation to one another	58–61

CHAPTER V.

THE PRODUCTS OF THOUGHT. — II. CONCEPTS.

§ 34–38. Formation and Essential Nature of Concepts	62–65
§ 39. Relations to Objects and to Language	65–72
§ 40–44. Quantity of Concepts: — Extensive and Intensive	72–78
§ 45–50. Relations of Concepts in Extension	78–86
§ 51–54. Relations of Concepts in Comprehension	86–90

CHAPTER VI.

THE PRODUCTS OF THOUGHT. — III. REASONINGS.

§ 55–58. Nature, Denominations, and Divisions of Reasonings	91–94
§ 59–65. Immediate Reasonings: — Conversion; Quantitative Restriction; Modal Restriction; Transference; Disjunction; Composition	94–102

CONTENTS.

§ 66–70. Categorical Syllogisms: — Deductive; Inductive 102–118
§ 71–77. Conditional Syllogisms: — Ponent and Tollent; Hypothetical; Dilemma; Disjunctive 118–128
§ 78–80. Polysyllogism: — Epichirema; Sorites . . 128–131

PART II.

METHODOLOGY.

CHAPTER I.

METHOD IN GENERAL.

§ 81. Nature of Method 132, 133
§ 82–87. Threefold Perfection of Science: — Material; Formal; Verbal 133–146

CHAPTER II.

METHOD IN SPECIAL. — METHODOLOGY OF JUDGMENTS.

§ 88. The Three Conditions of Perfection in Judgments 147–149
§ 89–95. Special Rules of Judgments . . . 149–156

CHAPTER III.

METHODOLOGY OF CONCEPTS.

§ 96. The Three Conditions of Perfection in Concepts . 157
§ 97. Objective Law of Concepts 157–163
§ 98–108. Subjective Law: — Logical Definition; Analysis 163–180
§ 109. Verbal Law 180–182

CHAPTER IV.

METHODOLOGY OF REASONINGS.

§ 110. Probation and Investigation . . . 183, 184
§ 111. Objective Law of Reasonings . . . 184, 185
§ 112–124. Subjective Law 185–206

PART III.
LOGICAL PRAXIS.

	PAGE
I. Exercises in Judgments	207–214
II. Exercises in Concepts	214
III. Exercises in Reasonings	214–222
Appendix A. Induction	223–227
" B. Origin of Language	227–231

INTRODUCTION.

DEFINITION OF LOGIC.

§ 1. LOGIC is the Science of the Laws of Thought as Thought.

Logic defined.

The name, Logic, is derived from λόγος, which word in Greek had a twofold meaning, denoting both thought and the expression of thought. To avoid the ambiguity thus arising, Aristotle limits the term, when applied to thought, by the definitive τὸν ἔσω — *that within* the mind; and when applied to the expression of thought, — to speech, by the definitive τὸν ἔξω — *that without.*

Origin of Name.

It has been a point much discussed whether Logic is a science, or an art, or neither, or both. " Plato and the Platonists received it as a science ; but with them Dialectic was coëxtensive with the Logic and Metaphysics of the Peripatetics taken together. By Aristotle himself, Logic is not defined. The Greek Aristotelians, and many philosophers since the revival of letters, deny it to be either science or art. The Stoics, in general, viewed it as a science ; and the same was done by the Arabian and Latin schoolmen. In more modern times, however, many Aristotelians, all the Ramists, and a majority of the Cartesians, maintained it to be an art; but a considerable party were found who defined it as both art and science. In Germany, since the time of Leibnitz, Logic has been almost universally regarded as a science."

Logic a Science.

By a science, is meant only a branch of knowledge, unfolded in systematic method. It would seem superfluous to attempt a formal vindication of the claims of Logic to be thus regarded.

The object-matter of Logic is Thought, strictly so called,
Its Object-Matter. as the product of the Discursive Faculty, otherwise called the Faculty of Comparison, the Understanding, and by Hamilton, the Elaborative Faculty. This term, *thought,* has been used to include any act of consciousness, whether a cognition, a feeling, or a volition. It has been more commonly used to include any act of the Intelligence — any cognitive act. But as the object-matter of Logic, it is used in a still more restricted meaning to denote only an act of the Discursive Faculty — the Faculty of mediate cognition. Logic, accordingly, takes no account of the faculties of original cognition — the Presentative Faculties of Perception, Self-Consciousness, and Intuition; nor of the Faculties of Representative Knowledge — Memory and Imagination. The range of Thought proper, then, is far more limited than the bounds of the Intelligence, as a department of mental activity coördinate with the feelings and the will. And of the several Faculties of the Intelligence, it is restricted to the operations of but one — the Discursive Faculty, or Faculty of Comparison.

The distinctive nature of Thought may be indicated in a general way thus: The Faculties of original cognition first, as a condition to the exercise of Thought, present to the mind one or another of their several objects. These objects, as apprehended, become, as cognitions, the materials upon which the Faculty of Thought then commences its operations. If, for example, the Faculty of Perception present any object, as a Tree, the object is first apprehended vaguely and simply by itself. But as the attention is concentrated upon it, it is apprehended as standing in certain relations — either in external relations to other objects which with it make up a certain sphere of knowledge to us, or in internal relations to some of its own parts or properties.

The object, thus viewed in relation to the object without or to the part or property within, is said to be *thought*. Before, the tree was simply perceived — known simply in itself; now it is known relatively to something else — to some object external to itself, or to some internal part of itself: for instance, externally, as distant from some other external object; or, internally, as broadly-branched, as covered with foliage, as fruit-bearing, or as having some other property or character. Thought, then, is a cognition, not immediate and irrelative, as is a perception, an intuition, an imagination, but mediate and relative — a cognition of an object as related to something else. We *think* the tree, when we apprehend it as distant, as branching, and the like — as having some attribute.

Logic, thus, as the science of Thought, is limited to a single department of our cognitive functions — to the function of relative cognitions. Its more precise nature will be exhibited in the sequel.

§ 2. The utility of Logical Science may be estimated from the inherent excellence and interest of the Science itself, and from its value as a Mental Discipline and Instrument of Knowledge. *Utility of Logic.*

Objectively, as a science to be acquired and understood, Logic claims a twofold consideration. First, in respect of its object-matter, Human Thought, no science presents more commanding inducements to its investigation and study. The mechanism of Thought, its parts, its springs, its movements, its products, its guides and principles, — no subject certainly possesses a prior claim to the consideration of Thought itself than this its own mechanism. All science, all our systematic, methodical knowing, is the product of Thought. Thought introduces into the Temple of Truth. The first truth we gain is given us by Thought, and all subsequent truth is equally her gift. Perception and Self-Consciousness give us objects of knowledge, furnish the rude materials of Thought. But their products are, in themselves, but the most meagre, vaguest cognitions. *(a) Objective; — 1. As Science of Thought.*

They are only impressions. It is the prerogative of Thought to attribute to these vague impressions reality, to determine their relations to the universe of truth around, to mark the inner properties which characterize and qualify them.

It is under the prompting and guidance of Thought, indeed, that Perception itself moves on from the most indeterminate observations to full and definite cognitions. Without the aid of Thought, it stumbles and falls at the very threshold of knowledge. The keenest eye and the most laborious delving in the earth can at best uncover but little of the story of the antediluvian world. Out of a single fragment of a fossil, geological Thought reads a voluminous history of life, habits, conditions, laws, belonging to ages before the flood. The mere observer might sweep his eye over volumes of an ancient language, and be little wiser as to its history and connections, its laws and structure; while a single page furnishes all the conditions necessary to enable the disciplined Thought of the philologist to determine all. The great part of astronomical facts, of such as are attainable without Thought, were known to the early Oriental shepherds. Thought, out of those few observations, has constructed that magnificent structure of modern astronomy. Indeed, human Intelligence would be little elevated and expanded above and beyond that of the brute without the Faculty of Thought. By the comparative excellence of the object-matter of Logical Science may we, thus, estimate its own importance and value.

2. As Pure Science.
But Logic presents another peculiar attraction, as a *Pure Science*. Its matter lies in the mind itself; and it treats only of that which is necessary in that matter. It has this feature in common with Mathematical Science. They both found themselves upon the operations of the same faculty — the Discursive Faculty, which, if viewed in its essential characteristics, and exclusively of its conditions and accessories, is simply an identifying faculty, ever and only recognizing *the same* and *the different*. In

Mathematical Science, its identities are those which are found only in the forms in which Being enters into our experience — the forms of Space and Time, and are only those of *the equal, the more* and *the less*, in magnitude and number. In Logical Science, the identities in Being itself, as it comes into our experience, — *the same* and *the different* there, are in addition brought into view. Now, as only what transpires within its own realm can be accepted by Thought as strictly necessary, as what is given to thought must be ever taken only as given, — must be assumed, and so viewed as only problematical — all necessary matter lies in thought ; and as Logic, like Mathematics, takes into view only the necessary in thought itself, it is, as conversant only with the necessary, a Pure Science. Mathematics and Logic are, thus, as the only sciences of pure thought, the only sciences of necessary truth. No other science possesses properly the character of necessary matter, except so far as pure thought enters into and characterizes it ; and wherever, in whatever department of knowledge, pure thought enters, there is necessary truth. There is here discovered an eminent incidental utility of Logical Science that it enables us to discriminate readily what is necessary from what is at best but contingent in any department of knowledge, while it claims to itself all those distinctive attractions and excellencies which properly belong to Pure Science.

Subjectively, however, as Instrument of Knowledge and of Mental Discipline, Logic claims the highest consideration as a useful science. *(b) Subjective Utility of Logic.*

It is, indeed, in a certain restricted sense, only a Formal Instrument of Knowledge. It can of itself effect no new discovery in the field of matter from which it derives the conditions of its operations. We cannot begin with our thought, and out of that evolve being — construct sciences of the world external to thought. It is but gross self-imposture to assume a mere form of thought, an empty formula, and then, out of this, educe outward, objective reality. It is no function of

Thought, of itself to amplify any science in respect to the proper object-matter of that science. So far as it attempts this, it invades the territory of the Presentative Faculties, and its attempts are suicidal.

Still, Logic is true Instrument of Knowledge. It prompts and guides the proper Presentative Faculties. Except as these lead on to Thought, and except as Thought elaborates their rude and indeterminate cognitions, they themselves seem to lose spring and motive to exertion. They are, to a great extent at least, blind, also, and need to be directed as to the proper objects which they are to apprehend and to present to Thought. How much of modern astronomical discovery has been prompted and guided by Thought? Certain relations in the solar system, obtained by pure, scientific Thought, indicated the existence of planetary worlds here or there in space; and the telescope, guided by these indications of Thought, brought the unknown worlds into view. Indeed, a large proportion of the new discoveries that are made in the progress of every science have originated in what have been vaguely called analogies, which have been furnished by Thought. And it is the province of Logic to unfold the laws that govern these analogies, determine their conditions, test their soundness and validity.

1. As Aid to Discovery.

Further, all proper science is the product of Thought, and lies wholly within the domain of the Discursive Faculty of the human Intelligence. The cognitions of Perception, as already remarked, are vague and indefinite; the cognitions of the pure Reason, or, as it has been called, the Regulative Faculty, are equally without limitation and without relation. Science is relative and defined cognition. It is the proper province of Logic to acquaint us with the laws of all science, or all relative cognition, and thus, in the intelligent application of these laws, to conduct us to assured knowledge.

2. As Builder of Science.

While Thought deals only with cognitions, with what is already in the mind, and thus, strictly speaking, originates no *material* knowledge, we must not take in too narrow an application the truth that it is but the Formal Instrument of Knowledge. Mathematics, like Logic, is a Formal Science, yet our knowledge of the heavenly bodies has been chiefly furnished to us by Mathematics. The facts given in observation are comparatively meagre. Astronomy has in fact made most of its growth since the time of Kepler and Newton, and that growth has been effected chiefly by mathematicians, not by observers. What Mathematics is to the outer world, Logic is to the inner world of truth. Neither can do anything for any object of science, till the object is given to it; neither can start forth and from its own underived and unacquired resources construct any system of knowledge. But matter being given it in very meagre amounts, and each,' in its sphere, can build up vast structures of true knowledge; for the essential qualities of any object of knowledge are very few in comparison with the relative. While the observed attributes increase arithmetically, the relations of thought increase with the rate of permutation and combination. When a fragment of a bone was presented to Cuvier, he was enabled in thought to read in it the size, age, habits, the specific characteristics of the animal to which it belonged. So Thought, out of a fragment of fact, interprets rich and vast treasures of truth through its relations, internal and external. It is true that Logic is not Thought; it is true, also, that men think without Logic. So Mathematics is not Astronomy; and men can compute without arithmetical rules. But how extremely limited is all such computation, all such thought; and at best how uncertain are its results, and even although correct, how little assurance do these results give to the ignorant calculator and thinker?

The absolute impotence of Logic, of Thought, to construct a science in any department, without the matter of that science being previously given in experience, is now every where recognized. Not so distinctly recognized is its dependence on the other faculty or source of knowledge — the

Regulative Faculty — the Reason — Common Sense. But if not its absolute impotence, still its impotence to any thing valuable or worthy, is just as real without the ideas of the Reason, as without the facts of experience. Of what worth would science be to us, even were it possible, that proceeded independently of our ideas of Space and Time; of Being, Substance, Cause; of Truth, Beauty, Rectitude, and Goodness? Logic can venture forth not one step in safety, or in promise of attaining any worthy result, except as these great ideas of the Reason guide and animate, as its processes are upon and through these fundamental *data* of the Intelligence. But in turn, these grand ideas are of little worth to us, except as Thought apprehends them, scans them in their manifold relations, and then determines and indicates these relations.

Logic, indeed, is not Thought; it is only Thought applied to Thought; the science of Thought, or still more precisely, the science of the necessary in Thought. But this very limitation of Logic suggests its immeasurable utility to the spirit of man, whose dignity consists so much in Thought. If Logic is not Thought, it yet presides over Thought, and prescribes its function and its sphere. It preserves us, thus, from illusions and phantoms, which are for the most part occasioned by the confounding of experiences and thoughts; and the consequent imposition of thoughts for objects.

Logic, moreover, opens the way for Thought, and by presenting occasions, calls it forth into exercise. It teaches how it may fasten upon an object of experience, or an idea of the Reason; trace out its relations; determine its properties, its conditions, its bearings. The chief obstacle to thinking is ignorance how to think. Matter enough is given in every outlook upon the external world, in every glance turned inward upon our mental experience, to provoke and to sustain endless thought. Thought does not go forth as this gate of occasion opens to it, because it does not see. Logic opens its eyes upon the relations in their diversity, through which it may go forth to its work.

Logic, further, completes and perfects Thought. Thought necessarily remains feeble and immature, except as it is developed and matured by Logic. As Mathematics enables Thought to carry its computations to indefinite limits, and to pace off the measureless skies, while the savage can only compute but several scores, and can measure only where the foot can tread; so Logic not only carries Thought forward in every particular direction to its remotest bounds, but also carries it over the entire field of its explorations, so that no part shall be overlooked.

Logic is useful, also, in correcting our knowledge. It has been justly termed *a medicine of the mind*, as it helps to purge it from errors which impair and vitiate its healthful activity. It does not directly heal the imperfection or error that may have crept into its operations at the original presentation of its matter. But when, by its sure procedure, it discovers that the original *datum* as presented to it has led to results that are not in harmony with its already ascertained truths, or that involve contradictory relations, or that do not admit of being perfectly brought under the complete and necessary conditions of thought, by detecting the fact of error and its probable source, it guides and helps to the needful correction by the proper presentative faculty; precisely as Mathematics, although like Logic a purely formal science, can show that there is error somewhere in the original measurement, or the running of the lines of a survey, if the bearings and distances as given will not admit of being plotted into a bounded field, and may indicate also, possibly, where the error originated, so that it may be corrected by new survey. 3. As Corrective of Error.

Logic, still further, is of eminent utility in furnishing the proper assurance of Truth. If it is much to know, it is often more to know that we know; to be reasonably assured that what we accept as true is indeed true, as verified by the only possible criteria of truth within the reach of the human mind. Confidence in the correctness of the 4. As assuring truth.

procedures of Thought, confidence in the validity of the results of Thought, is one of the leading conditions of success in all thinking. To be in doubt whether we are on the road to truth, whether we are in possession of the requisite means of attaining it, whether what we at last have reached is the truth we seek, is very mental imbecility. It is the prerogative and proper function of Logic, as the Science of the Laws of Thought, to remove the grounds of such doubt, to indicate and so to assure as certain the way to truth, and to impart credibility to the results of Thought. It is true that, in large departments of our knowledge, what we know can have at best but the character of probable truth, never that of absolute certainty. But it is the part of Logic to point out just where the lines that separate probable from absolute certainty run, and also to discover just where the contingency in imperfect knowledge attaches; the nature, the source, the extent, the means, if any, of removal of all that impairs our knowledge. Such is the assurance that Logic gives to our thinking.

"But it is not only by affording knowledge and skill that Logic is thus useful; it is perhaps equally conducive to the same end by bestowing power. The retortion of thought upon itself — the thinking of thought — is a vigorous effort, and, consequently, an invigorating exercise of the Understanding; and as the Understanding is the instrument of all scientific, of all philosophical speculation, Logic, by preëminently cultivating the understanding, in this respect likewise vindicates its ancient title to be viewed as the best preparatory discipline for Philosophy and the sciences at large.

5. As Invigorating the Understanding.

"But Logic is further useful as affording a Nomenclature of the laws by which legitimate thinking is governed, and of the violations of these laws, through which thought becomes vicious or null.

6. As affording a scientific Nomenclature.

"Words do not give thoughts; but without words, thoughts could not be fixed, limited, and expressed. They are, therefore, in general, the essential condition of all thinking worthy of the name. Now, what is true of human thought in general, is true of Logic and Rhetoric in particular. The nomenclature in these sciences is the nomenclature of certain general analyses and distinctions, which express to the initiated, in a single word, what the uninitiated could (supposing, what is not probable, that he could perform the relative processes) neither understand nor express without a tedious and vague periphrasis; while, in his hands, it would assume only the appearance of a particular observation, instead of a particular instance of a general and acknowledged rule. To take a very simple example: there is in Logic a certain sophism, or act of illegal inference, by which two things are, perhaps in a very concealed and circuitous manner, made to prove each other. Now, the man unacquainted with Logic may perhaps detect and be convinced of the fallacy; but how will he expose it? He must enter upon a long statement and explanation, and after much labor to himself and others he probably does not make his objection clear and demonstrative after all. But between those acquainted with Logic the whole matter would be settled in two words. It would be enough to say and show that the inference in question involved a circle, and the refutation is at once understood and admitted. It is in like manner that one lawyer will express to another the *ratio decidendi* of a case in a single technical expression; while their clients will only perplex themselves and others in their attempts to set forth the merits of their cause. Now, if Logic did nothing more than establish a certain number of decided and decisive rules in reasoning, and afford us brief and precise expressions by which to bring particular cases under these general rules, it would confer on all who in any way employ their intellect — that is, on the cultivators of every human science — the most important obligation. For it is only in the possession of such established rules, and of such a technical nomenclature, that we can accomplish, with facility, and to an adequate extent, a criticism of any work of reasoning. Logical language is thus, to the general reasoner, what the notation of Arithmetic, and still more of Algebra, is to the mathematician. Both enable us to comprehend and express, in a few significant symbols, what would otherwise overpower by their complexity; and thus it is that nothing would contribute more to facilitate and extend the faculty of thinking, than a general acquaintance with the rules and language of Logic."

§ 3. Logic may be divided on different principles of division into different sets of species, of which the more important are the three following:

Divisions of Logic.

1. Objective and Subjective.

First, in reference to the mind or thinking subject, Logic is divided into Objective *(Logica Systematica)* and Subjective *(Logica Habitualis).*

" By Objective or Systematic Logic is meant that complement of doctrines of which the science of Logic is made up; by Subjective or Habitual Logic is meant the speculative knowledge of these doctrines which any individual, as Socrates, Plato, Aristotle, may possess, and the practical dexterity with which he is able to apply them.

" Now, it is evident that both these Logics, or rather, Logic considered in this twofold relation, ought to be proposed to himself by an academical instructor. We must, therefore, neglect neither. Logic considered as a system of rules, is only valuable as a mean toward Logic considered as a habit of the mind; and, therefore, a logical instructor ought to do what in him lies to induce his pupils, by logical exercise, to digest what is presented to them as an objective system into a subjective habit. Logic in both these relations belongs to us, and neither can be neglected without compromising the utility of the study.

§ 4. " In the second place, by relation to its application or non-application to objects, Logic is divided into Abstract or General, and into Concrete or Special.

2. Abstract or General, and Concrete or Special.

" Abstract Logic considers the laws of thought as potentially applicable to the objects of all arts and sciences, but as not actually applied to those of any; Concrete Logic considers these laws in their actual and immediate application to the object-matter of this or that particular science. The former of these is one, and alone belongs to philosophy, whereas the latter is as multiform as the arts and sciences to which it is relative.

"This division of Logic does not remount to Aristotle, but it is found in his most ancient commentator, Alexander the Aphrodisian, and, after him, in most of the other Greek Logicians. Alexander illustrates the opposition of the logic divorced from things, to the logic applied to things, by a simile. "The former," he says, "may be resembled to a geometrical figure, say a triangle, when considered abstractly and in itself; whereas the latter may be resembled to the same triangle, as concretely existing in this or that particular matter: for a triangle considered in itself is ever one and the same; but viewed in relation to its matter, it varies according to the variety of that matter; for it is different as it is of silver, gold, lead — as it is of wood, of stone, etc. The same holds good of Logic. General or Abstract Logic is always one and the same; but as applied to this or to that object of consideration, it appears multiform.' So far Alexander. This appearance of multiformity, however, is not real; for the mind has truly only one mode of thinking, one mode of reasoning, one mode of conducting itself in the investigation of truth, whatever may be the object on which it exercises itself. Logic may, therefore, be again well compared to the authority of a universal empire — of an empire governing the world by common laws. In such a dominion there are many provinces, various regions, and different præfectures. There is one præfect in Asia, another in Europe, a third in Africa, and each is decorated by different titles; but each governs and is governed by the common laws of the empire confided to his administration.[1] The nature of General Logic may likewise be illustrated by another comparison. The Thames, for instance, in passing London, is a single river — is one water — but is there applied to many and different uses. It is employed for drinking, for cooking, for brewing, for washing, for irrigation, for navigation, etc. In like manner, Logic in itself is one: as a science or an art, it is single; but in its applications, it is of various and multiform use in the various branches of knowledge, conversant be it with necessary, or be it with contingent matter. Or further, to take the example of a cognate science, if any one were to lay down different grammars of a tongue, as that may be applied to the different purposes of life, he would be justly derided by all grammarians, indeed by all men; for who is there so ignorant as not to know that there is but one grammar of the same language in all its various applications?

"Thus, likewise, there is only one method of reasoning, which all the sciences indifferently employ; and although men are severally occupied in different pursuits, and although one is, therefore, entitled a Theologian, another a Jurist, a third a Physician, and so on, each employs the same processes, and is governed by the same laws, of thought. Logic itself is, therefore, widely different from the use — the application of Logic. For Logic is astricted to no determinate matter, but is extended to all that is the object of reason and intelligence. The use of Logic, on the contrary, although potentially applicable to every matter, is always actually manifested by special reference to some one. In point of fact, Logic, in its particular applications, no longer remains logic, but becomes part and parcel of the art or science in which it is applied. Thus Logic, applied to the objects of geometry, is nothing else than Geometry; Logic, applied to the objects of physics, nothing else than Natural Philosophy. We have, indeed, certain treatises of Logic in reference to different sciences, which may be viewed as something more than these sciences themselves. For example: we have treatises on Legal Logic, etc.; but such treatises are only introductions — only methodologies of the art or science to which they relate. For such special logics only exhibit the mode in which a determinate matter or object of science, the knowledge of which is presupposed, must be treated, the conditions which regulate the certainty of inferences in that matter, and the methods by which our knowledge of it may be constructed into a scientific whole. Special Logic is thus not a single discipline, not the science of the universal laws of thought, but a congeries of disciplines, as numerous as there are special sciences in which it may be applied. Abstract or General Logic, on the contrary, in virtue of its universal character, can only and alone be one; and can exclusively pretend to the dignity of an independent science. This, therefore, likewise exclusively concerns us.

§ 5. "In the third place, considered by reference to the circumstances under which it can come into exercise by us, Logic is divided into Pure and Modified. Pure Logic considers the laws of thought proper, as contained *a priori* in the nature of pure intelligence itself. Modified Logic exhibits these laws as modified in their actual applications by certain general circumstances external and internal, contingent in themselves, but by which human thought is always more or less influenced in its manifestations. 3. Pure and Modified.

"Pure Logic considers Thought Proper simply and in itself, and apart from the various circumstances by which it may be affected in its actual application. Pure Logic.
Human thought, it is evident, is not exerted except by men and individual men. By men, thought is not exerted out of connection with the other constituents of their intellectual and moral character, and, in each individual, this character is variously modified by various contingent conditions of different original genius, and of different circumstances contributing to develop different faculties and habits. Now, there may be conceived a science which considers thought not merely as determined by its necessary Modified Logic.

and universal laws, but as contingently affected by the empirical conditions under which thought is actually exerted; which shows what these conditions are, how they impede, and, in general, modify, the act of thinking; and how, in fine, their influence may be counteracted. This science is Modified or Concrete Logic. It is identical with what Kant and other philosophers have denominated Applied Logic.

"Modified Logic, however, is neither an essential part nor an independent species of General Logic, but a mere mixture of Logic and Psychology, and may, therefore, be called Logical Psychology or Psychological Logic. There is thus in truth only one Logic, that is, Pure or Abstract Logic."

§ 6. Pure Logic may be most conveniently distributed into two parts;— the one of which shall expound the conditions of thinking in itself, irrespectively of the proper end of thinking; the other shall set forth the conditions of thinking in order to the attainment of truth or science, as the proper end of all thinking. In the first part, accordingly, should be exhibited the elements of thought in itself, the Absolute Conditions of Thought; and in the second part, the elements of thought in its relations to Truth or Science, the Relative Conditions of Thought.

Parts of Pure Logic.

PURE LOGIC, then, will embrace the two parts of—

I. The Doctrine of the Essential Elements of Thought; and,

II. The Doctrine of Method or Methodology.

To these two Parts of Systematic Logic should be added another of Subjective Logic, in the form of a Logical Praxis.

PURE LOGIC.

PART I.

THE ELEMENTS OF THOUGHT.

CHAPTER I.

THE NATURE OF THOUGHT.

§ 7. THE First Part of Logical Doctrine embraces the Doctrine of the Elements of Thought. These Elements consist of the necessary Conditions of Thought, and the Products of Thought. This first part of Logic accordingly comprehends two leading departments, treating severally —

I. Of the LAWS OF THOUGHT;
II. Of the PRODUCTS OF THOUGHT.

In order, however, to the more exact determination of the nature and validity of these Laws of Thought, and of the characters and relationships of these Products of Thought, it will be necessary to define, more precisely than we have yet done, the nature of Thought itself, so far as Logic takes cognizance of it.

§ 8. Thought, in its limited import, as denoting the product of the Discursive Intelligence, is a relative cognition. *Thought a relative cognition.*

In Perception, the cognition is immediate and independent; the knowledge is of something considered directly and in itself. When I see an individual object thus, — say Bucephalus, or Highflyer, — or when I represent him in imagination, I have a direct and immediate apprehension of a certain object in and through itself. There is no relation in such a cognition as a mere perception. But such is the nature of the complex activity of the human mind, and such the connection between its several energies, that while the activity is always first awakened by a perception, every perception draws on, as by a necessity, the exertion of other energies. Thus, when I perceive Bucephalus, I at once have awakened in my mind the intuitive idea of existence. There are thus present in the mind at the same time the two cognitions; that of Perception — Bucephalus — and that of Intuition — Existence. These two cognitions are accordingly viewed in relation, each to the other; and the recognition of this relation is clearly distinguishable from the two prior cognitions. It is a new cognition, — a cognition not of Bucephalus by himself, not of Existence by itself, but of Bucephalus as existing. This is a thought, a judgment; and is manifestly a relative cognition or knowledge; a cognition, not of objects by or in themselves, but of objects in relation to each other; a cognition, in fact, of related cognitions, not of related external objects.

The second cognition into relation with which the cognition of Bucephalus is thus brought through the restless and diverse energy of the mind, is not, necessarily and always, it should be noticed, an Intuitive cognition. It may be another Perception; as, for instance, on perceiving Bucephalus, I may also perceive a part or a property belonging to him, as that he is *four-footed — quadruped*. As before, the cognition of *Existence*, so now that of quadruped is brought into relation with the cognition of Bucephalus; and the relative cognition, the *thought* of Bucephalus as quadruped comes up in the mind.

It is obvious that thought, as thus a relative cognition — a cognition of cognitions related to each other — necessarily respects two cognitions, and two only; inasmuch as, although either one may be itself complex, the relation can properly subsist between two only. If, in the combinations of thought and in abbreviations of verbal expression, more than two factors seem to be brought into relation, they can always be reduced to two. Thought is, accordingly, ever and essentially a cognition of a duality.

In the instances given, the second cognition in each case is one that is *internal* in relation to the first; *existence* and *quadruped* being qualities recognized as belonging to Bucephalus. In these cases, *Bucephalus* is viewed as a whole, of which *existence* and *quadruped* are severally parts. But the second cognition may be *external* to the first; Bucephalus being viewed as a part in relation to some other object, as to Alexander. The thought then arises, *Bucephalus is Alexander's.* The relation recognized in thought between the first and second cognitions, which are its objects, may thus be either internal or external to the first. But the judgment in all cases is a relative cognition; and the judgment, as will be shown hereafter, is the primitive form of thought from which the two others, the concept and the reasoning, are derived. All thought thus is a relative cognition.

Still further, it is apparent that, when I think any thing, I view it in relation to one only of many other possible cognitions. I may think Bucephalus as *existing*, or as *four-footed*, or as *Alexander's*, and so on indefinitely. There are so many different modes of thought. As I cannot think any thing without thinking it in some particular mode, that is, in relation to some attribute, so these modes, possible to thought, are of unlimited diversity.

Logicians have designated these modes by different terms, which it will be of convenience to present and explain in connection.

§ 9. "When we think a thing, this is done by conceiving it as possessed of certain modes of being, or qualities, and the sum of these qualities constitutes a *concept* or *notion* (νόημα, ἔννοια, ἐπίνοια, *conceptum*, *conceptus*, *notio*). As these qualities or modes (ποιότητες, *qualitates*, *modi*) are only identified

<small>The various terms by which the modes of cogitable existence are designated.</small>

with the thing by a mental attribution, they are called *attributes* (κατηγορούμενα, *attributa*); as it is only in or through them that we say or enounce aught of a thing, they are called *predicates, predicables,* and *predicaments,* or *categories,* these words being here used in their more extensive signification (κατηγορίαι, κατηγορήματα, κατηγορούμενα, *prædicata, prædicabilia, prædicamenta*); as it is only in and through them that we recognize a thing for what it is, they are called *notes, signs, marks, characters (notæ, signa, characteres, discrimina)*; finally, as it is only in and through them that we become aware that a thing is possessed of a peculiar and determinate existence, they are called *properties, differences, determinations (proprietates, determinationes).* As consequent on, or resulting from, the existence of a thing, they have likewise obtained the name of *consequents* (ἑπόμενα, *consequentia,* etc). What in reality has no qualities, has no existence in thought — it is a logical nonentity; hence, *e converso,* the scholastic aphorism — *non-entis nulla sunt prædicata.* What, again, has no qualities attributed to it, though attributable, is said to be *indetermined* (ἀδιόριστον, *indeterminatum*); it is only a possible object of thought."

CHAPTER II.

THE LAWS OF THOUGHT.

§ 10. THE Fundamental Laws of Thought, or the conditions of the thinkable, are four: 1. The Law of Identity; 2. The Law of Contradiction; 3. The Law of Disjunction; and 4. The Law of Exclusion or Excluded Middle.

The ground of these Laws is furnished in the essential nature of the Discursive Faculty, or the Faculty of Thought. The primitive and essential gradation in the operations of this faculty is the Judgment. Now an act of Judgment, in its positive import, is nothing more nor less than the identification of one object with another. When I affirm or judge, on perceiving Bucephalus, that he *is*, or that he is a *quadruped*, I only identify *existence* in the one case, or the attribute of *four-footed* in the other, with *Bucephalus*, as a part of the characters which make up the whole mental object — Bucephalus. If I should affirm all the attributes which I recognize in the perception as belonging to him, the predicate would be exactly equivalent to the subject. Such an affirmation would be difficult or impossible, however, in the case of an individual object, as Bucephalus; but in relation to the object of thought, denoted by the term *horse*, it is not so difficult, as in the judgment — *horse is a single-hoofed, non-ruminant quadruped.* In this judgment the terms — that is, the subject, or that of which we think, and the predicate, or that which we think of the subject — are in thought exactly equivalent, the impressions which they make being precisely identical and indistinguishable. As will be shown hereafter, this judgment may be read or interpreted in two ways: 1. In what is called its Comprehensive Quantity, thus: the notion, *horse*, contains or is made up of the three characters, *single-hoofed, non-ruminant, quadruped*. 2. In its Extensive Quantity, thus: the notion, *horse*, is the *single-hoofed, non-ruminant* part of the class of animals called *quadruped*.

In this example, the two terms, the subject and the predicate, are completely equivalent or identical. But in the more common class of judgments the identity affirmed between the terms is not complete or total, but only partial; as when it is affirmed *the concept, horse, is single-hoofed*. In this judgment it is only affirmed that, of the characters which make up the notion, *horse*, one is that of being *single-hoofed*. The identification is as real as before; but it is only partial, only respects one of the plurality of characters embraced in the subject.

The essential nature of a judgment is thus an identification, total or partial, between its terms. Hence springs its one comprehensive law — that of *Identity*. The force and import of this law, is, simply, that every positive judgment, to be a judgment, must identify — must affirm an identity between its terms.

From this cursory analytic view of the nature of an act of thought we can better proceed to determine more exactly the ground, the validity, and the special phases of the Laws of Thought, by a view of the manner in which thought takes place in the mind.

The Reason, under its specific law of causality, compels us to suppose that mental activity is first awakened by the presentation of some object from without as its necessary condition. Let us suppose this to be some impression on the sense — some sensation occasioning a perception. There are involved in this act two elements, a mind perceiving and an object perceived. The faculty of Thought, now, from the necessities of its nature, as necessarily self-active when the proper conditions of its acting are brought to it, recognizes these two terms both as existing and also as different from each other. The idea of existence is an idea of the Reason ; a necessary, primitive idea. It is, accordingly, brought in the mind face to face with each of the two factors in the perception — the perceiving subject, and the perceived object. Thought now, in the first place, necessarily affirms this idea given by the Reason — Existence, both of the perceiving mind and of the external object — in other words, identifies each of them as existing. In the next place, with an equal necessity, it affirms that the perceiving mind is not the object perceived; in other words, it denies that they are identical. This is the necessary negative phase of the thought, as the former is the necessary positive phase. They constitute the two phases of the first, comprehensive, essential law of thought, called from its positive phase, the Law of Identity.

It is necessarily involved in this act of mind — the act of thought, as it has now been regarded — that to recognize the perceiving mind and the perceived object as the same in all respects, that is, to recognize the different as the same, *to identify the non-identical*, is the very contrary of thought — is not thought. In this view is founded the second of the Necessary Laws of Thought — the Law of Non-Contradiction, more commonly called for the sake of brevity, the Law of Contradiction.

Still further, in order that thought may thus identify or difference, it is plain there must be assumed as the necessary condition of its acting that there is that in the nature of its objects which admits of their being thus identified or differenced in thought. In other words, thought begins with the Postulate: Of all possible objects of thought, any two are, in respect of each other, either the same or different; and so far as apprehended at all in thought must be apprehended either as the one or the other — either as the same or different. This is the third Law of Thought, and is called the Law of Disjunction. The negative phase of this law, which excludes from thought every other mode of apprehending its objects, constitutes the Fourth Law of Thought, called the Law of Exclusion, or Excluded Middle.

The first two laws are founded immediately in the nature of thought; the last two, in the relation of objects to thought. The pairs are related to each other as subjective to objective; the two in each pair are related to each other as positive to negative.

§ 11. The First General Law of Thought is *the Law of Identity*, or as it might more adequately be denominated, *the Law of the Same and Different*. It prescribes as the primary condition of all true and valid thought that there ever enter into it as its constituents in its positive form, the Same, and in its negative form, the Different. Its formula is: $a = a$.

The Law of Identity.

This fundamental Law of Thought has the characters of an Axiom. It validates itself, as it is involved in the nature of thought. Its sanction is, that unless obeyed, Thought cannot be.

The application of the law is universal, and of like force to each of the several products of thought, but, as will be seen, in modes peculiar to each.

§ 12. The Second General Law of Thought is *the Law of Contradiction*, or, as it may more adequately be denominated, the Law of Non-Contradiction. It prescribes that the elements which enter into any one thought be not thought both as same and as different. Its formula is: *A is not non-A*, or $A - A = 0$.

The Law of Contradiction.

This law is but the negative form of the First, and has the same self-evidencing character and universal validity in Thought. It has been expressed in the formula: Whatever is contradictory is unthinkable. Its sanction is, that unless obeyed, Thought is destroyed. Just so far as disregarded, just so far as the contradictory creeps into thought, thought ceases to be valid — becomes a zero.

§ 13. The Third General Law of Thought is *the Law of Disjunction*. It prescribes that when two objects are presented to Thought, it recognizes them either as identical or as non-identical — as the same or as different. Its formula is: *A either is B or is not B.*

The ground of this law is, as already indicated, in the nature of all objects possible to thought. Thought necessarily moves when the conditions are supplied, and these conditions are the presence in the mind of any two objects of thought, necessarily assumed in their nature either as same or as different. Its sanction is that, unless obeyed, the very conditions of thought are disowned, and any act of thought is vain and impotent.

§ 14. The Fourth General Law of Thought is *the Law of Disjunctive Exclusion*, also called *Excluded Middle*, and more briefly *Exclusion*. It prescribes that no third thing be attempted in thought beyond the identical and the non-identical, the same and the different. Its formula is: *A is not other than B or non-B. A — (B or non-B) = O.* <small>The Law of Exclusion.</small>

This law is the prohibitory or negative side of the Law of Disjunction. Like that, it is grounded on the essential nature of things as possible to thought. Its sanction is that, unless obeyed, the Faculty of Thought departs from its sphere, and its movements are invalid and illusory.

The Third and the Fourth Law stand in the same relation to each other as the First and the Second, constituting like them a Duad composed of two elements, a Positive and a Negative.

The first Duad, the Laws of Identity and Contradiction, indicate the positive or actual characters of all true Thought; they are the Subjective Laws of Thought. The second, those of Disjunction and Exclusion, express the predetermining conditions of all actual thought; they are the Objective Laws of Thought.

§ 15. From what has been said in respect to the nature of thought, it appears that in every thought there are two terms or factors; as when I think Bucephalus as existing, there are the two terms <small>Relations of Quantity — kinds of wholes.</small>

Bucephalus, and *Existing*. They are parts of the thought. This judgment is thus a Whole in relation to the terms, and the terms are complementary to each other. If I think at all of any subject, I must think some predicate of it; so if I think of any predicate, I must think some subject. In every thought, accordingly, is necessarily the double relationship, that of Whole and Parts, and that of Parts which are complementary of each other — the relation of Quantity. As the thought takes in more subjects or more predicates, becomes more composite, the Quantity becomes increased, and the relationships between the parts are multiplied, without, however, destroying or obliterating the primitive duality which characterizes all thought. Instead of one part being exactly complementary of another part, it may be but jointly with others so complementary — partly complementary of it. All proper thought, however complicated, being essentially founded on this one principle of Identity, thus of its own nature unfolding itself into all the complications of Quantity, or the manifold relations of Whole to all or any one of its Parts, and of a Part to any one or more complementary Parts, it becomes necessary to present here a summary view of the different kinds of Wholes which exact and effective thought requires should be readily discriminated. This will be done in the next chapter.

CHAPTER III.

THE WHOLES IN THOUGHT. — LOGICAL POSTULATE.

§ 16. Wholes may first be divided into two *genera* — into
I. A Whole by itself, *(totum per se);*
II. A Whole by accident, *(totum per accidens).*

I. Of the first kind of Wholes, there are Five Species: (a) Whole by itself.

1. *The Whole of Thought* — *the Dianoetic Whole.* Every thought includes a positive and a negative. If we think explicitly *A is B,* we also think implicitly *A is not non-B.* The two make up the whole of the thought in the relation of *A* to *B*. 1. Dianoetic Whole.

2. *The Whole of the necessary Forms in which Being enters into thought* — *the Integrate or Mathematical Whole.* This species has two varieties: (1.) The *Numerical,* or that of Time. (2.) The *Geometrical,* or that of Space. As applied to Bodies in Time and Space, these become respectively *Collective* and *Mass Wholes;* a Collective Whole being constituted of parts numerically different from one another, as *a heap* of stones, *a forest* of trees; a Mass Whole being constituted of parts specially different from one another, as *a gallon* of water, *a block* of wood. In this kind of Whole, the Mathematical or Integral, the parts lie out of one another, and their relation to the Whole is expressed by the preposition *of.* 2. Integrate or Mathematical Whole.

3. *A Whole of Being* — *an Essential Whole.* This includes two species: (1.) *A Whole of Substance, composed of substance and attributes* — *a Substantial Whole.* (2.) *A Whole of Cause, composed of Cause and* 3. Essential Whole.

its Effects — a Causal Whole. Substance and Attribute on the one hand, and Cause and Effect on the other, are respectively complementary of each other in our thought, so that we cannot think the one without thinking the other; just as we cannot think a positive without thinking a negative in a Dianoetic Whole, or a part of a Mathematical Whole, as the half of a number, or the half of a surface, without thinking the other half.

4. *A Logical Whole,* being the artificial whole of the Discursive Faculty, embracing the two species of

<small>4. Logical Whole.</small>

1. *The Extensive Whole, or the Whole of Extension.* which is the whole of the objects embraced under a notion, 2. The *Intensive* or *Comprehensive Whole,* or *Whole of Comprehension,* which is the whole made up of the characters or attributes that make up a notion.

Thus the notion *man* is regarded as a whole, containing two kinds of parts. One kind of parts embraces such as the varieties — Asiatic, African, European, American, or the individuals that make up the race. The notion is then said to be taken in its Extensive Quantity, or the Quantity of Extension. It is an Extensive Whole. The other kind of parts includes such as Rational, Animal, Intelligent, Susceptible, Moral. The notion is then said to be taken in its Comprehensive or Intensive Quantity or the Quantity of Comprehension. It is an Intensive or Comprehensive Whole.

When a notion is taken in Extensive Quantity, it is said to contain its parts *under* it. As the whole *man* taken extensively contains under it the parts *Asiatic, African, European, American, Socrates, Plato, Demosthenes, Cæsar,* &c.. Or if the part be made the subject, the parts, *Asiatic,* &c., are contained under the whole, *man.* Such parts are called Extensive Parts.

When, on the other hand, a notion is taken in Comprehensive Quantity, it is said to contain its parts *in* it. Thus, the whole, *man,* taken comprehensively, contains *in* it the attributes or characters *Rational, Animal, Intelligent, Susceptible,*

Moral; or the characters *Rational,* &c., are contained *in* the notion, *man.* Such parts are called Intensive or Comprehensive Parts.

This kind of Wholes is called Logical, because they are *thought* Wholes; that is, they are Wholes constructed by the mind for its own convenience and use, and not necessarily *actual* wholes. The mind can construct as many of these kinds of Whole as it finds necessary; and, although its classifications will be founded on correspondencies in the actual world, at least, will not designedly contradict them; yet they are, in number and in kind, determined not by the actual, but by the conveniencies of science or knowledge.

As will appear hereafter, an Extensive Whole is composed of the subjects of Judgments, and a Comprehensive Whole of the predicates of Judgments.

5. A *Corporate or Representative Whole,* called also, and more properly a *Formal* or *Æsthetic Whole,* is made up of the matter and the form in every individual object of imagination, or more exactly, and more comprehensively, it is a Whole made up of idea, and the matter in which the idea is embodied. 5. Corporate Wholes.

§ 17. II. WHOLES BY ACCIDENT include such as the relative *Whole of Degree,* as, Mankind is made up of *the poor and the rich;* of *Position,* as *northern and southern;* of *Affinity,* as *parent and child,* and the like. (b) Wholes by Accident.

§ 18. "The only postulate of Logic which requires an articulate enouncement, is the demand that before dealing with a judgment, concept, or reasoning, expressed in language, its import should be fully understood; in other words, Logic postulates to be allowed to state explicitly in language all that is implicitly contained in the thought. The Logical Postulate.

This postulate can not be refused. In point of fact, Logic has always proceeded on it, in overtly expressing all the steps of the mental process in reasoning — all the propositions of a syllogism; whereas, in common parlance, one at least of these steps or propositions is usually left unexpressed. This postulate, though a fundamental condition of Logic, has not been consistently acted on by logicians in their development of the science; and from this omission have arisen much confusion and deficiency and error in our present system of Logic. Aristotle, however, states of syllogistic — and, of course, his statement applies to Logic in general — that the doctrine of syllogism deals, not with the external expression of reasoning in ordinary language, but with the internal reasoning of the mind itself."

CHAPTER IV.

THE PRODUCTS OF THOUGHT. — 1. JUDGMENTS.

§ 19. THE primitive and essential gradation of thought we have indicated to be the Judgment. In accordance with what has been said, a Judgment may be defined to be *a recognition of the identity or non-identity between any two objects presented to the Faculty of Thought.* Judgment defined.
As expressed in words, a Judgment is called a *Proposition*, or in grammatical nomenclature, a *Sentence.*

Besides the Judgment, there are two other products of thought, both derivatives from the Judgment. The one is the *Concept*, which is derived from several Judgments by an act of *Conceiving* — taking together, in other words, by an act of synthesis. The other is the *Reasoning*, which is derived from one or more Judgments by an act of analysis or separation. As all thought is essentially a movement in Quantity, and as variations in Quantity can be effected only in the one or the other of these two directions, synthesis and analysis, the Concept and the Reasoning are the only conceivable derivatives from a Judgment, except such as consist only in variations of form, that do not affect the identity of the thought.

In explication of this definition of a Judgment, it will be necessary simply to recall what has been already said in the exposition of the general nature of thought. As we have seen, a judgment necessarily supposes two objects; and its essential characteristic, as an act of Intelligence, consists in this: that it is a cognition of this particular relation of identity or non-identity between the two objects. These two objects of a judgment are given to it by some other faculty of the Intelligence, as of Perception, Intuition, Memory, or by the Discursive Faculty itself, in some previous exercise. It may be some object of Perception, as *Bucephalus*. As thus given by the Perceptive Faculty, the cognition is of an object by itself, without relation either to other objects or to the parts of the object itself. Color is not in the perception itself distinguished from figure; neither color nor figure from the position or the time in which it is perceived; and neither of these from the useful qualities of the object. All the perceptible qualities are given together without distinction in the presentation itself of the object. But when thus given, the mind at once, and by a kind of necessity of its being as essentially active and reflective, exerts its activity on it, first, by apprehending it as a part of a multiplicity of objects around, to each of which it stands in relation, and also, as a whole, containing parts in itself. This is the primitive and conditional gradation in all thought — the apprehension of an object as a part or as a whole — in other words, in the relation of Quantity. Simultaneously with this, it apprehends some other object of thought given to it by Perception, or by some other Faculty of the Intelligence, or in some previous exercise of the Judgment, and thus comes to view the two objects thus given in relation to each other, as the same or not the same. Its act then becomes complete; and a perfected product of thought, a Judgment, is the result. Thus the second object may be given in the Perception itself, as *black*, or *four-footed*, and the Judgment recognizes this color or this form as belonging to Bucephalus — that is, as identical with one of the parts or characters that make up the whole perception. Or the second object may be given by the Regulative Faculty, or Faculty of Intuition, as of Being, of Space, of Time, or other idea of the proper Reason; and then the Judgment identifies Bucephalus with Existence, with some part of Space, of Time; or in other words, affirms Bucephalus *to be, to be in such a place, at such a time,* and the like. The second object of thought may, in like manner, be given to the Judging Faculty by the Memory. We may identify Bucephalus as now perceived with the Bucephalus perceived yesterday; with the black color, the four-footed figure, before perceived in some other object.

The essential nature of a Judgment, thus, is seen to be an identification of one object with another, either totally or partially — in some one or in all respects. It is accordingly a *relative* cognition; and in the relation which it involves are necessarily contained three elements: 1. The object of thought identified with some other. 2. The object with which it is identified, either in whole or in part. And, 3. The mental act which identifies. The first two constitute *the matter of thought*, the *datum;* the last is the Thought itself, the identifying cognition — the Judgment.

§ 20. To the several parts, or to different aspects of the complex procedure in all Thought as thus exemplified in one of its gradations — the Judgment — Psychology has assigned distinctive names, which it may not be inexpedient here to recall.

Inasmuch as the original *datum* or object of thought is given in an indefinite vagueness as one and undivided, and as, in order to be cognized in thought, *Analysis.* it must be viewed in relation to some part, it becomes necessary to loosen up, to analyze or separate it as a whole into its parts. This part of the process is called *Analysis.*

The next step is to select the part out of the whole for separate apprehension, and to draw it away, as it were, to abstract it from the other parts. This part of the movement in Thought is called *Abstraction.* The term, however, it is proper to add, is applied in various ways *Abstraction.* by different writers or on different occasions, but with the same result. Thus it may be applied to the mind itself; so that in Abstraction the mind, when confining its view to certain parts of an object, is regarded as being abstracted or drawn away from the parts that are to be excluded from view; and this, it may be observed, is in strictness the most correct view. But in a looser sense the term may be applied to the part itself that is selected, and then such part is regarded as being abstracted from the other parts. Or, in the third place, it may be applied to those other excluded parts themselves, and then they are regarded as being abstracted or drawn away either from the other parts or from the mind's consideration. The result is the same in any view, that one part is separated from the other parts for exclusive consideration, and it is therefore a matter of indifference, so far as the result is concerned, which of these different views is entertained.

When thus one part is separated from the rest for exclusive consideration by the mind, the act of mind in which it concentrates its notice upon it is called *Attention*.

<small>Attention.</small>

In the next place, the two objects are brought up and viewed face to face with each other in order that their identity or non-identity may be apprehended. This part of the process is called *Comparison*.

Finally, the last part of the complex process, in which the thought is perfected by bringing together the two objects attended to into one relative cognition, is called an act of *Synthesis*.

<small>Synthesis.</small>

All Thought thus begins with an Analysis, it proceeds by Abstraction, Attention, and Comparison, it ends with a Synthesis. And this is to be understood in a sense more or less full and complete, in modes varying with the nature of the particular gradation of all the acts of thought, whether in judging, conceiving, or reasoning. The two essential elements of thought are analysis and synthesis. With one it necessarily begins, with the other it necessarily ends. For its very function is to lead to truth, to a unity in the intelligence, which supposes an undistinguished manifold as its condition, and a gathering into a unity as its result. The other parts of the complex process, abstraction, attention, and comparison, are the means by which the mind passes from the multiform given in the analysis to the unity in the synthesis.

Inasmuch as in a Judgment an object is regarded only in one of manifold relations, the act is appropriately called *a determination* of the object — a limiting down to some specified relationship. And, accordingly, the object which is identified with another is called the *determined* element of the judgment, and that with which it is identified, is called the *determining* element.

§ 21. Of the two objects of thought identified in a Judgment, one is necessarily viewed as the primitive which is to be identified with the other, or is determined by it. This so viewed primitive or determined object is called the *Subject;* which may be defined to be that of which we judge. The other, viewed as the determining element, is called the *Predicate,* which may be defined to be that which is judged of the subject. The Subject and the Predicate make up the matter of thought or the *datum* to thought. They are called the *Terms* of a Proposition, (*termini,* ὅροι.) The act of thought itself which recognizes the identity between the two terms is called the *Copula,* which may be defined to be the identification of two objects of thought. It was called by Aristotle, in reference to the two terms, an *Interval,* (διάστημα).

<small>Parts of a Judgment.</small>

Thus, in the proposition, *iron is magnetic,* we have *iron* for the Subject, *magnetic* for the Predicate, and *is* for the Copula. It is not always the case, however, that in propositions the copula is expressed by *is,* or in a distinct word from the predicate.

In fact the copula is expressed separately thus only when the subject is apprehended as substance and the Judgment identifies one of its parts as a quality. As in the example, *iron is magnetic,* the meaning is that one of the qualities of the subject, *iron,* is the quality magnetic — iron, in one respect, is magnetic, the identification being partial. But in the proposition, *iron magnetizes,* the subject, *iron,* is apprehended as cause. In this expression the copula is merged in the predicate. In the English Language there are no longer verbs expressing simply quality, like, perhaps, the Latin *albet, rubet,* and as in the obsolete English of Wickliffe, "Thou maddist." They all express action, and require that the subject be apprehended as cause. And the meaning of the proposition, *iron magnetizes,* is that it identifies a part of the causal agency of iron with magnetizing. Here, also, the identification is partial. There is, perhaps, one exception to this general remark in regard to English verbs. The so-called substantive verb, *to be,* is used often to express the quality of *Existence,* as: *God is; there is a God.* There are manifold other ways of expressing the copula, which will, so far as necessary, be indicated hereafter.

§ 22. The word *Term,* as used technically in Logic, it should be observed, is applied either to the subject or to the predicate of a proposition. It may embrace one or more principal notions; thus in the proposition, *The greatest vicissitude of things among men is the vicissitude of sects,* there are three principal notions or objects of thought in the subject, *vicissitudes, things, men;* but with the other modifying and relative words they make but one logical *Term.* So the predicate contains two notions or objects of thought. In a single proposition, there can be but two Terms — one subject and one predicate. In a compound proposition there are, of course, as many Terms as there are distinct subjects affirmed of, and distinct predicates affirmed. In the proposition, *James and John are related,* there is but one affirmation, one subject, one predicate, and, accordingly, two Terms. In the proposition, *James and John are learned and virtuous,* there are distinguishable four affirmations, four subjects, four predicates, and eight Terms, inasmuch as it may be decomposed into the four single propositions: *Jams is learned, John is learned, James is virtuous, John is virtuous.* It should be added that the judgment may be compounded of two or more copulas.

The Terms of a Judgment.

The Terms of a Judgment are ever to be viewed as objects of thought. Even when a Term is presented as an original primitive *datum* by another Faculty, as the Perceptive, and so far as thus given, affords only a simple, irrelative cognition, so soon as it is accepted by the Faculty of Thought, it assumes a new character; it is no longer simple, but a relative cognition. Thus in the judgment, *Bucephalus is four-footed*, the subject, *Bucephalus*, is in the thought apprehended either as an individual — as one of many four-footed things; as a part of a whole — or as a whole containing one of many parts, which here are attributes or characters, as that of four-footed, that is, as one of many other attributes that belong to Bucephalus as a substance.

As objects of thought, the Terms of a Judgment are thus ever cognitions, not real objects. In the Judgment, *Bucephalus is four-footed*, the subject is Bucephalus, as known, as already introduced into the mind by the Perceptive Faculty, and entertained there not as actual, but only as known. This observation has been made sufficiently prominent, perhaps, in the exposition already given of the nature of Thought; but it cannot well be too forcibly impressed on the mind, in the study of the elements of thought, that they are all *cognitions*; and not only that, but they are also all essentially *relative cognitions*. A Term, thus, is not a simple *representation*, as Hamilton seems to teach, but a relative *cognition*, partaking at once, as soon as accepted by thought, of the relativeness that is characteristic of all thought.

The Terms of a judgment may be conveniently distributed into three classes, distinguished by the re- Terms of three grades or classes. spective modes in which they are thought, or more exactly, by the different stages at which they are respectively accepted as objects in the elaborative process bestowed by thought on the original *datum*. At the first stage is this primitive *datum* itself, as accepted from the Perceptive or Intuitive Faculties, and invested with the character of relativeness attaching to all thought; of this class are all individual and simple cognitions, as *Bucephalus, Mars, Socrates, Space, Time, Being, Identical,* and the like.

At the next stage are the products of a synthesis of these terms of the first class, to be hereafter more fully described, called *Concepts,* which, as modified or not, make up the larger part of the Terms used in discourse.

At the third stage are Judgments themselves used as Terms in other Judgments; as, *That men are free is a doctrine of general recognition; If virtue is voluntary, vice is voluntary.* A Judgment thus used as a Term is called a *Clause.* *That men are free,* is thus a Clause.

§ 23. Besides the Terms, — the Subject and the Predicate, — as we have seen, there is another element in the Judgment, namely, the Copula, a reciprocal relation between these Terms as determining and determined. This is the pure Thought-element. It is important here to investigate its precise nature or character. We have already found that all thought is relative — that it ever proceeds under the relations of Quantity. Now there are two kinds of relationship, equally primitive and equally necessary, involved in this general relation of Whole and Parts. There is first the relation of Whole to Part, with its converse of Part to Whole. There is next, the relation of Part to Part; as we cannot think a Part without thinking its Complementary Part. These two, then, are the primitive channels of thought, inasmuch as it moves ever between the Whole and the Part, or between the Part and the Complementary Part. The Copula determines indifferently in either of these two relations. It identifies the Whole as containing the Part, and identifies one Part as complementary of the other. This is its positive form. It denies, however, as well as affirms; it differences as well as identifies. Accordingly in one relation it differences in one view the Whole from the Part, as well as in another view it identifies them; and in the other relation, it differences the one Part from the Complementary Part in one view, as in another it identifies them. This is the negative form of thought.

The Copula of a Judgment.

Language furnishes modes of Expression for marking these diverse movements of thought in the Copula. It represents the relation of Whole and Part by such terms as *contains, comprehends, comprises,* and the like; while it represents the relation recognized between Part and Part, by such words as *implies, involves,* and the like. The words, *determine, condition,* and others also express the Copula in its various relations.

In that stricter analysis of thought and expression which is necessary in the training of the mind to accurate thinking and representation, and which is also required for the critical examination of discourse, this diverse mode of determining in thought, and of expressing the determination in language, needs to be familiarly known. It will of course be understood that such expressions as *Virtue is Free,* or *Virtue contains Freedom,* and *Virtue implies Vice,* when interpreted in their proper logical significance, mean: Virtue in one of its parts is identical with Freedom; and Virtue is identical with Vice in some one respect, that is, as being free.

§ 24. Judgments may be distributed into different sets of species, on several distinct principles of division. As a judgment is made up of internal form and matter, of thought proper, which is a purely subjective element, and the *datum* to thought, which is a purely objective element, the former of which constitutes the *copula* and the latter the *terms* of the judgment, we should anticipate finding in each of these constituents of all thought, one or more grounds of distinction. And accordingly, looking first to the subjective element, the copula, we find that there are three different principles of division given in it. *Division of Judgments.*

First, the judgment may vary in respect to its own internal and essential nature and irrespectively of its necessary relations to its matter and expression. This is the proper quality of a judgment; and in *1. In respect of the Copula. (1.) As to its Quality.*

respect to its Quality, as we have seen, while a Judgment *may be* affirmative or negative, it *must be* one or the other. Strictly speaking, the necessity of judging, when two objects of thought are given, either that they are or that they are not identical, is imposed upon the Faculty of Thought as a pre-determining condition, as the objective Law of Thought; while its own proper function lies in taking the one or the other of these alternatives — of affirming or denying. We may accordingly ground the first division of Judgments on their essential Quality. This distinction will give, 1. The simple Affirmative and Negative; 2. The Disjunctive; — the first being grounded on the Subjective Laws of Identity and Contradiction; the second on the Objective Laws of Disjunction and Exclusion. The first may be distinguished as of Simple Quality; the last as of Disjunctive Quality. Further, the first named species move more freely and characteristically in the relation of Whole and Part; the second in that of Part and Complementary Part.

Secondly, the Judgment may be combined or not with a recognition of the ground of its determination. If not so combined, the Judgment is pure, simple, or unmodified. It is then denominated an Assertory Judgment, as it is a mere assertion unmixed with any extraneous element. But the Judgment may take up with itself into the same act of consciousness the ground of its determination; it thus becomes so far modified. It is then denominated, in distinction from the pure or unmodified — that is, in distinction from the Assertory Judgment — a Modal Judgment.

(2.) Its Modality.

This principle of distinction in Judgments is what is known as the Modality of Judgments.

The Assertory Judgment, it is obvious, cannot be further subdivided in respect to this principle. But the Modal Judgment can be still further distinguished in respect to the particular grounds that may be recognized by the Judgment in its determination. These grounds may either lie wholly within the sphere of thought, or out of it, that is, in the matter, the *datum* of thought. If the ground of the Judgment be recognized as lying wholly within the sphere of thought, then there emerges the Necessary or Apodictic Judgment. If the ground of the Judgment be recognized, and as lying not in the thought, but in the matter of the thought, then emerges the Contingent or Problematic Judgment.

There may obviously be distinguished subdivisions of the Problematic Judgment. The higher grades of these subdivisions, indicated by such modals as *probably, possibly*, are, not unsuitably, recognized in Logical Science. Aristotle in his Treatise on Interpretation, enumerates four kinds of propositions grounded on their modality: Possible, Contingent, Impossible, and Necessary. In his Prior Analytics, he speaks only of the Necessary and the Contingent in distinction from Pure Propositions. These three primary distinctions are all that it seems important to notice here.

The characters of Judgments that are determined by this principle of modality, which respects the grounds on which the Judgment is recognized, should be carefully distinguished from such characters as those of *clear, vague, obscure*, which only look to the degree of consciousness, the mental force or energy involved in the Judgment.

It may further be observed, that the character of *necessary* belongs properly, that is, primarily and strictly, only to that truth or certainty, the ground of which lies in the thought itself exclusively. Thought must ever accept its own product as valid and beyond question; while all beyond that, even its own product so far as combined with matter which is not of pure thought, it must ever hold as not necessary, only problematical. Only the contradictory of pure thought can be called *absurd* in the highest sense. As thought originates cognitions, which cognitions may themselves be made the object of thought, such cognitions constitute what is called Necessary Matter, or as thought, Necessary Truth. All other cognitions constitute what is called Contingent Matter or Contingent Truth. As these latter cognitions approach more or less nearly to the character of necessary matter, they receive in loose unscientific discourse the denominations properly belonging to thought alone. We may, indeed, classify cognitions in respect to this approximation to Necessary Truth. In the first and highest class, we should have, thus, the pure products of thought, embracing all the relations in the Same and Different, the More and the Less, the Whole and the Part, the Part and the Complementary Parts, so far as these relations are kept pure from matter external to thought. Here, accordingly, lie all the truths of Pure Logic in the relations of Judgments to one another; of Concepts, also, whether of genus to species, or of attribute to involved attribute; and, moreover, of Reasonings. For a single exemplification in this department of Necessary Truth, *that an attribute, which is the constituent of another more comprehensive attribute belonging to a class, belongs to each individual of the class,* is a Necessary Truth. Here lie, too, all the Truths of Pure Mathematics — of Magnitude in Geometrical Science, and of Number in Arithmetic and Algebra, and in Higher Quantitative Analysis. All these are necessary Truths, inasmuch as they are absolute in thought, whether there be any extended being to be measured, any real objects to be numbered, or not; whatever may be believed in respect to the nature of Space and Time, whether they are realities or mere conditions or forms of the Intelligence. Here lie, moreover, manifold truths which are applicable to objects only so far as they are proper Being — the relations of Substance and Quality, of Cause and Effect. These are necessary truths for thought, whether external Being be a reality or only an idea.

In the class of Contingent Matter, but more nearly approximating the character of Necessary Truth, are the truths involved in the relations between the cognitions given in Perception and Self-Consciousness and those given in Intuition. That, for instance, *the body which is cognized by perception through the senses exists, is real,* and that *the mind which perceives it also exists, is real,* are truths which we loosely call necessary truths. They are, obviously, not strictly so, for the contradictories of these propositions are not absurdities.

In the same class, but further removed from the class of necessary truths, are those expressing relations between any two cognitions of Perception. Thus, that *the sun is bright,* is a contingent truth of a lower class in the respect of modality than the truth that *the sun exists.*

We have, thus, the manifold gradations of modality, ranging from the faintest possibility up through all the degrees of probability and of certainty to the truths of thought, where only we find that which is apodictic or absolutely necessary.

Some logicians, including Sir William Hamilton, have excluded from the science this division of Judgments, in respect of their modality, as well as the principle upon which it is founded, as not of proper logical consideration. Sir William Hamilton adduces two arguments for this exclusion. One is from Example. He takes the proposition, "Alexander conquered Darius honorably," and asserts that it may be resolved into the proposition, "Alexander was the honorable conqueror of Darius." By separating thus the word containing the copula into its two parts, the copula part *was,* and the predicate part *conqueror,* and thus showing that the modal word, *honorably,* really belonged to the predicate, he fancied he showed a universal fact in regard to all forms of expressing modality, that they belong properly to the predicate, not to the copula — to the matter, consequently, not to the form of the thought. But *honorably* is never a copula modal; and therefore his whole argument is fallacious. His other argument is, that in order to determine the modality of a Judgment, we must go to the matter, for so those logicians who have admitted modality as of proper logical consideration have taught. This argument is valid only against those who have taught thus erroneously.

But the modality regarded by logicians attaches to the

copula, not to the predicate; to the form of the thought, consequently, not to the matter. And the reasoning by which it is excluded would equally exclude the distinction between Affirmative and Negative Judgments; for it is just as easy and just as legitimate to remove the negative from the copula to the predicate, as to remove thus the proper copula modal, as, indeed, is freely allowed even by those who exclude modality, as they expressly but most erroneously teach that the proposition *A is not B*, is exactly equivalent to *A is non-B*. But proper logical modality, as we have seen, like proper logical quality, lies in the thought itself, not in the matter. We may say, indeed, *Alexander possibly conquered Darius*, or *Alexander was a possible conqueror of Darius*, and mean nearly the same thing. Still, *possible conqueror* and *non-B* are *data* presented to thought, while *possibly was*, like *is not*, is of the essence of the thought itself. One form of expression may, under some restrictions, be derived from the other; but to confound them is to confound form with matter, thought itself with the mere *datum* to thought.

Thirdly, a Judgment may vary according to the degree of identity recognized between the terms. As this identification is total or partial, the distinction gives the two species of — 1. Judgments of Total Identity; and, 2. Those of Partial Identity, with their subdivisions.

(3.) Its Degree.

This distinction, although at first view it might seem to lie rather in the Terms, may yet be not improperly recognized as a subjective element, lying in the thought itself. For, unlike the distinctions that are founded in the matter of the thought, this is created in the Thought-process itself — in the very act of judging. In the case of the others, the objects or terms are presented to the Judgment already distinguished, either as objects or as truths, as Comprehensive or Extensive Wholes, as Integrate, Substantial, or Causal. But here the Judgment itself originates the distinction. The two objects are given it simply as wholes. Thought itself then recognizes them in relation to their respective parts, and identifies some part of one thus recognized with the whole or some part of the other. There is, it is true, a seeming impropriety in founding this distinction on the copula. But it is only seeming; for it should be borne in mind that by the copula is properly meant the entire product of the judging activity in accepting and identifying the *data*. Whether the Judgment shall identify, for instance, a given object with more or less of its parts, is determined, not by the *datum*, but by the thought itself.

Looking next to the objective element in a Judgment, the matter or the Terms, we find given in it also a threefold distinction. First, the matter as *thought*, — and it is not matter in itself, but only as it is thought, that can be here regarded, — may be either itself a Judgment or a simple object of thought. In the latter case emerges the proper Categorical; in the former, the so-called Hypothetical, Judgment. *2. In respect of the Terms. (1.) Their Form.*

Secondly, the matter may be thought as in the one or the other of the two kinds of Logical Quantity, giving rise to the distinction of Extensive and Comprehensive Judgments, according as the terms are thought in Extensive or Comprehensive Quantity. *(2.) Their Logical Quantity.*

Thirdly, the matter may be thought in either of the kinds of Whole, in which Being is thought, giving rise to the distinction of the three kinds of Judgments — the Integrate, the Substantial, and the Causal. This principle of distinction may be denominated that of Material or Metaphysical Quantity. *(3.) Their Material Quantity.*

It might at first be supposed that, in making or accepting these distinctions, Logic was transcending its sphere as a purely Formal Science, and corrupting its own purity by admitting what concerns properly the matter of thought. But it should be borne in mind that if we think at all we must think something — Thought must have an object out of itself that is given, presented to it; and it must think that object as it is, not as it is not. It must, therefore, accept the matter as it is given. It, however, thinks what is given it only in its own proper relations — those of Identity and of

Whole and Part. It is of interest to Logic, accordingly, to regard the peculiarities of the objects given to Thought only so far as they affect the relations of Identity, or of Whole and Part. If these peculiarities affect the nature of the Whole, Logic must of necessity regard them, or its processes of thought become at once invalidated. The purely Formal Science of Mathematics presents a perfect analogy in its treatment of the wholes or magnitudes in space. It distinguishes a Linear Whole from a Superficial Whole, and both from a Solid. Were it to confound these, its procedures would be invalid and worthless. So it must accept the distinctions between a Right Line and a Curve; between Rectilinear Surfaces and Curved Surfaces. It must do this because the relations of Whole and Part in these several cases are different. The sum of the angles in a Rectilinear Triangle does not correspond with the sum of the angles in a Spherical Triangle. Any Formal Science must, therefore, be able to distinguish such peculiarities in its matter as affect the purity and validity of its formal processes. In other words, Logic, although, or perhaps more accurately, because, a Formal Science, must evolve its principles in such a way as to meet the peculiarities of the matter to which it is to apply its formal procedures.

At the same time, Logic does not scrutinize the reality of the matter given it to be thought, except, at least, to see that it does or does not correspond with its own principles, as whatever contradicts those it is bound to reject. It does not affect its Laws or the integrity and validity of its processes whether there be, in point of fact, any such distinctions in the matter as are given to it; as Mathematics does not inquire whether there be in nature Lines, Surfaces, Solids, its procedures being just as legitimate and sure, if there were nothing in reality in the outer world to correspond to these distinctions. It is sufficient to vindicate the propriety and the necessity of regarding these cogitable distinctions in matter, simply to consider that these distinctions are, in fact, cogitable — that they are possible to thought.

JUDGMENTS. 47

The limits to be placed in regard to the extent to which these distinctions should be admitted are to be determined by the proposed objects and uses of the Science. A system of general Logic should admit only the most general distinctions. It should not certainly stop short of those which are found in the two forms in which Being is known to us — Substance and Cause.

These six Divisions of Judgments, it should be observed, are, in reference to one another, Cross Divisions or Condivisions, and intersect one another. The same Proposition, thus, may be Affirmative, Assertory, Partial, Categorical, Comprehensive, and Substantial.

With these general views, in regard to the grounds of the distinctions to be recognized in Logical Judgments, we proceed to a particular consideration of them in order, presenting first the following tabular view: —

Judgments are divided,
- In respect of I. The Copula,
    1. As to its Quality, into (1.) Simple Affirmative and Negative; (2.) Disjunctive.
    2. As to its Modality, into (1.) Assertory; (2.) Problematic; (3.) Apodictic.
    3. As to its Degree, into (1.) Identical; (2.) Partial.
- II. The Terms.
    1. As to their Form, into (1.) Categorical; (2.) Hypothetical.
    2. As to their Logical Quantity, into (1.) Comprehensive; (2.) Extensive.
    3. As to their Material Quantity, into (1.) Integrate; (2.) Substantial; (3.) Causal.

§ 25. The First General Division of Judgments is founded on the Quality of the Copula, and gives as its results the two kinds of — 1. *Simple Affirmative* and *Negative;* and, 2. *Disjunctive Judgments.*

1. First Division of Judgments — as to Quality.

An Affirmative Judgment is a product of positive thought recognizing sameness between the Terms; as *A is B; Virtue is Manliness; The Skies are Blue.*

(1.) Affirmative.

The copula in the simple Affirmative Proposition is expressed in Mathematical Science by the symbol of Equality or Identity ($=$) as $a = b$. In common discourse, the inflections of the verb *to be* are used to express the simple copula.

A Negative Judgment is a product of negative thought recognizing difference between the Terms; as *A is not B; Virtue is not Necessity; The Skies are not Cloudy.*

(2.) Negative.

A Disjunctive Judgment is a necessitated product of thought, identifying an object with another, or with its different, as *A either is or is not B; virtue is either voluntary or involuntary; the skies are either light or dark; the flower is either blue or purple.*

(3.) Disjunctive.

The copula is expressed with the aid of the disjunctive particles, as *is either — or.* The first of this pair of particles is often omitted, and then the expression is equivocal, for the *or* may indicate an alternative in the words only and none in the thought, as in the proposition, *the electricity was vitreous or positive.*

There are three distinct forms of this species of Judgment, founded on the diverse kind of difference, or, as logicians designate it, of Opposition, that may be thought in the Judgment. First, the primitive form is where the opposition or difference lies in the copula itself; as *A is B or is not B; virtue either is voluntary or is not voluntary.* This must be regarded as a single judgment, not a compound, for it is a single act of thought, although embracing more

Logical opposition.

than one element or factor. In this case we have what is called *Pure Contradictory Opposition*. The Law of Exclusion forbids any negative Judgment of this form.

But an immediate derivative from this is effected by the transfer of the negation or sign of difference to the predicate — a transfer which although not always, yet is often legitimate in thought, as will be shown hereafter. So that from this primitive Judgment we obtain the form, *A is B or not B; Virtue is voluntary or involuntary*. In this form, while the opposition is no longer in the copula, but in the predicate, the opposition is between only two parts or members of the predicate, and is of such a nature that one by the necessities of thought excludes the other. This is called *Contradictory Opposition;* but, evidently, it is not necessarily *pure*, or of the thought merely; it is only accepted or assumed as contradictory. To assure perfect thought, it will be necessary often to reduce the Judgment to pure contradictory opposition. The fallacy arising from accepting opposition in the terms for opposition in the copula, is a very common one.

From this second form of a Disjunctive Judgment, there springs a third, in which the opposition between the parts of the predicate is not of such directly contradictory character, as that the one of necessity excludes the other, as in the proposition: *The flower is either blue or purple.* If the *flower* be not *blue*, it does not necessarily follow that it is *purple;* it may be of some other color, although it cannot be, at the same time at least and in the same part, both blue and purple. This kind of opposition in the terms of a Judgment is called *Contrary Opposition*. We have thus the following distinctions: —

§ 26. Disjunction in Thought may be either in the Copula or in the Terms. If it be in the Copula, we have *Pure Contradictory Opposition*. Its kinds: 1. Contradictory; 2. Contrary.

If it be in the Terms, it is either of *Contradictory* or of *Contrary Opposition*.

THE OPPOSITION IS CONTRADICTORY when it lies between two objects of thought, one of which necessarily, that is, in strict thought, excludes the other.

IT IS CONTRARY when it lies between two or more objects, so that the denial of one does not directly and necessarily imply the admission of the other, or the reverse.

It will have been observed that these several forms of Disjunction really work so many gradations in the logical rigor of the Thought. Only the first, which indeed the Definition properly respects, is a disjunction of strict logical necessity. The form *A is B or is not B*, holds necessarily true universally, as no two objects can be brought before the mind in regard to which Thought is not necessitated to affirm that they are either the same or are not the same. But the second form or gradation does not hold universally; for we cannot say *Sweetness is voluntary or involuntary*, since it is neither. Only when this form can be reduced to the first is it of necessary cogency. The third form or gradation is still further removed from the character of a necessary logical form. To insure for it this character, it must be reduced through the second to the first.

It is remarkable that logicians, who have been most rigid in insisting that Logic must be held to the pure form of Thought to the utter exclusion of all consideration of the matter of Thought, have admitted the second of these forms of Disjunction without a question, and have overlooked entirely the first, which is the only one that lies in the pure form of the Thought.

The examples given express a disjunction only in the predicate of the Judgment. But it may lie equally well in the subject; thus, *either A or B is C*, is just as legitimate a Judgment as *C is A or B*. So the negative form is equally competent. Examples in concrete matter are: *either John or James is guilty; neither James nor John is guilty*. This negative form corresponds with what has been called the *Remotive* Judgment, which is classed as a species of Composite

Categorical Judgments.[1] A Judgment, also, Disjunctive in form, may be sometimes equivalent to what has been termed the *Divisive* Judgment, which has been classed as a species of Categorical Judgments;[1] as, *Triangles are either Equilateral, Isosceles,* or *Scalene,* which is equivalent to *Triangles are partly Equilateral, partly Isosceles, partly Scalene.*

§ 27. The Second General Division of Judgments is founded on the Modality of the copula or determining act in the Judgment. This distinction gives the three species of — Second Division of Judgments as to their Modality.

1. *The Assertory.*
2. *The Problematic.*
3. *The Apodictic,* or *Necessary.*

An ASSERTORY JUDGMENT simply affirms or denies: as, *A is B; A is not B; A is either B or C.* (1.) Assertory.

A PROBLEMATIC JUDGMENT affirms or denies under the modification of Contingency: as *A may be B; A may be either B or C.* (2.) Problematic.

An APODICTIC OR NECESSARY JUDGMENT affirms or denies under the modification of Necessity: as, *A must be B; A must be either B or C; A is necessarily B.* (3.) Apodictic.

The Modality of a Judgment may be expressed by modals, or, as they are sometimes called, modal adverbs, as well as by the mood inflections of the verb *to be.* Thus *probably, possibly, contingently, perhaps, by chance, it may be,* and the like adverbial expressions, are Copula Modals appropriate to the Problematic Judgment. The characteristic of this Judgment is that in it the ground of the identification of the terms is accepted or assumed as in the matter, and not contained in the Thought itself. As in the second and third forms of the Disjunctive Judgment, so here, the problematic in the matter may be taken or assumed as partaking of the character of necessity, which properly comes from the Thought alone. This assumption is not, however, of strict right, but, so to speak, only by courtesy.

[1] Drobisch, *Logik.* §§ 44, 45. Leipzig, 1851.

The modals which are appropriate to Apodictic Judgments are such as *necessarily, unavoidably, of* or *by necessity.*

<small>Third Division of Judgments, as to their Degree of Identity.</small> § 28. The Third General Division of Judgments is founded on the Degree of Identity predicated. This Identity may be Total or Partial, giving rise to the two species of—

1. *Judgments of Total Identity.*
2. *Judgments of Partial Identity.*

These varieties of Judgments have been termed *Substitutive* and *Attributive* — a denomination not pointing to the essential ground of the distinction. It is true that in those of the first species in which a total identity is affirmed between the subject and the predicate, the terms are convertible — may be substituted one for the other. But precisely so in every Judgment, so much of either term as is taken is exactly convertible with whatever part of the other is taken in the Judgment; and so far as the validity of the Judgment is concerned, it is a matter of entire indifference which is made the subject or which the predicate. It is the occasion of the use which ever determines this. And in regard to the name given to the other species, Attributive, all Judgments are attributive, since it is of their very essence that they attribute.

The first of these two species of Judgments regarded as expressed, that is, as Propositions, embraces two varieties. 1. The *Tautological*, in which the terms are expressed in the same verbal form, as, A *is* A. 2. Proper Identical, in which the Terms are expressed in different forms of words, as, *Virtue is manliness;* likewise in Algebraic Formulas, as, $a = b + c$; and in Exact Definitions, as, *Virtue is right action.*

Those of the other species make up the great body of propositions occurring in discourse. In them one of the terms is always affirmed to be related to the other as Part to a Whole. Thus in the Proposition *Man is two-footed*, the character *two-footed* is affirmed to be one of the characters that make up the whole notion, *man*. In the Proposition *Man is a biped*, man is affirmed to be a part of the class of objects called *bipeds;* or, what is an exactly equivalent explication in the former proposition, one of the parts of the whole notion, *man,* is identified with the character *two-footed;* in the latter, the part or species, *man,* is identified with one of the parts that make up the whole genus, *biped.*

It will be convenient, and will involve no serious liability to error, if we adopt the familiar designations of *Identical Judgments* and *Partial Judgments* for the two species of this class. We then have the following definitions.

An IDENTICAL JUDGMENT is one in which the subject is identified wholly with the predicate; as, $a = b;$ *Virtue is manliness; Man is rational animal.* (1.) Identical.

A PARTIAL JUDGMENT is one in which the subject is but partially identified with the Predicate, in which case the relation recognized between the Terms is that of Whole and Part; as, *Man is rational; Man is a biped.* (2.) Partial.

A TAUTOLOGICAL PROPOSITION is one in which the Terms are expressed in the same verbal form; as *a is a; Gold is gold.* (3.) Tautological.

§ 29. The Fourth General Division of Judgments is founded on the diverse character of the Terms. These we have found to be of three classes. 1. Individual or Simple Objects. 2. Concepts. And, 3. Judgments. Those Judgments which have for their Terms other Judgments, possess some peculiar characters which make it desirable to keep them distinct from the others. They have been in fact familiarly distinguished by the denomination of *Hypothetical,* while other Judgments have been called simply *Categorical.* We have thus the following definitions. Fourth Division of Judgments, as to the character of their Terms.

A CATEGORICAL JUDGMENT is one the Terms of which are Individual or Simple Objects or Concepts; as, *Bucephalus is a quadruped; Man is rational; Fire burns.* (1.) Categorical.

A HYPOTHETICAL JUDGMENT is one the Terms of which are Judgments; as, *If A is B, C is D; If virtue is voluntary, vice is voluntary; That A is B implies that C is D.*

(2.) Hypothetical.

This last species of Judgments has received its name from the verbal form in which they more commonly appear. They are ordinarily expressed under the form of an hypothesis or condition indicated by the conjunction *if*. It must not be supposed that this suppositive or conditional character reaches beyond the Terms of the Judgment, or affects at all the absolute nature of the Judgment itself. The relation of identity between the Terms is just as absolute as in any Judgment. But the assumed character of the *datum*, or matter, is here, through the imperfections of language, signalized by the conjunction prefixed to the term; as where a judgment is used as an object of thought, we ordinarily mark it as thus used by a grammatical conjunction, such as *if* and *that*.

It is to be noticed here that, as elsewhere more fully exhibited, there are two fundamental relationships in Thought as essentially regulated by Quantity; the one between the Whole and Part, the other between a Part and its Complementary Part. The first is the only relationship in which logicians have exhibited Thought; and all their teachings and their illustrations have been confined to that. Perhaps, for the sake of simplicity, it may be expedient to limit the illustrations, generally and introductorily, to a single and a more familiar relationship. But it would involve serious error if that should be throughout exhibited as the only relationship in Thought. And here, precisely, in their treatment of Hypothetical Judgments, logicians have experienced the evil consequences of partial and one-sided views, as their expositions of this product of Thought are discordant and confused. It should be distinctly noticed then, that under the common form of the Hypothetical Judgment, either of the two relationships of Quantity, of Whole to Part, or of Part to Complementary Part, may be indicated. Thus in the

Judgment, *If virtue is free, temperance is free,* the relationship is that of Whole to Part; while in the Judgment, *If virtue is free, vice is free,* it is that of Part and Complementary Part, *virtue* and *vice* being complementary parts of the whole — *free action.*

In either case the antecedent clause is said, indifferently, to *determine,* to *condition,* to *imply,* or to *involve* the consequent clause, or the reverse. For it is to be remarked, that the consequent or predicate clause may condition as well as be conditioned by the other. This is, however, not to be taken unqualifiedly and without explanation. For while in the case in which the movement of Thought is between Complementary Parts, the two clauses may, of course, — except as one is assumed as a positive, and the other as a negative, — stand in perfectly reciprocal relations; in the other case, the whole conditions the part otherwise than as the Part the Whole. Thus *vice,* as complementary part, conditions *virtue* as much and in the same way as *virtue* conditions *vice;* but *temperance* conditions *virtue* as containing it as one of its constituent characters, while *virtue* conditions *temperance* as being contained in it.

A hypothetical Judgment has both its Terms Judgments. If but one Term be a Judgment, as may be the case, the Judgment is classed as Categorical.

§ 30. The characteristics of the Hypothetical and the Disjunctive Judgment may both concur in the same Judgment; we then have the *Hypothetico-Disjunct-* Hypothetico-Disjunctive. *ive,* or, as it has been called, the *Dilemma ;* as, *If A is B it is either C or non-C; If an action be prohibited, it is prohibited by natural or by positive law.* The explication of this Judgment is easy. The former of these examples means: The truth that *A is B* contains or involves the truth that *A is either C or non-C.* The latter means: The truth that an action is prohibited involves the truth that it is prohibited by natural or by positive laws. We thus have the definition: —

A Hypothetico-Disjunctive Judgment is a Disjunctive Judgment with truths or judgments instead of simple objects for its Terms.

It may be remarked here that Judgments of different classes may be combined almost indefinitely; but this particular combination of the Disjunctive with the Hypothetical has attained a classical distinction from its use by old Grecian sophists.

§ 31. The Fifth General Division of Judgments is founded on the two kinds of Logical Quantity — Extensive and Comprehensive or Intensive — which give the two species of Extensive and Comprehensive or Intensive Judgments.

Fifth Division of Judgments, as to their Logical Quantity.

An Extensive Judgment is one in which the Terms are taken in the Quantity of Extension; as, *Bucephalus is a quadruped;* that is, Bucephalus is one of the class quadruped.

(1.) Extensive.

A Comprehensive or Intensive Judgment is one in which the Terms are taken in the Quantity of Comprehension; as, *Bucephalus is four-footed;* that is, Bucephalus in one of his attributes is four-footed, or Bucephalus contains the character four-footed.

(2.) Comprehensive or Intensive.

In an Extensive Judgment, when affirming only partial identity, the predicate is affirmed to stand in the relation of whole to the subject. In a Comprehensive Judgment, when of partial identity, the subject is the containing whole, and the predicate is the part affirmed in the Judgment to be contained in the subject.

Before Sir William Hamilton, logicians had generally viewed all propositions as being of Extensive Quantity only. They accordingly divided them into four species, viz: 1. *Universal*, in which the subject is taken in its entire sphere, as, *All men are mortal.* 2. *Particular*, as *Some men are learned.* 3. *Individual* or *Singular*, in which the subject is an individual. And, 4. *Indefinite*, in which the subject is not articulately declared to be either Universal, Particular, or Singular. Rejecting this division, Hamilton proposes that the subordinate divisions of Judgments in respect of their Extensive Quantity be those of — (1) a Determinate, and (2) those of an Indeterminate, Quantity; the former including the Universal as one species, and the Individual as the other species, and the latter class corresponding to the Particular.

The two kinds of Judgments determined in respect of their Quantity, as Universal and Particular, being combined with two determined by their simple Quality, the Affirmative and the Negative, in their diverse combinations give rise to four species: the Universal Affirmative, the Universal Negative, the Particular Affirmative, and the Particular Negative; and, to facilitate the statement and analysis of the syllogism, these four have by logicians been designated by the vowels A, E, I, O. The Universal Affirmative are designated by A; the Universal Negative by E; the Particular Affirmative by I; and the Particular Negative by O.

But this classification originating in an extremely limited view of the diverse character of Judgments, and overlooking the distinctions both of Logical and of Material or Metaphysical Quantity, as well as excluding all consideration of Disjunctive and Hypothetical Judgments, may well be discarded. It deserves mention only as of the past and as historical.

§ 32. The Sixth General Division of Judgments is founded on the Material or Metaphysical Quantity of the Terms, as forming Integrate, Substantial, or Causal Wholes. This distinction gives rise to the three species of *Integrate, Substantial,* and *Causal* Judgments. *Sixth Division of Judgments as to the kind of Whole in the Terms.*

An INTEGRATE JUDGMENT is one in which the Terms are regarded as Integrate Wholes; as, $a = b + c$; *Man is Soul and Body.* (1.) Integrate.

A SUBSTANTIAL JUDGMENT is one in which the Terms are viewed in the relations of a Substantial Whole, that is, of Substance and Attribute; as, *Man is rational.* (2.) Substantial.

A Causal Judgment is one in which the Terms are viewed in the relations of a Causal Whole, or of Cause and Effect; as, *John is studying ; The Sun illuminates the planets.*

(8.) Causal.

The Copula in the Integrate Judgment is variously expressed in language, as by *is, consists of, is composed of, is constituted of, is made up of equals, is equivalent to, is identical with, is the same as,* and the like.

In the Substantial Judgment it is expressed by *is, contains, comprehends, includes, involves, implies,* and the like.

In the Causal Judgment it is generally and distinctively expressed by inflections of verbs, as *illuminates, produces,* or by *is,* with participial forms, as, *is illuminating, is producing.*

The expressions vary according as the Whole or the Part is presented as the Subject in the Judgment. Thus when the Whole is the Subject, the forms in the Integrate species are: *Man is composed of soul and body; Virtue comprehends freedom; Heat expands bodies.* When the Part is the Subject, the forms are such as these: *Soul and Body compose man; Freedom is comprehended in virtue; Bodies are expanded by heat.*

The relations between the Whole and the Parts are indicated by prepositions: in the Integrate Whole by *of,* as, *Body and Soul are parts of man;* in the Substantial and in Comprehensive Quantity, by *in,* as, *Rational is contained in man;* in Extensive Quantity, by *under,* as, *African is contained under man;* in the Causal, by *through* or *by,* as, *Bodies are expanded by heat.*

§ 33. In their relation to one another, Judgments are distinguished in various ways. It will be sufficient to state in a summary manner such distinctions as have been more generally recognized.

Distinctions of Judgments in relation to one another.

The most important of these relations is that which arises from the transposition of the Terms, so that the Subject and the Predicate change places. This transposition is technically called *Conversion,* and the prop-

Conversion.

osition arising from the conversion is called, in relation to the proposition in its first form, *the Converse.* Thus, *Right free action is virtue* is the Converse of *Virtue is right free action.*

"When the matter and form of two Judgments are considered as the same, they are called *Identical, Convertible, Equal,* or *Equivalent (propositiones identicæ, pares, convertibiles, æquipollentes)*; on the opposite alternative, they are called *Different (pr. diversæ).* If considered in certain respects the same, in others different, they are called *Relatively Identical, Similar,* or *Cognate (pr. relative identicæ, similes, affines, cognatæ).* This resemblance may be either in the subject and comprehension, or in the predicate and extension. If they have a similar subject, their predicates are *Disparate (disparata)*; if a similar predicate, their subjects are *Disjunct (disjuncta).* Judgments Identical. Different. Relatively Identical. Disparate. Disjunct.

"When two judgments differ merely in their quantity of extension, and the one is, therefore, a particular, the other a general, they are said to be subordinated, and their relation is called *Subordination (subordinatio).* The subordinating (or as it might, perhaps, be more properly styled, the *superordinate*) judgment, is called the *Subalternant (subalternans)*; the subordinate judgment is called the *Subalternate (subalternatum).* Subalternant. Subalternate.

"When, of two or more judgments, the one affirms, the other denies, and when they are thus reciprocally different in quality, they are said to be *Opposed* or *Conflictive (pr. oppositæ, ἀντικείμεναι),* and their relation, in this respect, is called *Opposition (oppositio).* This opposition is either that of *Contradiction* or *Repugnance (contradictio, ἀντίφασις),* or that of *Contrariety (contrarietas, ἐναντιότης).* Opposition of Judgments.

"If neither contradiction nor contrariety exists, the judgments are called *Congruent (pr. congruentes, consonantes, consentientes).* In regard to this last state- Congruent Judgments.

Subcontrary opposition. ment it is stated in logical books, in general, that there is an opposition of what are called *Subcontraries (subcontraria)*, meaning by these particular propositions of different quality, as, for example, *some A are B, some A are not B*; or, *some men are learned, some men are not learned;* and they are called *Subcontraries*, as they stand subordinated to the universal contrary propositions — All A are B, no A is B; or, *All men are learned, no man is learned.* But this is a mistake; there is no opposition between Subcontraries; for both may at once be maintained, as both at once must be true if the *some* be a negation of *all*. They cannot, however, both be false. The opposition in this case is only apparent; and it was probably only laid down from a love of symmetry, in order to make out the opposition of all the corners in the square of Opposition, which may be found in many works on Logic.

"It may be proper to add certain distinctions of judgments
Distinction of Propositions not strictly logical. and propositions, which, though not strictly of a logical character, it is of importance should be known. Considered in a material point of view, all judgments are, in the first place, distinguished
Theoretical and Practical. into *Theoretical* and *Practical*. Theoretical are such as declare that a certain character belongs or does not belong to a certain object; *Practical*, such as declare that something can be or ought to be done — brought to bear.

"Theoretical, as well as practical judgments, are either
Indemonstrable and Demonstrable. *Indemonstrable*, when they are evident of themselves; when they do not require, and when they are incapable of proof: or they are *Demonstrable*, when they are not immediately apparent as true or false, but require some external reason to establish their truth or falsehood.

"Indemonstrable propositions are absolute principles (ἀρχαί, *principia*); that is, from which in the construction of a system of science, cognitions altogether certain not only are, but must be, derived. Demonstrable propositions, on the other hand, can, at best, constitute only relative principles; that is, such as, themselves requiring a higher principle for their warrant, may yet afford the basis of sundry other propositions.

"If the indemonstrable propositions be of a theoretical character, they are called *Axioms;* if of a practical character, *Postulates.* The former are principles of immediate certainty; the latter, principles of immediate application. Axioms and Postulates.

"Demonstrable propositions, if of a theoretical nature, are called *Theorems (theoremata)*; if of a practical, *Problems (problemata.)* The former, as propositions of a mediate certainty, require proof; they, therefore, consist of a *Thesis* and its *Demonstration;* the latter, as of mediate application, suppose a *Question (quæstio)* and its *Solution (resolutio).* Theorems and Problems.

"As species of the foregoing, there are, likewise, distinguished *Corollaries (consectaria, corollaria),* that is, propositions which flow, without a new proof, out of theorems or postulates previously demonstrated. Propositions, whose validity rests on observation or experiment, are called *Experiential, Experimental Propositions (empiremata, experientiæ, experimenta); Hypotheses,* that is, propositions which are assumed with probability, in order to explain or prove something else which cannot otherwise be explained or proved; *Lemmata,* that is, propositions borrowed from another science, or from another part of the science, in order to serve as subsidiary propositions in the science of which we treat; finally, *Scholia,* that is, propositions which only serve as illustrations of what is considered in chief. The clearest and most appropriate examples of these various kinds of propositions are given in mathematics." Corollaries. Experimental Propositions. Hypotheses. Lemmata. Scholia.

CHAPTER V.

THE PRODUCTS OF THOUGHT. — II. CONCEPTS.

§ 34. THE Second gradation of Thought is the *Concept*. It is derived from the primitive product, the Judgment, by an act of synthesis or composition. It accordingly presupposes two or more Judgments, and, if a valid product of Thought, can always be resolved back into them. It can, in fact, be verified only by being thus referred back to the Judgments from which it is derived. It is formed either by the synthesis of the Subjects of two or more Judgments, or by a synthesis of their Predicates — an alternative which gives rise to the two fundamental classes of Concepts. It may conduce to clearness to exemplify the process of forming the Concept in these two ways separately.

Formation of Concepts.

First, then, if we synthesize the subjects, the procedure will be as follows: The Judgments, out of which the Concept is to be formed, we will assume to be — *Socrates is rational; Cicero is rational; James is rational.* By uniting the subjects, we have *Socrates* and *Cicero* and *James,* and marking the union by a single term which shall embrace them all in one, we will say, MAN, we have the union signalized in language. This union of the differing subjects of several propositions having a common predicate is called a *Concept;* in this case a Concept in Extensive Quantity. The formula for the formation of all Concepts of this class is, accordingly: The Judgments, B *is* A, C *is* A, give the Concept $(B+C)$, or when signalized in language by one term, the Concept D; or in brief: The Judgments B *is* A, C *is* A, give $B+C=$ the Concept D.

The procedure in forming Concepts of the other class is analogous. Here the Subject remains the same, and the Concept arises from the synthesis of the Predicates which differ. Thus, the Predicates in the Judgments, *Socrates is rational, Socrates is animal*, being united, we have *rational and animal*, or signalizing the union by a single term, we have the Concept, *Man*. The term *Man* here, it will be observed, means a complement of attributes, as *rational, animal*, not, as before, of subjects, as *Socrates*, &c. This is a Concept in Comprehensive Quantity; the formula of which is: The Judgments A is B, A is C, give, by synthesis of the differing Predicates, the aggregate $(B+C)$, which signalized as one in Language is expressed by D. Or the Judgments A is B, A is C, give Concept $(B+C) = D$.

§ 35. A CONCEPT may be defined, accordingly, to be a product of Thought, resulting from the synthesis of the Subjects or of the Predicates in several Judgments. Definition of Concept.

The common Subject in a Predicate-Concept, or the common Predicate in a Subject-Concept, on which the Concept is formed, is called its *Base*.

The name, *Concept*, is derived from the Latin word *Conceptum*, meaning *something taken with another*. The corresponding word used to denote the act of forming a Concept is *Conception*, which is also in common discourse often used to denote the product. It is used, in fact, like other words of this kind, in the threefold import of *faculty, act*, and *product*.

§ 36. The Law of Identity, or as, in its fuller expression, it may be denominated, the Law of the Same and Different, it will have been seen, presides over this product of Thought, as over the Judgment. No valid Concept can be formed, unless from Judgments which have either identical subjects or identical predicates. The Concept arises from the Synthesis of the different under the same; of different subjects having the same predicate, or of different predicates having the same subject. In other words, Concepts under Law of Identity.

in the Base is to be found the identifying principle governing in the Concept.

§ 37. It will have been observed, moreover, from the mode of its formation, as given in § 34, that a Concept is essentially a *relative cognition*. It is not only the result of a synthesis, not only the aggregate of a plurality of Judgments, and accordingly of relative cognitions, but the cognitions that are brought together in this synthesis sustain a determined and peculiar relation to one another. If the Concepts be formed from the subjects of the Judgments, those Judgments must have a common — the same predicate; if from the predicates, the Judgments must have the same subject. Concepts are thus from their very nature relative cognitions, and the principle of relation is in the sameness of the term of the Judgment which is not synthesized into the Concept — in its Base.

<small>Concept a Relative Cognition.</small>

Concepts, however, differ from Judgments, as relative cognitions, in this respect: that in the Judgment the relation is explicit, while in the Concept it is only implied. Thus in the Judgment, *Man is rational animal*, the relation is articulately declared; but in the Concept, *Man*, the relation to the other term of the Judgment from which it is derived, although real, is not expressed, but only implied. The Base of the Concept, although real, is not expressed.

§ 38. Still further, a Concept is essentially a one-sided cognition. It is formed from but one side of a Judgment, from the Subject or from the Predicate. It may be regarded, indeed, as an aggregate of Judgments, that is, a synthesized or composite Judgment, with the single term — the Base, and the Copula dropped.

<small>Concept a one-sided Cognition.</small>

A Concept, however, always implies the Judgments from which it is derived; it implies the other term, which has been dropped, but which is the indispensable condition of its being formed, and is, therefore, appropriately denominated the Base of the Concept; and also implies that this Base has been identified with each of the terms which compose the Concept.

Although a Concept has this character of one-sidedness, it must not be supposed that it is properly an *inadequate* cognition, as some logicians have taught. Of all objects of thought, that of a Concept is most exactly and adequately embraced in the thought; of all object-cognitions, the cognition in a Concept is the most adequate. A Concept is not, indeed, an adequate cognition of any individual embraced under it, or of any simple attribute embraced in it. But these are not the objects thought in Concepts. A Concept is ever just the cognition of the subjects embraced under it or the predicates embraced in it; it is of course a perfectly adequate cognition of its proper object.

From the inadequacy of language to express perfectly and fully the characters of thought, a word expressing a Concept is for the most part at least used indifferently both for a subject-concept and also for a predicate-concept. *Man*, thus, both denotes an aggregate of subjects, as *Socrates*, &c., and also of predicates or attributes, as *rational*, &c. For accurate and valid Thought, it becomes necessary to distinguish these uses; or, out of the confusion, error will be likely to arise. This distinction is sometimes marked, when a Concept is used as a term of a Judgment, by some peculiarity in the form of expression. Thus in the propositions, *Man is two-footed*, *Man is a bi-ped*, in the former, the Concept, *Man*, is obviously a predicate-concept; in the latter, a subject-concept. Often the distinction emerges only in the more advanced progress of the thought, as in a course of reasoning. It is natural to anticipate that the confusion might, in continued discourse, bring in serious error which could not be corrected nor indeed be brought to light without the application of the distinction. This will, in the proper place, be fully exemplified. It is sufficient here to expose the reality and the probable importance of the distinction to correct and valid thought.

§ 39. It will occur to the reflecting mind, on this exposition of the mode in which Concepts are formed, that they are mere products of Thought, aggregates of Concepts not Realities

Subjects, or aggregates of Predicates, and do not imply necessarily any exactly corresponding aggregates in the reality of things. How many individual subjects of Judgments shall be combined, or how many predicates, are questions that will be determined by such considerations as those of extent of observation, practicability of aggregation, convenience of use, the needs of occasion, and the like. The extent of the aggregation, therefore, varies indefinitely with the occasions of Thought; and it is not to be supposed that the constitution of things around us fluctuates precisely with the fluctuations of Thought. As the mathematical analyst, in the progress of his demonstration, finds it convenient to substitute single letters or symbols to denote a number of quantities in some respect of like character, so Thought, for its own manifold conveniences, often aggregates like elements and signalizes them by single words. It does not thereby change the constituted system of things.

Concepts, thus, and so the words in which they are embodied and maintain their existence, are not fixed and constant as inhering in the stability and constancy of nature. They rise and sink with the ever-varying vicissitudes of occasion. They are not, however, any more than the assumed general symbols in a mathematical process, illusory and empty. They are ever significant; they ever suppose and express what is similar, or rather, express recognized identities in the objects of thought. They can, in fact, simply by reversing the process by which they were formed, ever be traced through the Judgments back to the realities from which they originally sprang, or, at least, to the primitive cognitions brought to Thought by the proper Presentative Faculties.

In our endeavors to realize a concept, that is, to ascertain what exactly of reality it expresses, what in the reality of things around exactly corresponds to it, how far and in what respects it is a true, trustworthy cognition of the realities to which it applies, we must not expect of course to find an object that is exactly commensurate with

<small>How to realize a Concept.</small>

the Concept; that is, an aggregation of just so many subjects, no more, no less, having the single predicate under which we have found the Concept, or an aggregation of just so many attributes belonging to the single subject under which they are conceived or brought together in thought. We must not expect, for instance, when we endeavor to realize the Concept, *Man*, to find an object that is *rational* and *animal*, nothing more, nothing less; — an object that is merely rational, with no attributes that determine this rationality more specifically — an object, for instance, that is not learned nor unlearned, prince nor savage; that is not tall nor short, black nor white, male nor female. The Concept did not arise, was not formed, in such a way as to authorize any such expectation. It was founded immediately, as we have seen, in a plurality of judgments; and these judgments were formed from what was presented to the thought. If this *datum* to the thought be, for example, supposed to have been presented by the Faculty of Perception, and the movement of Thought to have been from the whole to the parts, then, as we have seen, Thought took the *datum* as a whole, say *Socrates*, and one of its parts, say the composite attribute, *rational animal*, and affirmed this part of the whole, thus, *Socrates is rational animal*, leaving out of regard for the time, all other attributes or parts, as that he was *learned, modest, tall, white*, and the like. Other *data*, as *Cicero, James*, were presented and treated in the same way. Then these several judgments being thus in the mind, and having the same predicate, which was one of the many attributes originally given in the several subjects, *Socrates*, &c., were synthesized or aggregated, and the common predicate and copula being dropped, we attained the Concept, which we signalized in language as a unit, by the term *Man*. Now the only element of reality introduced by this process into the Concept is simply the attribute *rational animal*, given in the plurality of subjects, *Socrates, Cicero, James*. All of real, therefore, that we can expect to find in our endeavor to realize the Concept, *Man,* is simply *rational animal.* This complex attribute, if the Concept is valid, must be found, must be realized, in every subject embraced under the Concept in *Socrates, Cicero, James,* &c.; but it would be absurd to expect more as necessarily expressed by the Concept, unless the attribute under which as its necessary Base the Concept was formed as being identical in the plurality of subjects, embraced something more than *rational animal.*

Inasmuch as words expressing Concepts make up a great majority of the terms in use in language, it becomes an interesting question, how far and on what grounds we may assume such words to denote real objects. And, although the question in its full import transcends the proper sphere of logical science, yet as the exposition we have given of the genesis of the Concept enables us to indicate the conditions of such a correspondence, and as some knowledge of them is necessarily involved in logical methodology, where the question will again meet us, it may be proper here in a very summary way to indicate them.

1. The original *datum* to thought must be a true presentation of the real object, and this implies two things: (1) that objective reality may be apprehended by the human mind; and (2) that the mind rightly apprehends it.

2. The objective world must have in its parts likenesses or resemblances corresponding to the identities recognized in forming the Concept. This condition implies (1) that the objective world has parts corresponding to those apprehended in thought; (2) that these parts are in some respects identical one with another; and (3) that the identities recognized in Thought, in the Concept, are the same as those that exist in the real objects of thought.

In all thinking, and especially in all communication of thought, in all discourse, there are three elements which it is ever necessary to discriminate with careful vigilance. There are, first, the objects of which we think or speak; secondly, our cognitions or mental apprehensions of those objects; and, thirdly, the words in which these cognitions of these objects of our thought are expressed. Thought thus stands in a twofold relation to its object, and to its expression or embodiment; and there is accordingly a twofold liability to error, as we may, in the first place, confound our thoughts, our cognitions, with the objects of which we think; or, in the second place, confound these cognitions with the words in which they are expressed.

In respect to this second relation of thought, its relation to language, their reciprocal dependence on each other, and the imperfection of thought by reason of this dependence, the following general observations of Sir William Hamilton are particularly worthy of attention: —

"For Perception, indeed, for the mere consciousness of the similarities and dissimilarities in the objects perceived, for the apprehension of the causal connection of certain things, and for the application of this knowledge to the attainment of certain ends, no language is necessary; and it is only the exaggeration of a truth into an error, when philosophers maintain that language is the indispensable condition of even the simpler energies of knowledge. Language is the attribution of signs to our cognitions of things. But as a cognition must have been already there, before it could receive a sign, consequently that knowledge which is denoted by the formation and application of a word must have preceded the symbol which denotes it. Speech is thus not the mother, but the godmother, of knowledge. But though, in general, we must hold that language, as the product and correlative of thought, must be viewed as posterior to the act of thinking itself; on the other hand, it must be admitted, that we could never have risen above the very lowest degrees in the scale of thought, without the aid of signs. A sign is necessary to give stability to our intellectual progress — to establish each step in our advance as a new starting-point for our advance to another beyond.

"A country may be overrun by an armed host, but it is

only conquered by the establishment of fortresses. Words are the fortresses of thought. They enable us to realize our dominion over what we have already overrun in thought; to make every intellectual conquest the basis of operations for others still beyond. Or another illustration: All have heard of the process of tunneling, of tunneling through a sand-bank. In this operation it is impossible to succeed, unless every foot, nay almost every inch in our progress, be secured by an arch of masonry, before we attempt the excavation of another. Now, language is to the mind precisely what the arch is to the tunnel. The power of thinking and the power of excavation are not dependent on the word in the one case, or the mason-work in the other; but without these subsidiaries, neither process could be carried on beyond its rudimentary commencement. Though, therefore, we allow that every movement forward in language must be determined by an antecedent movement forward in thought; still, unless thought be accompanied at each point of its evolution by a corresponding evolution of language, its further development is arrested. Thus it is, that the higher exertions of the higher faculty of Understanding — the classification of the objects presented and represented by the subsidiary powers in the formation of a hierarchy of notions, the connection of these notions into judgments, the inference of one judgment from another, and, in general, all our consciousness of the relations of the universal to the particular, consequently all science strictly so denominated, and every inductive knowledge of the past and future from the laws of nature — not only these, but all ascent from the sphere of sense to the sphere of moral and religious intelligence, are, as experience proves, if not altogether impossible without a language, at least possible to a very low degree.

"Admitting even that the mind is capable of certain elementary concepts without the fixation and signature of language, still these are but sparks which would twinkle only to expire; and it requires words to give them prominence, and, by enabling us to collect and elaborate them into new concepts, to raise out of what would otherwise be only scattered and transitory scintillations a vivid and enduring light.

"As a notion or concept is the factitious whole or unity made up of a plurality of subjects or of attributes — a whole too often of a very complex multiplicity; and as this multiplicity is only mentally held together, inasmuch as the concept is fixed and ratified in a sign or word; it frequently happens that, in its employment, the word does not suggest the whole amount of thought for which it is the adequate expression, but, on the contrary, we frequently give and take the sign, either with an obscure or indistinct consciousness of its meaning, or even without an actual consciousness of its signification at all. In consequence of this, when a notion is of a very complex and heterogeneous composition, we are frequently wont to use the term by which it is denoted, without a clear or distinct consciousness of the various characters of which the notion is the sum; and thus it is, that we both give and take words without any, or, at least, without the adequate complement of thought. In countries where bank-notes have not superseded the use of the precious metals, large payments are made in bags of money, purporting to contain a certain number of a certain denomination of coin, or, at least, a certain amount in value. Now, these bags are often sealed up and passed from one person to another, without the tedious process, at each transference, of counting out their contents, and this upon the faith that, if examined, they will be found actually to contain the number of pieces for which they are marked, and for which they pass current. In this state of matters, it is, however, evident, that many errors or frauds may be committed, and that a bag may be given and taken in payment for one sum, which contains another, or which, in fact, may not even contain any money at all. Now the case is similar in regard to notions. As the sealed bag or *rouleau* testifies to the enumerated sum, and gives unity to what would otherwise be an unconnected multitude of pieces, each only representing its separate value; so the sign or word proves and ratifies the existence of a concept, that is, it vouches the tying up of a certain number of attributes or characters in a single concept — attributes which would otherwise exist to us only as a multitude of separate and unconnected representations of value. So far the analogy is manifest; but it is only general. The bag, the guaranteed sum, and the constituent coins, represent in a still more proximate manner the term, the concept, and the constituent characters. For in regard to each, we may do one of two things. On the one hand, we may test the bag, that is, open it, and ascertain the accuracy of its stated value, by counting out the pieces which it purports to contain; or we may accept and pass the bag, without such a critical enumeration. In the other case, we may test the general term, prove that it is valid for the amount and quality of thought of which it is the sign, by spreading out in consciousness the various characters of which the concept professes to be the complement; or we may take and give the term without such an evolution.

"It is evident from this, that notions or concepts are peculiarly liable to great vagueness and ambiguity, and that their symbols are liable to be passed about without the proper kind, or the adequate amount, of thought."

§ 40. Inasmuch, likewise, as a Concept is in its essential nature an aggregate resulting from the synthesis of the subjects or of the predicates in several Judgments, it is necessarily to be regarded as a Quantity. And in this, its most essential characteristic, we are to find the highest principle of Division in the distribution of Concepts. But inasmuch as a Concept may be a synthesis of Subjects or of Predicates, we have at once given us the primary distinction of Concepts into the two classes of Subject-Concepts and Predicate-Concepts. These two kinds of Quantity have been denominated by logicians *Extensive Quantity* and *Comprehensive* or *Intensive Quantity;* Extensive Quantity belonging to concepts in so far as formed of subjects, and *Comprehensive* Quantity belonging to them in so far as they are formed of predicates.

§ 41. The EXTENSIVE QUANTITY of a concept, otherwise called its *Extension*, also its *sphere* or *domain*, *sphæra, regio, quantitas, ambitus*, and by the Greek logicians, its *breadth* or *latitude*, πλάτος, respects the concept as a complement of subjects. Thus the concept, *man*, taken in its Extensive Quantity, denotes the aggregate of the individual subjects of which some common attributes may have been predicated in Judgments actually or impliedly made before, as *Socrates, Cicero, James*, and all other individuals judged as *rational animal*. {Extensive Quantity.}

In this Quantity the relation of the concept as a whole to the particular subjects which are its component parts, is expressed by the preposition *under;* thus, *Socrates* is said to be contained *under* the concept, *man*.

§ 42. The COMPREHENSIVE QUANTITY of a concept, otherwise called its *Intensive* or *Internal Quantity*, its *Comprehension, Intension, quantitas complexus*, also by the Greek logicians *depth*, βάθος, respects the concept as a complement of predicates or attributes; as thus the concept, *man*, taken in its Comprehensive Quantity, denotes the aggregate of the attributes that may have been predicated of the same subject in former actual or implied Judgments, as *rational* and *animal*, attributed severally to the same subject, *Socrates*. {Comprehensive or Intensive Quantity.}

In this Quantity, the relation of the concept as a whole to the particular attributes which are its component parts, is expressed by the preposition *in;* thus the concept, *man*, is said to contain *in* it the attribute *rational*.

§ 43. Nothing in the formation of a concept forbids a synthesis of terms that are themselves concepts. The primitive concepts, as the primitive Judgments, must be of terms that are individual; but these terms may be combined with other individual terms or {Amplification of Concepts.}

with concepts, or concepts may be combined with other concepts, and in either quantity, the Base ever remaining unchanged.

The logical process by which a term is amplified by being combined with other analogous terms, if in Extensive Quantity, is called *Generalization ;* if in Comprehensive Quantity, it is called *Determination.*

This process of amplifying a term or concept, may be thus exemplified. We will begin with a primitive consciousness in which an object of sight, say the *Moon,* is brought into it. The Judgment, when this cognition given by the Faculty of Perception and the Intuitive Cognition of Existence occasioned by the perception, present themselves before its view, at once affirms Existence both of the subject perceiving — the *Ego* — and also of the object perceived, *I am, The moon is,* the verb being used here substantively to include both the copula and the predicate of Existence. Under the common predicate, the subjects may be synthesized, and a concept emerges, which, by successive syntheses of subjects, becomes the concept *being,* comprehending all objects of Thought which agree in respect of this predicate. We can enlarge the contents of this concept taken in its Extensive Quantity, by bringing into it or under it any other subject of a Judgment having this predicate ; but we can add no existing subject to Being so as to form a higher class of subjects. We cannot, therefore, amplify the concept *being,* so that it shall become a higher genus. The limit to the amplification of a subject-concept, that is, of a concept in Extensive Quantity, is thus a perfectly simple predicate. But this predicate may be amplified if we find a subject having this and some other predicate. Thus in the Judgments *The Moon is existing, The Moon is material,* by combining the predicates there emerges the predicate-concept *Material Existence,* that is, *Matter.* We may go on to amplify this concept, taken in Comprehensive Quantity, by combining with it under some common subject another predicate, as *luminous,* and, still further, by adding to this new amplification, the predicate *by reflection*, till we reach the limit of amplification in this direction. It is obvious that as we thus amplify the comprehension of the concept, we are contracting the boundaries of the subject of which the concept may be affirmed, that is, we are *determining* it. Thus *existence* may be predicated of many objects; *material*, of fewer; *luminous*, of fewer still; *luminous by reflection*, of yet fewer objects. The process of amplifying the comprehension is called, therefore, *Determination*, as logical nomenclature has originated rather from the view of objects in their Extensive Quantity. It is also called *Concretion*.

On the other hand, if we begin with a subject having not a simple predicate as before, but one more or less amplified, we may amplify the Extension of this subject by combining with it subjects having some part of this predicate in common. Thus beginning with *Socrates* in any Judgment having a predicate not absolutely simple, as in the Judgment, *Socrates is of Athens*, we may add subjects in Judgments having the same predicate, as, *Plato is of Athens, Alcibiades is of Athens, Xenophon is of Athens*, &c., and we obtain the subject-concept *Athenian*, embracing under it many individuals. So, again, by combining *Athenian, Theban, Spartan*, under the common predicate of *Greece* or *Grecian*, we amplify the Extension still more, that is, we bring more subjects under it. This process, that of amplifying the Extension, is called *Generalization*.

It will be observed that, from the inadequacy of language to signalize all the modifications of Thought, these two quantities, notwithstanding they differ so much, are not always distinguished by peculiar forms of verbal expression. Indeed, almost every term may be used indifferently either as Subject or as Predicate, and accordingly in either Comprehension or Extension. The use in discourse alone can ordinarily indicate in which Quantity the term is used. Individuals, as such, can never, indeed, be predicates, except in Identical

Propositions; yet Language does not hesitate at its will to trample upon this high prerogative of individuality, and conscript it into the ranks of its predicates, as its wants require. It makes *Alexander* to serve as predicate of every ambitious military conqueror, and, proceeds thus to create a genus of *Alexanders* — restoring the subject-character, but robbing it of the individual prerogative. Hence the necessity to correct and valid Thought of a careful discrimination of this twofold significance of a term denoting a concept.

The ability to be acquired only by intelligent practice, readily, and, as it were, instinctively, to distinguish these two quantities in the import of concepts, is needed in order to the ready and correct interpretation of discourse; to facile criticism of discourse, also, and determination of its conformity to truth, and the detection and exposure of error. Discourse, moreover, becomes at once freighted with a double richness of meaning to the mind practiced and skillful in this discrimination. But vastly more needful is this dexterity in the construction of Discourse. In this the main and more essential labor consists in the right unfolding of knowledge, which for the most part is laid up in concepts. To unfold concepts in ignorance of their twofold quantity is not only difficult and slow, because in blindness as to the necessary path to be pursued, but, also, unavoidably liable to confusion, from which it has been truly said it is more difficult for truth to emerge than from absolute error.

It is pertinent to remark in this connection that obviously *common nouns*, or, as they might more properly be called, *class nouns*, are as really abstractions as any others. They do not stand for any actual concrete realities. There is, as has been shown, no real being answering to the concept *horse*, having the characters *solid-hoofed*, *non-ruminant*, *mammal*, and no others. The concept is a mere product of Thought, and is the result of abstraction. It is only by abstracting from other properties or characters, and thus limiting the attention to one or more, that we can form a thought of any class of subjects. Thus it happens, that any predicate, as it can be made a subject in a Judgment, so can be a class-noun. A concrete noun can differ from an abstract only in this respect, that in its use it is treated as a Subject-concept, while an abstract noun is treated as a predicate-concept.

"Such, in general, is what is meant by the two quantities of concepts — their Extension and Comprehension.

§ 44. "But these quantities are not only different, they are opposed, and so opposed, that though each supposes the other as the condition of its own existence, still, however, within the limits of conjunct, of correlative existence, they stand in an inverse ratio to each other — the maximum of the one being the minimum of the other. Intensive and Extensive Quantities are opposed to each other.

"A notion is extensively great in proportion to the greater number, and extensively small in proportion to the smaller number of subjects it contains under it. When the Extension of a concept becomes a minimum, that is, when it contains no other notions under it, it is called an *individual*.

"A notion is intensively great in proportion to the greater number, and intensively small in proportion to the smaller number of determinations or attributes contained in it. Is the Comprehension of a concept a minimum, that is, is the concept one in which a plurality of attributes can no longer be distinguished, it is called *simple*; whereas, inasmuch as its attributes still admit of discrimination, it is called *complex* or *compound*. Law regulating the mutual relations of Extension and Comprehension.

"These two quantities stand always in an inverse ratio to each other: for the greater the Comprehension of a concept, the less is its Extension; and the greater its Extension the less its Comprehension.

"When I take out of a concept, that is, abstract from it one or more of its attributes, I diminish its comprehension. Thus, when from the concept, *man*, equiva- Illustration.

lent to *rational animal*, I abstract the attribute or determination *rational*, I lessen its internal quantity. But by this diminution of its comprehension I give it a wider extension; for what remains is the concept, *animal*, and the Concept *animal* embraces under it a far greater number of subjects than the concept *man*."

§ 45. Concepts have been characterized by certain relations which they bear to one another. The most important of the different kinds of concepts as thus determined will best be exhibited separately under the two kinds of Quantity.

<small>Reciprocal Relations of Concepts.</small>

"As dependent upon Extension, concepts stand to each other in the five mutual relations: 1°. Of Exclusion; 2°. Of Coëxtension; 3°. Of Subordination; 4°. Of Coördination; and 5°. Of Intersection.

<small>Under Extension.</small>

"1. One concept excludes another when no part of the one coincides with any part of the other. 2. One concept is coëxtensive with another, when each has the same subordinate concepts under it. 3. One concept is subordinate to another (which may be called the *Superordinate*) when the former is included within, or makes a part of, the sphere or extension of the latter. 4. Two or more concepts are coördinated, when each excludes the other from its sphere, but when both go immediately to make up the extension of a third concept, to which they are co-subordinate. 5. Concepts intersect each other, when the sphere of the one is partially contained in the sphere of the other.

"Of Exclusion, *horse, syllogism,* are examples: there is no absolute exclusion.

"As examples of Coëxtension — the concepts *living being*, and *organized being*, may be given. For, using the term *life* as applicable to plants as well as animals, there is nothing living which is not organized, and nothing organized which is not living. This reciprocal relation will be represented by two circles covering each other, or by two lines of equal length and in positive relations.

<small>Examples of the five mutual relations of Concepts in Extension.</small>

"As examples of Subordination and Coördination — *man, dog, horse,* stand, as correlatives, in subordination to the concept *animal,* and, as reciprocal correlatives, in coördination with each other.

"What is called the reciprocal relation of Intersection, takes place between concepts when their spheres cross or cut each other, that is, fall partly within, partly without each other. Thus, the concept *black* and the concept *heavy* mutually intersect each other, for of these some black things are heavy, some not, and some heavy things are black, some not.

"Of these relations, those of Subordination and Coördination are of principal importance, as on them reposes the whole system of classification; and to them alone it is, therefore, necessary to accord a more particular consideration.

"Under the Subordination of notions, there are various terms to express the different modes of this relation; these it is necessary to bear in mind, for they form an essential part of the language of Logic, and will come frequently, in the sequel, to be employed in considering the analysis of Reasonings.

§ 46. "Of notions which stand to each other in the relations of Subordination — the one is the *Higher* or *Superior* (*notio, conceptus, superior*), the other the *Lower* or *Inferior* (*notio, conceptus, inferior*). The superior notion is likewise called the *Wider* or *Broader* (*latior*), the inferior is likewise called the *Narrower* (*angustior*). *[Superior and Inferior, Broader and Narrower, Notions.]*

"A notion is called the *higher* or *superior,* inasmuch as it is viewed as standing over another in the relation of subordination — as including it within its domain or sphere; and a correlative notion is called the *lower* or *inferior,* as thus standing under a superior. Again, the higher notion is called the *wider* or *broader,* as containing under it a greater number of things; the lower is called the *narrower,* as containing under it a smaller number.

"The higher or wider concept is called, also, in contrast to the lower or narrower, a *Universal* or *General Notion* (νόημα καθόλον, *notio, conceptus, universalis, generalis*) ; the lower or narrower concept, in contrast to the higher or wider, a *Particular Notion* (νόημα μερικόν, *notio, conceptus, particularis*).

<small>Universal and Particular Notions.</small>

"A notion is called *universal*, inasmuch as it is considered as binding up a multitude of parts or inferior concepts into the unity of a whole; for *universus* means *in unum versus*, or *ad unum versus*, that is, *many turned into one*, or *many regarded as one*, and *universal* is employed to denote the attribution of this relation to objects. A notion is called *particular*, inasmuch as it is considered as one of the parts of a higher concept or whole.

"A superior concept is also called a *General Notion* (νόημα καθόλον, *notio, conceptus, generalis*), or, in a single word, a *Genus* (γένος, *genus*): and an inferior concept, contained under a higher, is called a *Special Notion* (νόημα εἰδικόν, *notio, conceptus, specialis*), or, in a single word, a *Species* (εἶδος, *species*). The abstraction which carries up species into genera, is called, in that respect, *Generalization*. The determination which divides a genus into its species is called, in that respect, *Specification*. Genera and Species are both called *Classes ;* and the arrangement of things under them is, therefore, *Classification*.

<small>Genus and Species.</small>

"It is manifest that the distinction into Genera and Species is a merely relative distinction; as the same notion is, in one respect, a genus, in another respect, a species. For except a notion has no higher notion, that is, except it be itself the widest or most universal notion, it may always be regarded as subordinated to another; and, in so far as it is actually thus regarded, it is a species. Again, every notion, except that which has under it only individuals, is, in so far as it is thus viewed, a genus. For example, the notion, *triangle*, if viewed in relation to the notion of *rectilineal figure*, is a

<small>The distinction of Genus and Species merely relative.</small>

species, as is likewise *rectilineal figure* itself, as viewed in relation to *figure* simply. Again, the concept *triangle* is a genus, when viewed in reference to the concepts — *right-angled triangle, acute-angled triangle*, etc. A right-angled triangle is, however, only a species, and not possibly a genus, if under it be necessarily included individuals alone. But, in point of fact, it is impossible to reach in theory any lowest species; for we can always conceive some difference by which any concept may be divided *ad infinitum*. This, however, as it is only a speculative curiosity, like the infinitesimal divisibility of matter, may be thrown out of view in relation to practice; and, therefore, the definition, by Porphyry and logicians in general, of the lowest species, is practically correct, even though it cannot be vindicated against theoretical objections. On the other hand, we soon and easily reach the highest genus, which is given in τὸ ὄν, *ens aliquid, being, thing, something,* etc., which are only various expressions of the same absolute universality.

"In regard to the terms *Generalization* and *Specification*, these are limited expressions for the processes of Abstraction and Determination, considered in a particular relation. And first, in regard to Abstraction and Generification. In every complex notion, we can limit our attention to its constituent characters, to the exclusion of some one. We thus think away from this one — we abstract from it. Now, the concept which remains, that is, the fasciculus of thought *minus* the one character which we have thrown out, is in relation to the original — the entire concept, the next higher — the proximately superior notion. But a concept and a next higher concept are to each other as species and genus. The process of Abstraction, therefore, by which out of a proximately lower, we evolve a proximately higher, concept, is, when we speak with logical precision, called the process of *Generalization*.

Generification and Specification — what.

"Take, for example, the concept, *man.* This concept is proximately composed of the two concepts or constituent characters — *animal* and *rational being*. If we think either of these characters away from the other, we shall have in that other a proximately higher concept, to which the concept *man* stands in the relation of a species to its genus. If we abstract from *animal*, then *man* will stand as a species in subordination to the genus, *rational being*, and the concept, *animal*, will then afford only a difference to distinguish *man* as a coördinate species from *immaterial intelligences*. If, on the other hand, we abstract from *rational being*, then *man* will stand as a species in subordination to the genus *animal*, having for a coördinate species, *irrational animal*. Such is the process of Generalization. Now for the converse process of Specification.

"Every series of concepts which has been obtained by abstraction, may be reproduced in an inverted order, when, descending from the highest notion, we step by step add on the several characters from which we had abstracted in our ascent. This process, as has been stated, is called *Determination* — a very appropriate expression, inasmuch as by each character or attribute which we add on, we limit or determine, more and more, the abstract vagueness or extension of the notion; until, at last, if every attribute be annexed, the sum of attributes contained in the notion becomes convertible with the sum of attributes of which some concrete individual or reality is the complement. Now, when we determine any notion by adding on a subordinate concept, we divide it; for the extension of the higher concept is precisely equal to the extension of the added concept *plus* its negation. Thus, if to the concept, *animal*, we add on the next lower concept, *rational*, we divide its extension into two halves — the one equal to *rational animal*, the other equal to its negation, that is, to *irrational animal*. Thus an added concept and its negation always constitute the immediately lower notion, into which a higher notion is divided. But as a notion stands to the notions proximately subordinate to it in the immediate relation of a genus to its species, the process of Determination, by which a concept is thus divided, is, in logical language, appropriately denominated *Specification.*

"So much in general for the Subordination of notions, considered as Genera and Species. There are, however, various gradations of this relation, and certain terms by which these are denoted. The most important of these are comprehended in the following paragraph.

§ 47. "A Genus is of two degrees — a highest and a lower. In its highest degree, it is called the *Supreme* or *Most General Genus* (γένος γενικώτατον, *genus summum,* or *generalissimum*), and is defined, 'that which being a genus cannot become a species.' In its lower degree, it is called a *Subaltern* or *Intermediate* (γένος ὑπάλληλον, *genus subalternum* or *medium*), and is defined, 'that which being a genus can also become a species.' A Species, also, is of two degrees — a lowest and a higher. In its lowest degree, it is called a *Lowest* or *Most Special Species* (εἶδος εἰδικώτατον, *species infima, ultima,* or *specialissima*), and is defined, 'that which being a species cannot become a genus.' In its higher degree, it is called a *Subaltern* or *Intermediate Species* (εἶδος ὑπάλληλον, *species subalterna media*), and is defined, 'that which being a species may also become a genus.' Thus a Subaltern Genus and a Subaltern Species are convertible.

Gradations of Genera and Species, and their designations.

"These distinctions and definitions are taken from the celebrated *Introduction* of Porphyry to the *Categories* of Aristotle, and they have been generally adopted by logicians. It is evident that the only absolute distinction here established is that between the Highest or Supreme Genus and the Lowest Species; for the other classes — to wit, the Subaltern or Intermediate — are, all and each, either genera or species, according as we regard them in an ascending or a descending order — the same concept being a genus, if considered as a whole containing under it inferior concepts as parts, and a species, if considered as itself the part of a higher concept or whole. The distinction of concepts into Genus and Species, into Supreme and Intermediate Genus, into Lowest and Intermediate Species, is all that Logic takes into account; because these are all the distinctions of degree that are given necessarily in the form of thought, and as abstracted from all determinate matter.

"It may be remarked, by the way, that in the physical sciences of arrangement, the best instances of which are seen in the different departments of Natural History, it is found necessary, in order to mark the relative place of each step in the ascending and descending series of classes, to bestow on it a particular designation. Thus *kingdom, subkingdom, class, order, tribe, family, genus, subgenus, species, subspecies, variety*, and the like, are terms that serve conveniently to mark out the various degrees of generalization, in its application to the descriptive sciences of nature.

§ 48. "The character, or complement of characters, by which a lower genus or species is distinguished, both from the genus to which it is subordinate, and from the other genera or species with which it is coördinated, is called the *Generic* or the *Specific Difference*, διαφορὰ γενική, and διαφορὰ εἰδική, *differentia generica*, and *differentia specifica*. The sum of characters, again, by which a singular or individual thing is discriminated from the species under which it stands and from other individual things along with which it stands, is called the *Individual* or *Singular* or *Numerical Difference* (*differentia individualis* vel *singularis* vel *numerica*).

Generic, Specific, and Individual Difference.

"Two things are thus said to be generically different, inasmuch as they lie apart in two different genera; specifically different, inasmuch as they lie apart in two different species; individually or numerically different, inasmuch as they do not constitute one and the same reality. Thus, *animal* and *stone* may be said to be generically different; *horse* and *ox* to be specifically different; *Highflyer* and *Eclipse* to be numerically or individually different. It is evident, however, that as all genera and species,

Generic and Specific Difference.

except the highest of the one and the lowest of the other, may be styled indifferently either genera or species, *generic difference* and *specific difference* are in general only various expressions of the same thing; and, accordingly, the terms *heterogeneous* and *homogeneous*, which apply properly only to the correlation of genera, are usually applied equally to the correlation of species.

" Individual existence can only be perfectly discriminated in Perception, external or internal, and their numerical differences are endless; for of all possible contradictory attributes, the one or the other must, on the principles of Disjunction and Excluded Middle, be considered as belonging to each individual thing. On the other hand, species and genera may be perfectly discriminated by one or few characters. For example, *man* is distinguished from every genus or species of animal by the one character of *rationality; triangle*, from every other class of mathematical figures, by the single character of *trilaterality*. It is, therefore, far easier adequately to describe a genus or species than an individual existence; as in the latter case we must select, out of the infinite multitude of characters which an individual comprises, a few of the most prominent, or those by which the thing may most easily be recognized. But as those which we thus select are only a few, and are only selected with reference to our faculty of apprehension and our capacity of memory, they always constitute only a petty, and often not the most essential part of the numerical differences by which the individuality of the object is determined.

<small>Individual or Singular Difference.</small>

§ 49. " Notions, in so far as they are considered the coördinate species of the same genus, may be called *Conspecies;* and in so far as Conspecies are considered to be different but not contradictory, they are properly called *Discrete* or *Disjunct Notions* (*notiones discretæ* vel *disjunctæ*).

<small>Coördination of Concepts.</small>

§ 50. " The whole classification of things by Genera and

Species is governed by two laws. The one of these, the law of *Homogeneity* (*principium Homogeneitatis*), is — That how different soever may be any two concepts, they both still stand subordinated under some higher concept; in other words, things the most dissimilar must, in certain respects, be similar. The other, the law of *Heterogeneity* (*principium Heterogeneitatis*), is — That every concept contains other concepts under it; and, therefore, when divided proximately, we descend always to other concepts, but never to individuals; in other words, things the most homogeneous — similar — must, in certain respects, be heterogeneous — dissimilar.

[Side note: The two general laws by which Subordination and Coördination, under Extension, are regulated — viz., of Homogeneity and Heterogeneity.]

"Of these two laws, the former, as the principle which enables, and in fact compels, us to rise from species to genus, is that which determines the process of Generification; and the latter, as the principle which enables, and in fact compels, us to find always species under a genus, is that which regulates the process of Specification. The second of these laws, it is evident, is only true ideally, only true in theory. The infinite divisibility of concepts, like the infinite divisibility of space and time, exists only in speculation. And that it is theoretically valid, will be manifest, if we take two similar concepts, that is, two concepts with a small difference: let us then clearly represent to ourselves this difference, and we shall find that how small soever it may be, we can always conceive it still less, without being nothing, that is, we can divide it *ad infinitum;* but as each of these infinitesimally diverging differences affords always the condition of new species, it is evident that we can never end, that is, reach the individual, except *per saltum.*

§ 51. "When two or more concepts are compared together according to their Comprehension, they either coincide or they do not; that is, they either do or do not comprise the same characters. Notions are thus divided into *Identical* and *Different* (*conceptus identici et diversi*).

[Side note: Identical and Different Notions.]

The Identical are either absolutely or relatively the same. Of notions *Absolutely Identical* there are actually none; notions *Relatively Identical* are called, likewise, *Similar* or *Cognate* (*notiones similes, affines, cognatæ*); and if the common attributes, by which they are allied, be proximate and necessary, they are called *Reciprocating* or *Convertible* (*notiones reciprocæ, convertibiles*).

"In explanation of this paragraph, it is only necessary to say a word in regard to notions absolutely Identical. That such are impossible, is manifest. For, it being assumed that such exist, as absolutely identical, they necessarily have no differences by which they can be distinguished: but what are indiscernible can be known, neither as two concepts nor as two identical concepts; because we are, *ex hypothesi*, unable to discriminate the one from the other. They are, therefore, to us as one. Notions absolutely identical can only be admitted, if, abstracting our view altogether from the concepts, we denominate those notions *identical* which have reference to one and the same object, and which are conceived either by different minds, or by the same mind, but at different times. Their difference is, therefore, one not intrinsic and necessary, but only extrinsic and contingent. Taken in this sense, *Absolutely Identical* notions will be only a less correct expression for *Reciprocating* or *Convertible* notions.

_{Absolutely Identical Notions impossible.}

§ 52. "Considered under their Comprehension, concepts, again, in relation to each other, are said to be either *Congruent* or *Agreeing*, inasmuch as they may be connected in thought; or *Conflictive*, inasmuch as they cannot. The confliction constitutes the *Opposition* of notions (τὸ ἀντικεῖσθαι, *oppositio*). This is twofold: 1°. *Immediate* or *Contradictory Opposition*, called likewise *Repugnance* (τὸ ἀντιφατικῶς ἀντικεῖσθαι, ἀντίφασις, *oppositio immediata* sive *contradictoria, repugnantia*); and, 2°. *Mediate* or *Contrary Opposition* (τὸ ἐναντίως ἀντικεῖσθαι, ἐναντιότης, *oppositio mediata* vel *contraria*). The former emerges

_{Opposition of Concepts.}

when one concept abolishes (*tollit*), directly or by simple negation, what another establishes (*ponit*); the latter, when one concept does this not directly or by simple negation, but through the affirmation of something else.

<small>Identity and Agreement; Diversity and Confliction.</small> "Identity is not to be confounded with Agreement or Congruence, nor Diversity with Confliction. All identical concepts are, indeed, congruent; but all congruent notions are not identical. Thus *learning*, and *virtue*, *beauty* and *riches*, *magnanimity* and *stature*, are congruent notions, inasmuch as, in thinking a thing, they can easily be combined in the notion we form of it, although in themselves very different from each other. In like manner, all conflicting notions are diverse or different notions, for unless different, they could not be mutually conflictive, but on the other hand, all different concepts are not conflictive, but those only whose difference is so great that each involves the negation of the other; as, for example, *virtue* and *vice*, *beauty* and *deformity*, *wealth* and *poverty*. Thus these notions are by preëminence — κατ' ἐξοχὴν — said to be *opposed*, although it is true that, in thinking, we can oppose, or place in antithesis, not only different, but even identical, concepts.

<small>Contradictory and Contrary Opposition.</small> "To speak now of the distinction of Contradictory and Contrary Opposition, or of Contradiction and Contrariety; of these the former, Contradiction, is exemplified in the opposites — *yellow, not yellow; walking, not walking*. Here each notion is directly, immediately, and absolutely repugnant to the other — they are reciprocal negatives. This opposition is, therefore, properly called that of *Contradiction* or of *Repugnance;* and the opposing notions themselves are *contradictory* or *repugnant* notions — in a single word, *contradictories*. The latter, or Contrary Opposition, is exemplified in the opposites, *yellow, blue, red*, etc., *walking, standing, lying*, etc.

"In the case of Contradictory Opposition, there are only two conflictive attributes conceivable; and of these one or other must be predicated of the object thought. In the case of Contrary Opposition, on the other hand, more than two conflictive characters are possible, and it is not, therefore, necessary, that if one of these be not predicated of an object, any one other must. Thus, though I cannot at once sit and stand, and consequently *sitting* and *standing* are attributes each severally incompatible with the other; yet I may exist neither sitting nor standing — I may lie; but I must either sit or not sit, I must either stand or not stand, etc. Such, in general, are the oppositions of Contradiction and Contrariety."

§ 53. Concepts as compared with each other in respect of their Comprehension, are further distinguished into *Intrinsic* and *Extrinsic*. The former are made up of those attributes which are presented to Thought as its view is turned from the object inwardly to its parts. These attributes are of the proper, inner being or essence of the object; and, severally considered, are called *Essentials*, or *Internal Denominations* (οὐσιώδη, *essentialia, denominationes internæ, intrinsicæ*), and conjunctly, the *Essence* (οὐσία, *essentia*). The latter, on the contrary, consist of those attributes which are presented to thought as its view is turned outward from the object to other objects around. These attributes of external relation are styled *Accidents*, or *Extrinsic Denominations* (συμβεβηκότα, *accidentia, denominationes externæ* or *extrinsicæ*). Intrinsic Notions.

§ 54. "Further, in respect of their Comprehension, no less than of their Extension, notions stand to each other in a relation of Containing and Contained; and this relation, which, in the one quantity (extension) is styled that of *Subordination*, may in the other (comprehension), for distinction's sake, be styled that of *Involution*. *Co-ordination* is a term which may be applied in either quantity, being the relation alike in both of Part to Complementary Part. Involution and Coördination.

"In the quantity of comprehension, one notion is involved

in another, when it forms a part of the sum total of characters, which together constitute the comprehension of that other; and two notions are in this quantity coördinated, when, while neither comprehends the other, both are immediately comprehended in the same lower concept.

"Thus the notion of the individual *Socrates* contains in it, besides a multitude of others, the characters of *son of Sophroniscus, Athenian, Greek, European, man, animal, organized being,* etc. But these notions, these characters, are not all equally proximate and immediate; some are only given in and through others. Thus the character *Athenian* is applicable to Socrates only in and through that of *son of Sophroniscus* — the character of *Greek*, only in and through that of *Athenian* — the character of *European*, only in and through that of *Greek* — and so forth; in other words, Socrates is an Athenian only as the son of Sophroniscus, only a Greek as an Athenian, only a European as a Greek, only a man as a European, only an animal as a man, only an organized being as an animal. Those characters, therefore, that are given in and through others, stand to these others in relation of parts to wholes; and it is only on the principle — Part of the part is a part of the whole, that the remoter parts are the parts of the primary whole. Thus, if we know that the individual *Socrates* comprehends the character *son of Sophroniscus,* and that the character *son of Sophroniscus* comprehends the character *Athenian;* we are then warranted in saying that *Socrates* comprehends *Athenian,* in other words, that *Socrates* is an *Athenian*. The example here taken is too simple to show in what manner our notions are originally evolved out of the more complex into the more simple, and that the progress of science is nothing more than a progressive unfolding into distinct consciousness of the various elements comprehended in the characters, originally known to us in their vague or confused totality."

CHAPTER VI.

THE PRODUCTS OF THOUGHT. — III. REASONINGS.

§ 55. THE Third gradation of Thought is the Reasoning. Like the Concept, it is derived from the Judgment. It differs from the Concept in its form, as, unlike that, it retains the full forms of the Judgment, and accordingly, also, to a certain extent, it differs from it in the mode of its derivation. It differs from the Judgment proper in this respect, that it is a derivation from a Judgment — a traced movement of Thought, superadded to that which constitutes the Judgment. It is not the derived Judgment, not the mere terminus, the point at the end of the line over which the Thought has moved, but the line itself as traced in the movement of the Thought. When viewed as a resultant product of Thought, therefore, it must be regarded as the track of Thought left marked by the movement, not the mere attained object or goal of the movement, which is nothing more than a Judgment. We are carefully to distinguish, therefore, a Reasoning from the Conclusion — from the Judgment which is attained by the reasoning. *Reasoning — what it is.*

A REASONING, thus, is a derivation of a Judgment from another Judgment or Judgments.

§ 56. The term *Reasoning* is ambiguously employed to denote both the act, and, also, the product of the act. In its different gradations, this process of Thought has obtained a variety of other designations, which may here for convenience be summarily enumerated and explained. *Denominations of the process.*

" Considered as an act, Reasoning, or Discourse of Reason

(τὸ λογίζεσθαι, λογισμός, διάνοια, τὸ διανοεῖσθαι), is, likewise, called the act or process of *Argumentation (argumentationis),* of *Ratiocination (ratiocinationis,)* of *Inference* or *Illation (inferendi),* of *Collecting (colligendi),* of *Concluding (concludendi),* of *Syllogizing* (τοῦ συλλογίζεσθαι, barbarously *syllogisandi*). The term *Reasoning* is likewise given to the product of the act; and a reasoning in this sense (*ratiocinatio, ratiocinium*) is likewise called an *Argumentation (argumentatio)*; also, frequently, an *Argument (argumentum),* an *Inference* or *Illation (illatio),* a *Collection (collectio),* a *Conclusion (conclusio, συμπέρασμα),* and, finally, a *Syllogism* (συλλογισμός).

Terms by which the process of Reasoning is denominated.

Reasoning. Ratiocination.

"*Reasoning* is a modification from the French *raisonner* (and this a derivation from the Latin *ratio*), and corresponds to *ratiocinatio*, which has indeed been immediately transferred into our language under the form of *ratiocination*. *Ratiocination* denotes properly the process, but improperly, also, the product of reasoning; *Ratiocinium* marks exclusively the product. The original meaning of *ratio* was *computation*, and from the calculation of numbers it was transferred to the process of mediate comparison in general.

Discourse.

Discourse (discursus, διάνοια) indicates the operation of comparison, the running backward and forward between the characters or notes of objects (*discurrere inter notas,* διανοεῖσθαι). The terms *discourse* and *discursus,* διάνοια, are, however, often used for the reasoning process, strictly considered, and *discursive* is even applied to denote mediate, in opposition to intuitive, judgment, as is done by Milton. The compound term, *discourse of reason,* unambiguously marks its employment in this sense. *Argumentation* is derived from *argumentari*, which means *argumentis uti; argument* again, *argumentum* — what is assumed in order to argue something — is properly the middle notion in a reasoning — that through which the conclusion is established; and by the Latin Rhet-

Argumentation. Argument.

oricians it was defined, '*probabile inventum ad faciendam fidem.*' It is often, however, applied as coëxtensive with *argumentation*. *Inference* or *Illation* (from *infero*) indicates the carrying out into the last proposition what was virtually contained in the antecedent judgments. *To conclude* (*concludere*), again, signifies the act of connecting and shutting into the last proposition the two notions which stood apart in the two first. A *conclusion* (*conclusio*) is usually taken, in its strict or proper signification, to mean the last proposition of a reasoning; it is, sometimes, however, used to express the product of the whole process. *To syllogize* means to form syllogisms. *Syllogism* (συλλογισμός) seems originally, like *ratio*, to have denoted a *computation* — an *adding up;* and, like the greater part of the technical terms of Logic in general, was borrowed by Aristotle from the mathematicians. Συλλογισμός may, however, be considered as expressing only what the composition of the word denotes — *a collecting together;* for συλλογίζεσθαι comes from συλλέγειν, which signifies *to collect.* Finally, in Latin, a syllogism is called *collectio,* and to reason, *colligere.* This refers to the act of collecting, in the conclusion, the two notions scattered in the premises."

Inference.

To conclude.

Conclusion.

To Syllogize. Syllogism.

Collectio.

§ 57. A Reasoning is composed of two parts — the original Judgment or Judgments which are the original *datum* in the process, and the movement of the Thought in the process. As the *datum* is regarded as logically determining and preceding, it is called the *Antecedent*, and the other part, regarded as logically determined, or following, is called the *Consequent*. Its proper sign is *therefore*. These are the parts of a Reasoning regarded as an Integrate Whole.

Integrant Parts of a Reasoning. Antecedent and Consequent.

§ 58. The Antecedent in a Reasoning may consist of a single Judgment, or of a plurality of Judgments. If it consist of but one Judgment, the Reasoning is called an *Immediate Reasoning*. If the ante-

Divisions of Reasonings: Immediate; Mediate.

cedent consists of more than one Judgment, the Reasoning is called a *Mediate Reasoning*, or, more technically, a *Syllogism*.

Again, in a Mediate Reasoning, the Antecedent may consist of two, or of more than two, Judgments. In the former case there emerges the *Single Syllogism*; in the latter, the *Polysyllogism*, also called the *Sorites*.

<small>Syllogism; Sorites.</small>

Still further, in a Mediate Reasoning the derived Judgment may be mediated through the relations of the terms contained in the Antecedent, or through those of the copulas — that is, the reasoning may turn on proper Concepts as wholes and parts in relations to each other, or on proper Judgments. In the former case, there emerges the *Categorical Syllogism;* in the latter case, the so-called *Conditional Syllogism*.

<small>Categorical; Conditional.</small>

Once more, the reasoning may be fully expressed in the complete regular form of the Syllogism, or may be Elliptical, one or other of the several Judgments which form it being suppressed and only implied. A reasoning in which one of the Judgments is thus suppressed, is called an *Enthymeme*. This is the more common form of a reasoning in actual discourse. Accordingly, Aristotle tells us that the Enthymeme is the Rhetorical Syllogism.

<small>Enthymeme.</small>

An apparent relaxation of logical strictness characterizes this general division of Reasonings. It arises from the desire to retain the familiar nomenclature, while avoiding the error and confusion which attend it. Logicians have generally represented the Hypothetical and Disjunctive Syllogisms as differing from the Categorical in another respect than that here recognized. And this treatment has necessarily obscured and complicated the exposition of the proper characters of the several species. No real difficulty will, however, follow our continuing the old denominations; but certain explanations of the names will differ from those to be found in previous logical treatises.

§ 59. AN IMMEDIATE REASONING is an immediate derivation of a Judgment from another single Judgment; as, *Man is rational animal; therefore, Man is rational.* Immediate Reasonings.

The occasions and objects of our thinking often demand that the form of an attained Judgment be changed, so that the primitive Judgment shall be treated as a *datum*, or matter of Thought, yet matter having characters as a product of Thought that may be recognized as of its own originating, and therefore legitimate and valid for its further uses. It becomes important, therefore, to determine precisely the allowed limits and conditions of such transformation, so that the new Judgment must be recognized as valid. It will be expedient to recall here some of the fundamental principles and characters of Thought as already ascertained and expounded.

All Thought, then, proceeds under the relation of *Identity*. It is valid only as the principle of the Same and the Different — the Identical and the Non-identical validates it.

Moreover, as Thought is an activity continuing through time, as it moves on over the Same, the principle of repetition necessarily comes in, and, under the form of Synthesis, or its opposite, Analysis, exerts its sway over the movements of Thought. All valid Thought, accordingly, is under the relations of Quantity — of Whole and Parts, so that wheresoever these relations are given to Thought in any object or matter, Thought may move, and can move only when they are thus given. Quantity, in fact, is but identity identified — the result of repeated identifications.

Further, the only essential relationships in Quantity are the two relationships: (1) of Whole to Part, with its reciprocal of Part to Whole; and, (2) of Part to Part. All Thought must, to be valid or legitimate, proceed in one of these two relationships, in their positive or their negative forms; and all thought that is in these relations is so far valid — in other words, bears the character of necessary truth.

All relations, other than these two relations of Quantity — those of Whole to Part, and of Part to Part — are foreign to Thought; they are without its proper characters, the characters of necessary truth, and are termed, in distinction, Problematic, Contingent, Probable, Possible, according to the various degrees or kinds of modality. Hence the necessity of keeping in mind clearly the boundaries between the mere *datum*, or matter of Thought, and Thought itself. Only so far as we intelligently observe this distinction, can we accept any result in our thought as necessarily valid.

Once more, the *data*, the objects of Thought, are greatly diversified. The applications of Thought, therefore, to attain the objects of our thinking, must accept these diversities in the essential qualities of its matter. It can do this, however, only within the limitations of its own proper sphere; only, therefore, under the limitations of Quantity. It may, thus, assume the different kinds of Whole that are given to it, which, as we have seen, are the Integral, the Substantial, and the Causal; and in order to any trustworthy results in the interest of truth, it must be able to discriminate these different kinds of Whole, and thus avoid confounding them in its movements.

This recapitulation of the principles of Thought will guide us in the enumeration of the changes possible by thought in a given Judgment, that shall be legitimate changes, and so bear the characters of necessary truth.

§ 60. The first kind of Immediate Reasonings is that of *Conversion*, in which the terms of the original Judgment, its Subject and Predicate, are simply transposed. Its formula is: $A = B$; *therefore*, $B = A$. The primitive Judgment is called *the Convertend;* the derived Judgment, *the Converse.*

Conversion.

The validity of this Reasoning is too obvious to require extended proof or illustration. It has been already observed that it is not Thought itself, but the occasion or the design of Thought, which determines which of the two objects presented to it shall be viewed as subject and which as predicate. Thought itself only identifies the two. It is, consequently, indifferent to Thought which of the two be the occasion or starting point. The conversion of a Judgment cannot, accordingly, in any way affect its validity.

The Law of Identity, which presides over every movement of Thought, here prescribes that there be no change in the quality of the Judgment, and none in the kind of Whole, that is, in the quantity of either term. The specification of the diverse applications of this Law in the conversion of a Judgment, with the indications of the necessity for a peculiarly careful attention to it in certain cases, will properly come under consideration in 'the Second Part of Logical science — the Doctrine of Methodology.

§ 61. The second kind of Immediate Reasonings is that by *Quantitative Restriction*, in which one or both of the terms, regarded as wholes, are changed to a logical part or parts. Its formula is: *A is B, therefore some A is B.* The primitive Judgment is called *the Restringend;* the derived Judgment, *the Restricted.* <small>Quantitative Restriction.</small>

The logical validity of this form of Immediate Reasoning is equally obvious as that of the first kind by Conversion. Every whole is made up of like parts, each one of which may be recognized as identical, in some respect, with any other coördinate part. If the whole, therefore, is identified with another whole, any part may be identified with any like part of the second whole.

If the Restriction is confined to but one of the terms, either the Subject or the Predicate, it is called *Unilateral;* if extended to both terms, it is called *Bilateral.*

Examples of Unilateral Restriction in Quantity are —

1. Of Subject: *Man is rational animal; therefore, Socrates is rational animal.*

2. Of Predicate: *Man is rational animal; therefore, man is rational.*

Of Bilateral: *Man is rational animal; therefore, Socrates is rational.*

The Law that governs in this movement of Thought, is that of Identity as applied to the relation of Part to Whole. What is true of the Whole distributively is true of every part.

§ 62. The third kind of Immediate Reasonings is that by *Modal Restriction*, in which the modal energy of the Judgment is reduced; as, *A must be B; therefore, A is B.*

<small>Modal Restriction.</small>

Nothing need be said to illustrate the validity of this process of Thought. We have distinguished two kinds of Modified Judgment, — the Necessary, where the ground of the Judgment is given as lying in the Thought itself; and the Problematic, where the ground of the Judgment lies out of the proper sphere of Thought. The other kind of Judgment given by this distinction is, of course, the unmodified, or the simple Assertory. Now it is plain that the Necessary must always involve both the Problematic and the Assertory, inasmuch as if Thought has once identified, its identification being absolute and sovereign throughout the realms of Thought, the terms it has once identified in a necessary Judgment are ever and everywhere, whether simply or problematically, identified; as, $3 + 1 = 4$ being a necessary Judgment, these terms may with absolute validity be accepted as identical in any matter foreign to Thought — any contingent matter.

The governing Law in this process of Thought is, as in the last enumerated, that of Identity as applied to the relation of Part to Whole. Here the whole is one of Degree or Intensity, as it lies in the judging act, not in the matter judged. The stronger ever includes the weaker.

§ 63. The fourth kind of Immediate Reasonings is by *Transference*, in which some character of the Thought in the copula is transferred to the matter in the terms; as, *A is not B; therefore, A is non-B.*

<small>Transference.</small>

This process of Thought, although generally recognized by logicians as of unquestioned validity, evidently lacks the character of perfectly pure Thought. It is not necessarily valid, because it accepts the intermingling of Thought with its matter as legitimate, whereas to confound the qualities of the thought with those of its matter is precisely the grand source of error against which the Science of Logic chiefly seeks to guard. That such a transference is not of itself legitimate will be apparent from a single example. Substitute in the formula given, for *A*, *a stone*, and for *B*, *vertebrate;* we shall then have the reasoning: *A stone is not vertebrate; therefore, it is non-vertebrate;* that is, *invertebrate.* It is obvious that, in the transference, we have changed the Thought from being purely negative in its quality to one having something of a positive character. Our conclusion is a palpable falsity, as we have ranked *a stone* among the class of invertebrates. We must not at once conclude that this process is wholly extra-logical. It is assuredly a process of Thought; and nothing that concerns Thought can be regarded as extra-logical. It is the part of logic to separate the element of pure Thought from the hybrid process, and so indicate precisely what there is of logical validity in it. Certainly there is a semblance of legitimacy in the process, else logicians would not so universally have accepted it without question, for we find it thus accepted by logical purists of the first degree, who have insisted upon exterminating from the science every weed of matter, and upon keeping the field entirely free to the purest forms of Thought. It will not be difficult to discriminate the matter from the form here, and thus to attain the proper criteria for the validity of such a process in our thinking.

We have found the relations of Whole and Parts to be the proper relations of Thought. Any procedure under these relations is a legitimate and valid procedure of pure Thought. If, consequently, any matter given to Thought be given in these relations, then Thought can move on in necessary certainty as pure Thought. So far, then, as the transfer of a quality of the copula from it to either of the terms is within this relation of Whole and Part, it is valid. Thus, substituting for *B*, in the example given, a term thought as a Whole, of which *vertebrate* and *invertebrate* are logically Complementary Parts, and for *A*, a term given as a part of that Whole, say *butterfly*, then the transference of the negative becomes valid — we can conclude, *Butterfly is invertebrate*. We have now avoided the intermingling of thought and matter; the movement has been within the proper sphere of Thought; from the proper field of a Judgment, in fact, to that of a Concept. The obvious limitation on this mode of reasoning, thus, is that the first form (B) of the term to which the quality of the Judgment is transferred be recognized as a part complementary of the second form (non-B), and that the other term (A) be recognized as lesser part of one or the other of these complementary parts.

The logical validity of the Thought as thus regulated is obvious on the principle that in a given whole any one part is complementary of the rest, and reciprocally the rest is complementary of it; and that any lower part of that whole must belong to one of these complementary parts. If, thus, there be a whole *C*, of which *A* and *B* are parts, and *B* and *non-B* are the two complements of that whole, if *A* is not *B*, it necessarily is *non-B*. Otherwise; *A* being some part of *C*, and *B* and *non-B* being also complementary parts of *C*, if *A* is not *B*, it must be *non-B*.

This form of Immediate Reasoning, by transference of Quality from the copula to one of the terms, is legitimate in each species of Wholes. Thus, in a Spacial Whole, if by *A* and *B* in the formula given be understood respectively halves of a square bisected by a diagonal, we shall have: *This half* — *A* — *is not B; therefore, it is non-B.*

So in a Substantial Whole; if *rational* and *animal* be parts, making up the same whole, *man;* then *if* (*A*) *animal is not* (*B*) *rational, it is* (*non-B*) *non-rational;* or (*A*) an-

imal is not (*B*) *rational;* therefore, (*A*) *animal is* (*non-B*) *non-rational,* that is, *irrational.*

In the same way, in a Causal Whole, if a magnet be viewed as a cause acting, the parts through which are attraction and repulsion complementary of each other, so that *magnet* in this use of the term, as a cause only, attracts or repels, then we may reason: if this acting magnet does not attract, then it does *non-attract,* that is, *repel;* — *non-attracting* being here *repelling,* or the necessary alternative, that is, the complementary part of *attracting* in an acting magnet.

Reasonings by Transference are of two varieties. 1. The proper Quality of the copula may be transferred to one of the terms; as, *Mind is not material; therefore, it is immaterial; Necessity does not belong to rational being; therefore, non-necessity,* that is, *Freedom, belongs to rational being.*

Transference. 1. Qualitative; 2. Modal.

2. The Modality of the copula may be transferred to one of the terms; as, *Rain may fall to-morrow; therefore, Rain is a possible event to-morrow.*

The exposition given so far of this form of Immediate Reasoning has, for the sake of clearness, proceeded in forms of illustration appropriate strictly and throughout only to the first of these varieties. The movement of Thought we found to be valid, inasmuch as Thought did not move out of its own sphere — kept within its own proper relationships of Whole and Part, or more specifically within relations of Contradictory Disjunction. It is equally valid in the second variety, if only a proper modality of Thought be transferred. If the derived Judgment be interpreted as under a modality of Thought, the reasoning is obviously not universally, that is, necessarily, valid. Thus, in regions where rain is only in one part of the year, although a stranger ignorant of the peculiarities of the climate might reason with himself, so far as thought can go: *Rain may fall to-morrow; therefore, Rain is a possible event to-morrow,* it would be a false conclusion, if the modal word *possible* were to be interpreted as expressive of physical modality. Only so far as proper modality of thought, can modality, thus, be transferred from the copula to the terms — from the thought to the matter.

In order to effect the transference legitimately, it may be necessary to bring into the antecedent another Judgment, so that we shall have a Mediate Reasoning. Thus, in the first case, we may need to add for a logical antecedent to the Judgment, *A is not B*, the Judgment, *A is part of B, or of non-B*. Then the conclusion is legitimated.

§ 64. The fifth kind of Immediate Reasoning is that of *Disjunction*. From a Disjunctive Judgment we may immediately infer both, (1.) That the disjunct members are not the same; and, (2.) That the one is contradictory of the other. Thus from *A is either B or C*, we may immediately infer either, (1.) *That B is not C*; or, (2.) *That non-B is C*. Or *Angles are right, acute, or obtuse;* therefore, (1.) *Right angles are neither acute nor obtuse;* and, (2.) *No acute angle is either right or obtuse.*

<small>Disjunction.</small>

The validity of this reasoning is evident from the nature of Disjunction, which is the principle of the relation of Part and Complementary Part.

§ 65. The sixth kind of Immediate Reasoning is that of *Composition*, in which, from several Judgments with the same term either as subject or predicate, a Judgment may be derived in which, with this term remaining, the other term shall be the sum of the other terms. Thus, if *A is B*, and *C is B*, then $A + C$ *is B*; or, *If animals are organic and vegetables are organic, then animals and vegetables*, that is, *all living beings, are organic*. *If all body has length, and all body has breadth, and all body has depth; then all body has length, breadth, and depth*, that is, *is solid*.

<small>Composition.</small>

The principle of this kind of Immediate Reasoning is obviously that of the Concept. No further illustration of its nature or validity is necessary.

§ 66. Mediate Reasonings we have distinguished into two classes, according as they embrace or not new matter not in the primitive Judgment. Those of

<small>Categorical Syllogism.</small>

the first class in which new matter is introduced, if the new matter be in a single term of a single new Judgment, are called *Categorical Syllogisms*. We thus have the following definition : —

A SINGLE CATEGORICAL SYLLOGISM is one whose antecedent member contains two Judgments, to which but one term in each is common, the other being different ; as, *Man is mortal; Caius is a man; therefore, Caius is mortal.* Its Definition.

In this example, the first Judgment in the antecedent member of the Reasoning contains for its matter the terms *man* and *mortal;* the second Judgment contains, besides the term *man* in the first, new matter in the term *Caius.*

The nature of this movement of Thought it will not be difficult to render intelligible. A primitive condition of Thought we have found to be a Law imposing upon it, if it move at all, the necessity of recognizing the identity or the non-identity of any two objects presented to it. Now as the essential quality of Intelligence is clearness, it may be impossible for Thought to move at all, to recognize identity or non-identity, that is, affirm sameness or difference, for want of light. It necessarily, therefore, remains in doubt. A new cognition in the form of another Judgment may afford the requisite light, and enable the Thought to move from the state of doubt to that of a determinate Judgment.

This new enlightening Judgment, however, must stand in a certain definite relation to the two terms that were originally presented to be identified or differenced ; and this relation must be one that lies within the sphere of Thought ; — must be, in other words, a relation of Quantity — of Whole to Part, or of Part to Part. If the two original terms, say *A* and *C*, were, one of them, *A*, a whole of which another term *B* were a part, and *B* also were a whole of which *C* were a part, then Thought could at once move in its own sphere of Quantity and recognize *C*, inasmuch as it is a part of *B*, as also a part of *A* of which *B* is a part ; in other words conclude that, if C is a part of B, and B is a part of A, C is a part of A. This may perhaps be better illustrated in a concrete example. We may have the two objects of thought given to us, of *sponge* and *animal;* and may be unable for want of light to recognize any identity between them so as to be warranted in affirming that the sponge is an animal, or in affirming that a sponge is not an animal — we stand in doubt. But by the aid of new Judgments, as that the sponge is *sentient*, and that all sentient beings are animal, this doubt is removed, as we recognize that, the sponge being a part of sentient beings and sentient beings a part of animal, the sponge must be part also of animal — that sponge is identical with part of animal.

This illustration characterizes but one of the two great classes of Mediate Reasonings — the so-called *Deductive* Reasonings or Syllogisms. Logicians have generally limited their view to this species, giving but incidental consideration to the other. Indeed, many, like Dr. Whately, have endeavored to subordinate all forms of Reasoning to the Deductive Syllogism, and with him the terms Reasoning and Syllogism are convertible. Sir William Hamilton has exposed the error of those views, but has failed to elaborate any trustworthy scheme that should comprehend all reasoning. Indeed, he seems to have utterly overlooked one of the two fundamental relationships in Thought. While recognizing all Thought as necessarily proceeding in the relations of Quantity, he has seemed to regard but one specific relation among them, viz: that between the Whole and Part; or, more exactly, perhaps, he makes of this single relation two — that from the Whole to the Part, and the converse, from the Part to the Whole, forgetting that these two supposed relations are necessarily one in Thought, the movement being indifferent so far as Thought is concerned, in the one direction or in the other, and that it is the object or proposed aim in thinking, the occasion external to the thought, that determines the direction of the movement, whether from this goal or from that, from the Whole or from the Part. The relationship between the Whole and the Part, thus, is the same, whether we think that the Whole contains the Part, or that the Part is contained in the Whole ; and the distinction of Hamilton is fallacious or utterly futile. But there is another entirely distinguishable relation of Quantity — that of Part to Part. Only as we admit this relation between part and complementary part in every whole, can we admit any disjunction in Thought — any recognition of Same and Different. The very notion of Difference implies a necessary relationship between Parts. This relation between Part and Complementary part, given at once and necessarily with the relation of Whole and Part, permeates Thought everywhere as its validating condition.

§ 67. Categorical Syllogisms are divided into two classes in respect of the two different directions in which Thought may move. If the movement be between the two relatives of Quantity, Whole and Part, the Syllogism is called *Deductive*. If, on the other hand, the movement of Thought be between relative Part and Part, the Syllogism is called *Inductive*. A Syllogism of either class may alike proceed either in Comprehensive or in Extensive Quantity.

§ 68. A DEDUCTIVE SYLLOGISM is a Mediate Reasoning in which the movement of Thought is from a Whole to a Part, mediated through a middle term, which is, respectively, a part of that whole and a whole of that part; as, *Man is mortal; Caius is a man; therefore, Caius is mortal.*

As the Deductive Syllogism is a Mediate Reasoning, its *datum* must consist of two Judgments, which, as given to Thought, are not of course at all validated by the Reasoning. They must be regarded consequently as only assumed for the Reasoning, or must rest on evidence foreign to it. But the movement of Thought in itself may be valid, although the given Judgments are false; just as an arithmetical process may be correct, although applied to unreal objects.

These two given Judgments constitute the *Antecedent;* as

the derived Judgment is the *Consequent* of the Reasoning. From their naturally preceding the Consequent, they are called the *Premises* (*Propositiones præmissæ*).

As might be supposed, not any two Judgments taken fortuitously can be accepted as premises in the same Reasoning. In the first place, both of the Judgments must contain the same term in common, the other term in each being different. In the next place, this term that is common to the two Judgments, must be a *part* in relation to the remaining term in one Judgment, and, also, a *whole* in relation to the remaining term in the other Judgment. Thus, in the example given, the term *man* is a part of the class *mortal*, but a whole class of which *Caius* is part. From its bearing this twofold relation to the remaining terms in the premises, of part to one, and of whole to the other, this common term is called the *Middle Term;* and the other terms are called the *Extremes (extrema,* ἄκρα*).* When this relation exists, and only then, can two judgments be accepted as premises; and, to use the expression of Aristotle, " when the three terms are so related to one another that the last is in the middle as a whole, and the middle is or is not in the first as a whole, a perfect syllogism necessarily emerges."

Of the Extremes, that which as a whole contains the Middle Term is called the *Major Term;* and that which is contained in or under the Middle, is called the *Minor Term.*

A convenient mode of designating the Terms is by the use of the letters W, P, and M: W denoting the Major Term; P, the Minor; and M, the Middle.

The very nature of the process excludes the possibility of there being more than these three terms in a single Deductive Reasoning — the two Extremes being compared through the Middle Term. A Term, it must be recollected, may consist of several words; they must, however, constitute one object of thought, and so be capable of being used as a subject or as a predicate. On the other hand, if a single word be used in different meanings in the several propositions which compose the Syllogism, we have, under the guise of three, in reality more than three, terms. This is the nature of the fallacy of four terms, *quaternio terminorum*. As in the Syllogism:

Animals are void of reason;
Man is an animal;
Therefore, man is void of reason.

Here the middle term, *animal*, is used in the Major premise as synonymous with *brute*, a conspecies of *man*, and so excluding it. In the Minor premise it is used to denote a genus containing under it the two species, *rational* and *irrational;* — as, in other words, including *man*. There are, thus, really two different objects of thought, two logical terms presented in the two premises by the same word — *animal*.

In respect of the Propositions, it is equally clear that there must be one showing the relation between the Major term and the Middle term — a proper Sumption; that there must be another showing the relation between the Middle and the Minor — a proper Subsumption; and, moreover, a Conclusion, showing the relation between the Major and the Minor.

The Hindoo system seems to have recognized five propositions, called the Assertion, the Reason, the Proposition, the Assumption, and the Deduction in a Reasoning: as "1. The mountain has fire; 2. For it has smoke; 3. But all that has smoke has fire; 4. And the mountain has smoke; 5. Therefore, the mountain has fire." But it is apparent that the first proposition, which is called the Assertion, is the same as the fifth, the Deduction or Conclusion; and the second, called the Reason, is the same as the fourth, called the Assumption. There are, in fact, only three propositions entering into the Reasoning proper. The premises must be regarded for the Reasoning as assumed; they are the *data* to Thought in its movement.

Of the two premises, that one which enounces the relation of the Major term to the Middle, is called the *Major Premise*, also the *Sumption* (*propositio major, sumptio major, sumptio, thesis*). The other of the premises which enounces the relation of the Minor Term to the Middle, is called the *Minor Premise*, also the *Subsumption* (*propositio minor, assumptio, subsumptum, subsumptio, sumptio minor*). It is not, of course, the order in which the premises are placed in the Syllogism which determines the one to be the Major, the other to be the Minor Premise. The order is merely of the form, the verbal expression, and does not concern the thought. Which shall precede is, hence, a matter of indifference so far as the essential character of the reasoning is concerned.

The Consequent is the derived Judgment — the result or goal of the Reasoning. It enounces the relation of the Minor term to the Major, and is called the *Conclusion* (*conclúsio, collectio,* συμπέρασμα). It is usually, in formal and fully stated Syllogisms, designated by the Conjunction, *therefore*, or by synonymous expressions, as *consequently*, and the like.

Logicians, recognizing only Extensive Quantity, and having accepted the division of Propositions into the four kinds, Universal Affirmative, Particular Affirmative, Universal Negative, and Particular Negative, as their ruling division, have connected the consideration of Quantity with that of Quality in their formal treatment of the Syllogism. It has been, accordingly, prescribed by them that the Sumption must be definite, that is, universal or single, while the Subsumption may be in either Quantity, definite or indefinite. But this teaching is all unnecessary, and tends to confuse and to mislead. The one principle is that each term must in each several proposition be taken in the same meaning in respect of Quantity, as well as in respect of nature of object denoted by it. If the Minor term be restricted by any limiting word, as *some, few*, or the like, while it is yet recognized in the Syllogism as being contained unrestricted in the Middle, we have, in fact, a mixed reasoning — a proper mediate reasoning combined with an immediate reasoning of the Restrictive Class. It is clear we cannot reason : *Some men are learned ; Caius is a man ; therefore, Caius is learned,* simply because the

Middle term in the Sumption is not used in the same extent of meaning as in the Subsumption. There are really four terms. When we have a Subsumption in Particular Quantity, so-called, as, for example, *Man is mortal ; some rational beings are men;* obviously we cannot conclude : *therefore, rational beings are mortal;* for we have changed the meaning of the Minor term, using it in a wider extent in the Conclusion, and a narrower in the Subsumption. But commonly, if the Minor term be used in a wider extent of meaning in the Subsumption than in the Conclusion, as, *Man is mortal ; philosophers are men ; therefore, some philosophers are mortal,* we have a valid conclusion, it is true, but a mixed reasoning, as just stated.

Logicians have enounced the comprehensive rule for the conclusion, thus : The Conclusion must always follow the weaker or worser part, the negative and the particular being regarded as the weaker or the worser in respect of the affirmative and the universal.

The general relations of the several judgments which compose a Deductive Reasoning to one another, moreover, logicians have illustrated to the eye by means of three unequal circles, the largest of which represents the Major term, the smallest the Minor, and the intermediate the Middle term. If we call them respectively W, P, and M, then it will readily be seen if the largest circle, W, include the middle circle, M, and if, also, M include the least circle, P, the largest circle, W, must include the least circle, P.

§ 69. As the relation of Whole and Part may exist in either of the two kinds of Logical Quantity, Extension or Comprehension, it is obvious we may have two kinds of Deductive Syllogism, the *Extensive* and the *Comprehensive* or *Intensive*. Two kinds of Deductive Syllogism.

In the Extensive form, the Middle is said to be contained *under* the Major term, and to contain *under* it the Minor term. In the Intensive form, the Middle is said to be contained *in* the Major term, and to contain *in* it 1. Extensive.
2. Intensive.

the Minor term. The Syllogism, as ordinarily expressed, may be explicated in either Quantity. Thus in the Syllogism, *Man is mortal; Caius is a man; therefore, Caius is mortal,* if we explicate it as in Extensive Quantity, we shall have the following:

The Middle term, *man,* is contained under the Major term, *mortal;* that is, *man* is a part of the class *mortal:*

The Minor term, *Caius,* is contained under the Middle term, *man;* that is, *Caius* is a part of the class *man:*

Therefore, the Minor term, *Caius,* is contained under the Major term, *mortal;* that is, *Caius* is a part of the class *mortal.*

If, again, the Syllogism be construed as in Intensive Quantity, the explication will be as follows:

The Major term, *Caius,* contains in it the Middle Term, *man;* that is, the complement of attributes, *Caius,* contains in it, as part, the complement of attributes, *man:*

The Middle term, *man,* contains in it the Minor term, *mortal;* that is, the attribute, *man,* contains in it, as part, the attribute *mortal:*

Therefore, the Major term, *Caius,* contains in it the Minor term, *mortal;* that is, the complement of attributes, *Caius,* contains in it as part the attribute *mortal.*

It will be noticed that the term *man* is the Middle term in each explication; but the two other terms change places;— the Major term in the Extensive form becoming the Minor in the Intensive; and the Minor in the former becoming the Major in the latter. Accordingly, the Major premise, which in the Extensive form compares the Major term, *mortal,* with the Middle term, *man,* in the Intensive form compares *Caius,* as the Major term, with the Middle; and a corresponding change takes place in the Minor premise. In other words, the Premises change with the changed relations of the Extremes to the Middle term.

It will also be seen that the one may easily be converted into the other without affecting the validity of the reasoning. But the formula *W contains M; M contains P; therefore,*

W contains P, is the one universal formula for all Affirmative Categorical Syllogisms in either quantity. This, however, may be stated in the passive form, but then prepositions come into use, and the kind of quantity is at once indicated by them. Thus, in Extensive Quantity, it would be expressed: *M is contained under W; P is contained under M; therefore, P is contained under W.* While, in Intensive Quantity, we should have: *M is contained in W; P is contained in M; therefore, P is contained in W.*

In Extensive Quantity, it will be recollected, a term always denotes a class or a part of a class; while in Intensive Quantity it denotes an attribute or a complement of attributes. And the formula of the Categorical Deductive Syllogism would be explicated in Extensive Quantity thus:

1. *Affirmative:* The class W contains under it the class M; the class M contains under it the class or individual P; therefore, the class W contains under it the class or individual P.

2. *Negative:* The class W does not contain under it, entirely excludes, the class M; the class M contains under it the class or individual P; therefore, the class W does not contain under it the class or individual P.

In Intensive Quantity it would be explicated thus:

1. *Affirmative:* The attribute W contains in it as part the attribute M; the attribute M contains in it as part the attribute P; therefore, the attribute W contains in it as part the attribute P.

2. *Negative:* The attribute W contains in it the attribute M; the attribute M does not contain in it, entirely excludes, the attribute P; therefore, the attribute W does not contain the attribute P.

While the entire reasoning as expressed in the ordinary forms of discourse may be explicated in either quantity, it would plainly be incorrect to explicate a part of it in one quantity and the rest in the other quantity;— to explicate, for instance, one premise in Extensive Quantity, and the other premise or the conclusion in Intensive Quantity.

112 PURE LOGIC.

§ 70. An INDUCTIVE SYLLOGISM is a Mediate Reasoning, in which the movement of Thought is from a given part to its complementary part; as, *Affirmation is Thought; but negation is the complementary of affirmation; therefore, negation is Thought: P is W; C is complementary of P; therefore, C is W.*

Induction defined.

We have found two general relationships in Thought as a relative cognition, each equally primitive and necessary, coördinate, and, moreover, conditioning each the other. They stand, indeed, in this respect, precisely on the footing of the two Laws of Identity and Contradiction in their relations to the two Laws of Disjunction and Exclusion. The one relationship is that of Whole to Part; the other is that of Part to Part. That there is a part, involves the necessity of there being another part or parts, which one part or which several parts are the complement of the first. We have, then, standing side by side with the principle that the whole contains its parts, the coördinate principle that *a part necessitates in Thought its complementary part.*

Explication.

Now this complementary part is, in some respects, identical with the other part; in other respects it is different from it. Just so far as they are parts of the same whole they are identical; but so far as they are complementary of each other they are different. If two triangles are parts of the same square bisected through its opposite angles, they are identical in respect of length of sides, angles, surface; they are different in being complementary parts, the one lying in one direction from the bisecting line, the other in the opposite direction from that line; in short, they are as complementary to each other, related as positive or affirmative and negative in reference to the principle of bisection. What is thus evident in an Integrate Whole, is equally true in the Whole of Substance. If *rational* and *animal* are the component parts of *man*, then so far as they are parts of the same whole, they are identical; that is, if as a part of *man*, as *living substance, rational* is *living*, we necessarily infer that *animal*, as such part, is also *living*. As complementary of each other they are different; *animal* is the *irrational* part of *man*. In like manner, in a Causal Whole, if *ashes* and *smoke* are complementary parts of the effect of combustion conceived as a whole, then, in some respects — for instance, as products of combustion — they are identical; in other respects, as complementary, they are different; one is the solid, the other is the non-solid — the gaseous product of combustion. In a logical Whole of Extension, the two species which in the strict dichotomous division make up its parts, are of course complementary of each other. They are identical in so far as they participate in the whole; they are different in so far as they are conspecies. Interpreting *animal* thus in Extensive Quantity, that is, as denoting a class, we have, as two species contained under it, *rational animals* and *irrational animals*, that is, *men* and *brutes*. Now whatever is true of *men* so far as *animal*, is true of *brutes* so far as *animal*. This follows, indeed, necessarily, from the very nature of a Concept. On the other hand, in so far as they are conspecies, and accordingly complementary of each other, they are different. In so far as *man* is *rational*, *man* is different from *brute*. And it is plain that whatever part of what is merely *animal* is in *man* must belong to whatever like part is *animal* in *brute*; while whatever part of *rational* is found in *man* differs from whatever like part pertains to *brute*. And here, in strictly logical or dichotomous division, difference is contradiction; so that we may infer that if *man* has a digestive system necessarily as *animal*, *brute* has, as *animal*, a like system; and on the contrary, if as *rational* man is *free*, *brute* as *irrational* is *not free*. The same view holds good of Intensive Quantity so obviously as to require no distinct consideration. The validity of this kind of thought here discovers its ready and certain test. If our Concepts in which we reason are valid, our Induction is so likewise.

Such is the simple nature of all Induction as a process of

Thought. It is a clearly distinguishable process from Deduction, and is precisely coördinate with that process — its exact complement as a derivation of a Judgment. It gives the character of absolute, apodictic certainty to its result. Extremely simple as it is, it imparts all there is of certainty or of probability to that infinite diversity of inferences in scientific investigations, in art-contrivances, in common life, which we call by this name of Induction — a far wider movement of thought, as already observed, and far more important, every way, than its coördinate, Deduction. It is to that, what Addition is to Subtraction in Arithmetic; and the two, Induction and Deduction, are to all our multifarious thinking what Addition and Subtraction are to all the possible and complicated operations in the limitless sphere of numerical calculation. And as no such calculation has any validity except on the principle that *one* added to *one* equals *two*, so all our induction in its multifarious forms is valid only on the principle that *a part* necessitates its *complement*. We discover, here, moreover, an exact analogy to the logical process of Disjunction. While Logic strictly validates only Contradictory Opposition in Disjunction, as of absolute necessary certainty, yet it shows how Contrary Disjunction may be validated by reduction to Contradictory, and thus enables us to secure the character of truth to those concise and complicated movements in which Thought in common life generally proceeds, just as Multiplication is a concise complicated process of Addition. So in Induction, while Logic strictly accepts only the immediate relationship in thought of Part and its Complementary Part, it yet shows how far this movement may be validated in the relationship of any Part to any other of manifold Parts in the same Whole.

As in Deduction, in precise logical strictness, we can reason only step by step down the gradations of parts, in regular succession, and must always be able, in order to validate our reasoning, to indicate each gradation, but yet may reason to a remote part of a part — may leap down over many steps in a single movement of Thought: so in Induction, extremest logical rigor requires us to reason only to one complementary part; yet it allows us, while maintaining our ability to verify our procedure by a reference to this its single ultimate principle, to reason to remote gradations of complementary parts. Thus, as in Deduction, if *rational* be part of concept *man;* and *intelligent,* part of *rational;* and *discriminative,* part of *intelligent;* and *comparative,* part of *discriminative,* we may safely conclude that *man* is *comparative,* through any middle — *rational, intelligent, discriminative* — although to verify our procedure we must go through each successive gradation; so in Induction, if *rational* be complement of *animal;* and *intelligent,* as part of *rational,* be complement of *moral;* and *discriminative,* as part of *intelligent,* be complement of *intuitive;* then we may infer by induction that if *animal* is *living,* then the remote complement of a remote part of *rational,* which we have assumed to be the complement of *animal,* is also *living.* The principle is the same as in the process when limited to the first gradation, and validates as of absolute certainty the abbreviated process. Indeed, we have here, as it has been indicated to be with Multiplication in respect to Addition, only a compendious method of thought, which we can test and validate only by a full exposition of the process into the full and formal statements of the Syllogism.

All Induction, thus, is in its essential nature a Mediate Reasoning, in which the agreement or difference between two objects of thought is recognized through their respective relation to a third. While in Deduction the thought moves from Whole to Part, in Induction it moves from Part to Part. In strictest logical accuracy these two parts are exactly and fully complementary of each other, making up one whole of thought. But as we may have valid thought proceeding in contrary opposition as well as in contradictory which is the strictly logical opposition, so we may have valid thought in the relations of any part of one of these two primitive complementaries to any like part of the other. Indeed, as most of our thinking is in fact in contrary rather than in contradictory opposition, so likewise most of our thinking is in fact in the relationship between the lower gradations of parts. And as we validate thought in contrary opposition by reducing it to contradictory, so likewise we validate reasoning in the relations of the lower gradations of parts by reducing it to those between the two primitive complementaries.

Under the Postulate that has been enounced, § 18, all valid Induction may be expressed in the formal Inductive Syllogism. This, like the Deductive, contains three Propositions which have as their subjects and predicates three and only three terms.

Of these three Terms, two are parts that are complementary of each other; and one of these two is the mediating term of the reasoning, and may, hence, properly be called the *Middle Term*. *The other two are the Extremes*, that which denotes the whole being the *Major Term*, and that which denotes the part being the *Minor Term*. The terms may conveniently be indicated by the letters W, P, and C; of which W denotes the major term, P the minor, and C the middle term.

Of the three Propositions, two are given. They express the *data* to the thought in the Reasoning. They constitute the *antecedent* of the syllogism, and are called the *Premises*. The other expresses the derived judgment in the Reasoning, or the *Consequent*. It is called the *Conclusion*.

Of the two Premises, one expresses the relation between the middle term and that one of the extremes which expresses the whole. It may be called the *Major Premise*, or, better perhaps, *the Sumption*. The other premise expresses the relation between the middle term and the other extreme as its complementary. It may be called the *Minor Premise*, or the *Subsumption*.

The Conclusion expresses the relation between the extremes. It is signalized by the illative conjunction *therefore*, and its synonyms.

The formula of the Inductive Syllogism will thus be:
Sumption: *C is W;*
Subsumption: *P is complementary of C;*
Conclusion: *Therefore, P is W.*

Exemplifications in concrete matter, and in the two kinds of Quality, Affirmative and Negative, may be given thus:

I. AFFIRMATIVE INDUCTIVE SYLLOGISM.

Sumption: *The Inferior Planets (C) shine by reflected light (W);*
Subsumption: *The Superior Planets (P) are complementary of the Inferior Planets (C);*
Conclusion: *Therefore, the Superior Planets (P) shine by reflected light (W).*

This syllogism may be thus explicated: —

Sumption: The middle term (C) *Inferior Planets* is part of the major term (W), the whole class of *things shining by reflected light;*

Subsumption: The minor term (P) *Superior Planets* is complementary of the middle term (C) *Inferior Planets;*

Conclusion: Therefore, the minor term (P) *Superior Planets* is part of the major term (W), the whole class of *things shining by reflected light.*

II. NEGATIVE INDUCTIVE SYLLOGISM.

Sumption: *Venus does not revolve about the earth;*
Subsumption: *Uranus is a planet like Venus;*
Conclusion: *Therefore, Uranus does not revolve about the earth.*

The exposition which has thus far been given of the Inductive Syllogism has, for the sake of clearness and simplicity, recognized it as proceeding only in Extensive Quantity. But it is equally valid in Intensive Quantity; and the change is exactly correspondent to that already indicated in the Deductive Syllogism.

We have accordingly the two kinds of Inductive Reasoning distingished in respect of the logical quantity of the terms: The Extensive Inductive Syllogism, and the Intensive Deductive Syllogism.

It will not be necessary to give examples of the Intensive form; for those already given may be easily explicated in this kind of quantity.

From the fact that European logicians, perhaps by reason of the omission of Aristotle, the father of European logic, to elaborate any system of Inductive as he did of Deductive Reasoning, have recognized only Deductive in their expositions and illustrations, the formal characters of the Inductive Reasoning are not so familiar to our minds as those of the Deductive. Indeed, but for the disproportionate elaboration of Deduction during the rise and early progress of European literature, shaping and coloring all its forms of expression, the full form of the Deductive Syllogism would undoubtedly be as strange to us as that of the Inductive; for our ordinary thought does not flow in full logical forms—one of the premises being generally omitted in reasoning. In Inductive reasoning, the Subsumption is hardly ever expressed. It is the proper function of Logical Science to supply what is thus implied, thereby to validate the Thought.

Induction, moreover, is used rather in the investigation of truth than in probation, which is more closely allied to Deduction. Its nature and validity will accordingly be more particularly illustrated under Methodology. See also Appendix.

§ 71. The second class of Mediate Reasonings we have in *Conditional Syllogisms: —what.* general terms distinguished from the first or Categorical class, by this peculiarity, viz: that in this second class the derivation of the new Judgment is effected through a Judgment as such — through the copula; while in the first class, the derivation is through Concepts as such, in the channel of their reciprocal relations as Wholes and Parts. The Categorical Deductive Syllogism thus derives the new Judgment through the relation of its terms as respectively whole and part in respect to another term called by virtue of this twofold relation, *middle*, and the Categorical Inductive Syllogism derives the new Judgment through the relations of its terms as respectively the whole and the complementary of another term which is called by virtue of this relation *middle*. In the Categorical Syllogism, thus, the reasoning is mediated through a term — a Concept. But, as we might anticipate as altogether a probable result, the mediation of the new Judgment may be effected through the proper essence of the Judgment; so that instead of a Concept, a Judgment may form the proper *middle* of a reasoning; and two Judgments, in so far as Judgments, and out of all regard to the relations of their terms, may stand in such relations to each other, that Thought, under its own proper law of Identity in its diverse phases, may legitimately move to a new Judgment. Such is the case in that class of Reasonings called *Conditional*. The name, it may be observed, is inadequate. It points only to one species of this class of Reasonings, called in the Greek, Hypothetical, a word rendered in Latin, Conditional. If, however, it be borne in mind that the denomination is not commensurate with what is denoted by the name, that it is, as in many other cases in language, founded on only a part of the object meant, no serious evil will arise from continuing the use of the appellation; probably less evil, indeed, than would arise from attempting an innovation on a received nomenclature.

A CONDITIONAL SYLLOGISM, then, is one in which the new Judgment or Consequent is derived through the relation of the copulas of the Antecedent Judgments; as, *If A is, B is; but A is, therefore B is; A is B or C; but A is B; therefore A is not C.*

§ 72. Inasmuch as every Judgment is essentially an Affirmative or a Negative, it might be anticipated that there would be two modes of mediating a conclusion through the copula according as it should be affirmative or negative. There are, in fact, accordingly, two modes of reasoning through the copula — the one is called the *Affirmative, the Ponent,* or the *Constructive,* as, *If A is, B is; but A is; therefore B is;* the other, the *Negative,* the *Tollent,* or

<small>Their two modes.</small>

the *Destructive*, as, *If A is, B is ; but B is not ; therefore, A is not.*

§ 73. We have distinguished two kinds of Quality:—
<small>Their two kinds: Hypothetical and Disjunctive.</small>
Simple Quality, the two complementary kinds of which are Affirmative and Negative; and Disjunctive Quality. On this distinction in Quality is grounded a distinction of Conditional Syllogisms into the two kinds of *Hypothetical* and *Disjunctive.* A Hypothetical reasoning, like a Categorical, thus, always moves in Simple Quality; while, at the same time, it differs from a categorical reasoning in that it is mediated through a Judgment, not through a Concept. A Disjunctive Reasoning, on the other hand, differs from both in that it moves characteristically in Disjunctive Quality.

§ 74. A HYPOTHETICAL SYLLOGISM is a Mediate Reason-
<small>Hypothetical Syllogism: its general nature.</small>
ing in which a new Judgment is mediated from a Hypothetical through the copula of a Conditioning Judgment.

The Sumption in this kind of Syllogism is a Hypothetical Judgment, or one in which the subject and predicate are Judgments, and which accordingly affirms that these two Judgments stand in the relation of logical Whole and Part, or of Part to Complementary Part to each other, that is, as *conditioning* and *conditioned.* The Subsumption may affirm or deny the Conditioning Judgment; accordingly the Reasoning may be in either one of two modes, the Affirmative or Negative. And the Conclusion will be, accordingly, an affirmation or negation of one of the members of the Sumption, as in the following example:—

Common Sumption — *If A is, then B is.*

PONENT MODE.   TOLLENT MODE.

Subsumption: *But A is ;*   Subsumption: *But B is not ;*
Conclusion: *Therefore, B is.*   Conclusion: *Therefore A is not.*

REASONINGS.

Common Sumption: *If Socrates is virtuous, he merits esteem.*

PONENT MODE.
But Socrates is virtuous;
Therefore, he merits esteem.

TOLLENT MODE.
But Socrates does not merit esteem;
Therefore, he is not virtuous.

In the Ponent or Affirmative Mode the conclusion is from the truth of the antecedent to the truth of the consequent; while in the Tollent or Negative Mode the conclusion is from the denial of the consequent to the denial of the antecedent.

We cannot conversely conclude either from the denial of the antecedent to the denial of the consequent, or from the affirmative of the consequent to the affirmative of the antecedent, as will be apparent from an example. From the Hypothetical Sumption: *If the sun has risen it is light in the hall;* we cannot conclude from a denial of the antecedent member *that the sun has risen*, that it *is not light in the hall;* for the hall may be light from some other luminary. Neither can we any more by affirming the consequent member, *it is light in the hall*, conclude by affirming the antecedent member, *the sun has risen*.

It appears, then, that the antecedent clause conditions or determines only positively, while the consequent clause conditions only negatively. The reason of this is, that the Sumption must affirm a determination of the consequent by the antecedent, or there would be only a negative — a zero — upon which to suspend the reasoning. But it is of the very nature of this determination that the consequent is conditioned by the antecedent. If no consequent is conditioned there can be no antecedent conditioning. To deny the consequent is, accordingly, to deny the antecedent. But the Sumption does not condition the antecedent upon the consequent member; consequently, we are not authorized from affirming the consequent to affirm the antecedent.

A regular and perfect Hypothetical Syllogism must contain three propositions: a Sumption, Subsumption, and Conclusion. The Sumption must be an affirmative Hypothetical Proposition, affirming the agreement between two judgments. The Subsumption may be affirmative or negative; but it must either affirm the truth of the antecedent member of the Sumption, or deny the truth of the consequent member. If the Subsumption be affirmative, the conclusion must affirm the truth of the consequent member of the Sumption — the Ponent mode; if the Subsumption be negative, the conclusion must deny the antecedent member of the Sumption — the Tollent mode.

§ 75. As a Hypothetical Judgment may be either simple or disjunctive, so the sumption of a Hypothetical Syllogism may be either simple or disjunctive. This gives rise to a division into the two classes distinguished in reference to this quality in the sumption: 1. The proper *Hypothetical*, of which we have just given an exposition, and, 2. The *Hypothetico-Disjunctive*, otherwise called the *Dilemma*, as, *Whether A is B or is C, D is E; but A is B or is C; therefore, D is E.*

Two kinds of Hypothetical Syllogism.

The Dilemma was a great favorite with the Sophists, as from the complexity of elements that enter into it, a fallacy may easily be disguised or veiled from the notice of an adversary. It has also received very prominent attention from logicians, who, however, have erred in ranking it as a coördinate class with Hypothetical and Disjunctive Reasonings. In so far as it is a reasoning, it is purely Hypothetical, the derived judgment being mediated independently of the disjunction; it is, consequently, to be ranked as a subdivision of Hypothetical Reasonings.

§ 76. If, when the characteristics of the Hypothetical and of the Disjunctive Judgment are combined, the disjunction appears only in the consequent or predicate member, as in the form, *If an action be prohibited, it is prohibited either by natural or by positive law,* the variation from the proper hypothetical is not for any purposes in thought sufficiently important to demand any special treat-

The Dilemma.

ment. But if the disjunction appear in the antecedent or subject member, we have a class of judgments of peculiar interest and importance. This species is called the *Dilemmatic Judgment*, being used in the famous reasoning known as the Dilemma. Its form is, *Whether A is B or C is D, E is F; whether it melt or freeze, the road will be rough*. We have here a disjunction of judgments, not of concepts; and it is the truth of one or the other of the alternative judgments constituting the antecedent on which the truth of the whole judgment rests. The meaning is, either alternative judgment, *that it will melt* or *that it will freeze*, involves the judgment that *the road will be rough*.

This Judgment is properly signalized by the conjunction *whether*, synonymous with *if — or*.

Its forms are various. In the first place, the disjunction may be extended to more than two members. If it be carried to three, the reasoning is called a *Trilemma;* if to four, a *Tetralemma;* or if to any number more than two, generally a *Polylemma*. The term *dilemma*, is, however, applied to all, whatever the number of disjunct members in the sumption.

In the next place, the disjunction may be either in the subject or in the predicate of the sumption, or in both subject and predicate.

In the third place, the reasoning may be either in the Ponent or the Tollent modes.

In any of the forms, the Subsumption, as in the proper Hypothetical Syllogism, either posits the antecedent in order in the conclusion to posit the consequent, or sublates the consequent in order to sublate the antecedent. The reasoning accordingly turns on a judgment, and is mediated through that. It is thus a mediate conditional reasoning.

The *true* historical Dilemma, as a reasoning which offers to an adversary an alternative of propositions, the so-called "horns of a dilemma," one of which he must take, is that in which the subsumption is a disjunctive proposition. The first and the fourth of the forms given below, are examples.

The following are exemplifications of different forms of the Dilemma.

1. *Ponent Dilemma with disjunct antecedent:*—" Whether the blest in heaven have no desires or have desires that are fully gratified, they will be perfectly content ; but they either will have no desires or will have them fully gratified; therefore, they will be perfectly content." The reasoning presented in this full syllogistic form, would, in ordinary discourse, be expressed in some such compendious way as the following : "The blest in heaven, will either have no desires, or if they have desires, must have them fully gratified, so that in either case they will be perfectly content." The formula of this form is, *Whether A is B or C, D is E; but A is B or C; therefore, D is E.*

2. *Tollent Dilemma with disjunct antecedent :* — " If it had rained, or if there had been a heavy dew, the walks would be wet; but the walks are not wet; therefore, there was neither rain nor dew." *If A is B or C, D is E; but D is not E; therefore, A is neither B nor C.*

3. *Ponent Dilemma with disjunct consequent:* — " If the parallelogram be not equal to the triangle, it must be either greater or less; but it is not equal; therefore, it is either greater or less." *If A is B, C is D or E; but A is B; therefore, C is D or E.*

4. *Tollent Dilemma with disjunct consequent :* — " If man is incapable of progress towards perfection, he must be either a divinity or a brute ; but man is neither divinity nor brute; therefore, he is not incapable ($=$ is capable) of progress towards perfection." *If A is B, C is D or E; but C is neither D nor E; therefore, A is not B.*

5. *Tollent Trilemma:* — " If mind and matter are not essentially diverse, then either they must be absolutely identical, or there is no such existence as mind, or no such existence as matter ; but neither of these three suppositions

is tenable; therefore, mind and matter are essentially distinct." *If A is B, then C is D, or E, or F; but C is neither D, nor E, nor F; therefore, A is not B.*

§ 77. A DISJUNCTIVE SYLLOGISM is a Mediate Reasoning in which a new judgment is mediated through a new judgment removing the disjunction; as, *A is B or is C; but A is B; therefore, A is not C.*   Disjunctive Syllogism.

It comes immediately under the second pair of the four fundamental Laws of Thought — those of Disjunction and of Exclusion. In this respect, it differs from Categorical as well as from Hypothetical Syllogisms, neither of which classes directly recognizes this pair of Laws.

It is composed of three propositions, of which the Sumption is a Disjunctive Proposition; the Subsumption removes the disjunction in the Sumption, which may be effected in either of the two ways of affirming or denying, giving rise to two modes, the *Ponent* or *Affirmative*, and the *Tollent* or *Negative;* and the conclusion denies or affirms the member not subsumed.

The Sumption of a Disjunctive Syllogism, as ever a Disjunctive Proposition, admits of the three gradations of logical opposition: 1. Pure logical contradiction, lying in the copula, as, *A is B or is not B;* 2. The looser logical contradiction, in which the opposition lies in the terms, as, *A is B or non-B; animals are vertebrate or invertebrate;* and, 3. Contrary opposition, as, *A is B or C.*

The Sumption is necessarily always affirmative, as we can conclude nothing from a mere zero of thought; much less from an impossibility in thought, as is the case in the pure Contradictory Disjunctive.

Now, as a Disjunctive Proposition, from its very nature, in its strictest form respects two members, either of which may, supposably, but only one of which can, actually, be recognized as true, it is clear that the new judgment — the conclusion — may be mediated through the removal of the disjunction either by affirming, *positing,* or by denying, *sublating,* one of the two disjunct members. We may, from the

Disjunctive Sumption *A is B or is not B*, either conclude by affirming — positing one member to a denial — a sublation of the other, or conversely, by sublating one to a positing of the other. There emerge, thus, two distinct kinds of Disjunctive Syllogisms.

1. The *Affirmative, Ponent,* or *Positing, (modus ponens, modus ponendo tollens,)* in which one of the disjunct members is posited in the Subsumption and the other sublated in the Conclusion, as, *A is B or C; but A is B; therefore, A is not C.*

2. The *Negative, Tollent, or Sublating, (modus tollens, modus tollendo ponens,)* in which one of the disjunct members is sublated in the Subsumption and the other posited in the Conclusion; as, *A is B or C; but A is not B; therefore, A is C.*

It is obvious that either of the disjunct members may be posited or sublated in the Subsumption; and that the number of disjunct members need not be restricted to two. But in case there are more than two, they must be taken as constituting but two parts, one part of them being the complementary of the other. Thus, if we have a Sumption in the form *A is B, or C, or D, or E,* and, in the Subsumption, posit B, we sublate C, D, and E, which three together make up the complementary of B. Or, if we posit B and C, then we sublate D and E, which are the complementary of the posited part of the disjunct members. The general principle in all disjunctive reasoning is that *by positing one part we sublate the complementary part, and by sublating the one part we posit the complementary part.*

It will be seen from this exposition of the nature of a disjunctive reasoning, that the removal of the disjunction in the sumption is essential. Consequently if there be no such removal of the disjunction, although the sumption may be a Disjunctive Proposition, we have no disjunctive reasoning. Thus the following is not a Disjunctive but a Categorical Syllogism: *A is B or C; but D is A; therefore, D is B or C.*

The Disjunctive Syllogism, moreover, may proceed in either quantity, Extensive or Intensive. Unless the special forms appropriated to the one or the other of these two kinds of logical quantity are employed, the reasoning may generally be explicated in either with equal facility.

The following examples, one in abstract, the other in concrete matter, will sufficiently illustrate the peculiar character of a disjunctive reasoning when expounded in the complete form of a Disjunctive Syllogism: —

Common Sumption: *A is either B or C or D.*

PONENT MODE.

Subsumption: *But A is B; Or, A is either B or C.*
Conclusion: *Therefore, A is neither C nor D; Or, Therefore, A is not D.*

TOLLENT MODE.

Subsumption: *But A is not B; Or, A is neither B nor C.*
Conclusion: *Therefore, A is either C or D; Or, Therefore, A is D.*

Common Sumption: *The ancients were in genius either superior to the moderns, or inferior, or equal.*

PONENT MODE.

Subsumption: *But the ancients were superior to the moderns.*
Conclusion: *Therefore, they were neither inferior nor equal.*

OR,

Subsumption: *But the ancients were either superior or equal.*
Conclusion: *Therefore, they were not inferior.*

TOLLENT MODE.

Subsumption: *But the ancients were not inferior.*
Conclusion: *Therefore, they were either superior or equal.*

OR,

Subsumption: *But the ancients were neither inferior nor equal.*
Conclusion: *Therefore, they were superior.*

It is plain that we may explicate the syllogism in either Quantity with equal readiness; thus, in Extensive Quantity, the class *ancients* is contained under the class *superior to the moderns*, or under the class *inferior*, &c.; in Intensive Quantity, the attribute notion *ancients* contains in it the attribute *superior to the moderns*, or the attribute *inferior*, &c.

§ 78. When the antecedent of a mediate reasoning consists of more than two judgments related to each other as wholes and parts, or as parts and complementary parts, the reasoning is called a *Polysyllogism*, also, a *Chain of Reasoning;* in respect to which other mediate reasonings are called *Monosyllogisms*. The Polysyllogism.

A Polysyllogism is, in truth, only a series of single syllogisms, and may always be resolved into as many single reasonings as there are middle terms in the series. Thus the Polysyllogism *C is D; B is C; A is B; therefore, A is D;* consists of two single syllogisms, there being two middle terms B and C, thus: 1°. *C is D; B is C; therefore, B is D.* 2°. *B is D; A is B; therefore, A is D.* Or, in concrete matter, the Polysyllogism: *An animal is a substance; a quadruped is an animal; a horse is a quadruped; therefore, a horse is a substance,* may be thus resolved into two monosyllogisms; there being two middle terms, *animal* and *quadruped*. 1°. *An animal is a substance; a quadruped is an animal; therefore, a quadruped is a substance.* 2°. *A quadruped is a substance; a horse is a quadruped; therefore, a horse is a substance.*

It appears from this illustration that the polysyllogism is equally valid as the single syllogism. It differs, in fact, from a series of single syllogisms in which the conclusion of one becomes a premise in another of the series, only in the particular that it omits the useless mention of this connecting proposition. If, in the example, we simply leave out of the single syllogisms the connecting proposition which is the conclusion of the first and the sumption of the second — *a quadruped is a substance* — we have the polysyllogism as in the first presented.

It is obvious, also, that the polysyllogism may equally as the monosyllogism move in either quantity, Extensive or Intensive.

Moreover, the reasoning may be *progressive* or *regressive*. That is, the single syllogisms which make up the chain may either of them be placed first; the order of statement being as truly immaterial as in the case of the premises of a single syllogism. If the conditioning syllogism be placed first, we have the Progressive chain; if the dependent syllogism be placed first, we have the Regressive chain. In truth, according as we explicate the reasoning in the one or the other quantity, we have the Progressive or the Regressive series. Thus, if we explicate the example in Extensive Quantity, we have the Progressive series: *An animal is part of the class substance; a quadruped is part of the class animal; a horse is part of the class quadruped; therefore, a horse is part of the class substance.* The first single syllogism here furnishes the sumption for the second. But explicated in Intensive Quantity, the reasoning, in the order in which its parts are stated, is Regressive. Thus: 1. *Animal contains the attribute substance; quadruped contains the attribute animal; therefore, quadruped contains the attribute substance.* 2. *Quadruped contains the attribute substance; horse contains the attribute quadruped; therefore, horse contains the attribute substance.* Here the conclusion of the first syllogism furnishes the subsumption of the second. In other words, the order of the two single syllogisms is in this last explication reversed, inasmuch as the subsumption is placed before the sumption, while in the more natural order it should be placed after the sumption. Whether the series is Progressive or Regressive, is a matter of no moment, so far as the validity of the reasoning is concerned.

§ 79. The Polysyllogism has been distinguished in respect of the form of statement, into two kinds: the *Epichirema* and the *Sorites*.

The EPICHIREMA is a polysyllogism in which one or more

of the single syllogisms which compose it is immediately attached to one of the premises, thus: *Animal is a substance; a horse is an animal, for it is a quadruped; therefore, a horse is a substance;* or, *A quadruped is a substance, for it is an animal; but a horse is a quadruped; therefore, a horse is a substance.*

The attached syllogism, which as in reasoning generally is presented elliptically and not in the full verbal form into which every thought may be required by our fundamental Postulate to be explicated, may obviously be joined to either premise or to both, and may itself be a polysyllogism or only single.

The Sorites is a Polysyllogism in which the single syllogisms which compose it are presented in equally independent relationship to the whole series. It is sufficiently exemplified in the examples given of the Polysyllogism. Indeed, it is the regular form, while the Epichirema is the irregular form of the Polysyllogism, into which the former may always be changed without affecting the nature of the reasoning.

§ 80. The Polysyllogism, further, may be Categorical or Conditional, which may, moreover, be in either form — the Sorites or the Epichirema.

The Categorical species has been sufficiently treated in the general exposition already given of the Polysyllogism.

The Conditional Polysyllogism embraces the two varieties of the Hypothetical and the Disjunctive.

It will be sufficient to give exemplifications of these varieties without more extended explanations. It is only necessary to add, that they may proceed in either Quantity — Extensive or Intensive; that they may be Ponent or Tollent; that the series may be Progressive or Regressive; that the number of links in the chain is limited only by the considerations of clearness and facility of expression; and that they respectively come under the control of the principles which regulate the higher classes of reasoning to which they severally belong, and may always be resolved into single syllogisms.

HYPOTHETICAL SORITES: *If Harpagon be avaricious, he is discontented; if he is discontented he is unhappy; now Harpagon is avaricious; therefore, he is unhappy.*

HYPOTHETICAL EPICHIREMA: *If Harpagon is avaricious, he is intent on gain; if he is intent on gain he is unhappy, for he is discontented; now Harpagon is avaricious; therefore, he is unhappy.*

DISJUNCTIVE SORITES: *A Science is either Pure or Inductive; a Pure Science is either Mathematical or Logical; but Astrology is neither Mathematical, nor Logical, nor Inductive; therefore, Astrology is not a Science.*

DISJUNCTIVE EPICHIREMA: *All Science is either Pure or Inductive; a Pure Science is either Mathematical or Logical, for it treats either of the Conditions of Thought or the Elements of Thought; but Astrology is neither Mathematical, nor Logical, nor Inductive; therefore, Astrology is not a Science.*

PURE LOGIC.

PART II.
METHODOLOGY.

CHAPTER I.
METHOD IN GENERAL.

Method — what.

§ 81. "METHOD in general is the regulated procedure towards a certain end; that is, a process governed by rules, which guide us by the shortest way straight towards a certain point, and guard us against devious aberrations. Now the end of Thought is Truth, Knowledge, Science — expressions which may here be considered as convertible. Science, therefore, may be regarded as the perfection of thought, and to the accomplishment of this perfection the Methodology of Logic must be accommodated and be conducive."

But while Science, thus, is the proper end of all Thought, and Logical Method must have reference to Thought as its one end, it is still to be regarded only as the immediate end, which may, itself, be modified and controlled by still higher ends. In fact, Science or Truth may have its end either in itself — in the True, or in the Beautiful, or in the Right and Good; and the Method of Thought will vary in some respects with this specific remoter end. Still further, the Method of Thought will vary with the more specific ends under each of these higher governing ends. We may deal with Thought for the purpose of acquiring knowledge, or for the purpose of communicating knowledge; and the Method requisite for the Investigation of Truth will so far vary from the Method requisite for the Communication of Truth.

In like manner the Method of Thought, as governed by the higher end of guiding to the Beautiful, will vary specifically, as the particular end is the Contemplation or the Creation of the Beautiful.

So, too, we have a specific variation in the Method of Thought, where the governing idea is the Right or the Good, according as Subjective or Objective Rectitude or Goodness is the particular end.

It is sufficient to point out here these modifications of Logical Method in respect to these several general ends in thinking. The full, detailed consideration of them belongs either to Modified Logic or to Applied or Special Logic. Pure Logic confines itself to the domain of Truth in itself — Science for its own sake.

§ 82. Science, farther, as true or certain knowledge, supposes two conditions. Of these, the first has a relation to the object known; the second, to the knowing subject. Moreover, it cannot be accepted as fully perfected until properly embodied in Language. We have thus determined to us the threefold Perfection of Science — Material, Formal, and Verbal. *Threefold Perfection of Science: Material, Formal, and Verbal.*

Now as Logic is a Science exclusively conversant about the form of thought, it would seem that it could take into account only the former of these two elements — the formal perfection of thought. And in a certain sense this is a correct inference. Only, in fact, so far as the form is necessarily dependent on the object of thought, only so far as its formal perfection must of necessity regard the matter, does Pure Logic look to the matter of Thought. Were Logic to shut out from its view all consideration of the matter of Thought, it would be reduced to such meagre proportions as to be unworthy of the name of a science, and barren of all utility; much as would be the case with Geometrical Science if, because a pure formal Science, it were to exclude from its consideration all distinctions of its object, such as Lines, Surfaces, and Solids, Rectilineal and Curvilinear Surfaces, and the like. The truth, the objective reality of its matter, indeed, a purely formal Science does not regard. The conclusions of Mathematical Science are equally sound whether there be space or not; whether space be a proper entity or a mere form of our thinking; whether there be, indeed, extension, that is, extended matter in space or not. It only *supposes* this or that in regard to its matter, — space, extension, — assumes it or accepts it as given to it. So Logic only assumes its matter or accepts it as given to it by other sciences. Yet inasmuch as, if we think, we must think of something, and that something must be viewed as standing in a necessary relation to our thought, so thought must be necessarily different, if carried beyond the most shadowy abstractions, as its object differs. Logic will then so far regard the matter of thought as to see that it is possible to think it and to think it correctly. As Thought regards Being as its object, and as Being is necessarily apprehended in the two aspects of Substance and Cause, and, if apprehended at all, must be apprehended in one of these two aspects, the proper Logical Perfection of Thought requires that this twofold consideration be taken of Being. Logic does not assume it into her province to prove the reality of Being as either Substance or Cause. She only assumes or accepts it as given to her, and deals with it as if real. Her laws are, consequently, just as valid to the pure Idealist as to the Realist. But she necessarily demands that what is given her be so given as that her capacities of receiving may lay hold of it; and so far she must assure herself in regard to Being that it is shaped to her capacities, conformed to her nature. Being, even ideal Being, can be nothing to Logic, except as apprehended in this seen correlation to her proper functions, which are simply and characteristically functions of Quantity, moving only in the relations of Whole and Parts. Farther than this, Logic needs to apprehend Being in order to verify, to illustrate, to apply her laws. Her growth, if growth she could be supposed to have, would be only the shadow of an abstraction unless allowed in Being. There could be no illustration, no exemplification. Moreover, the utility of Logic, and well-nigh its whole worth to man, lies in the possibility of its being applied to the objects with which he is conversant. If not so developed as to be readily and habitually applied to the realities of human life, logical science could only be regarded as a toy, a bubble, brilliant and beautiful it may be, but worthless, instead of being, as it should be, the chiefest guide and helper to all intellectual growth and culture.

Logic, then, must so far deal with the matter of Thought as to be able to verify its applications to Being, both as Substance and as Cause. It must view them, indeed, only in the relations of proper Identity and Quantity — of Whole and Parts. But it must view the parts of Substance in a somewhat different light from the parts of Cause. It must regard the parts of the former as Attributes in the narrower sense, and those of the latter as Effects — Effects in its fullest sense. As Thought proceeds differently, although under the self-same laws, when applied to the two respectively, Logic must be able to follow these different procedures with assurance of being right in its regulation of them.

Logical Science has, for the most part, regarded only Substance, and although it has used the term *attribute* to denote whatever can be predicated of a subject, it has in its illustrations identified the term with the parts of a Substance, and has seemed to ignore utterly the parts of a Cause. Indeed, the reputed father of the Science, Aristotle, himself seems to think Substance and Cause convertible in all predication; and in this he has been followed by subsequent logicians. Thus the proposition, " The Romans conquered," is alleged to be convertible with the proposition, " The Romans were victorious." But this is to confound " action " with " quality," the one being predicable only of " Cause," the other only of

"Substance." And the obscurities and errors which have followed from the confusion have been not less, nor of less importance, than those which have followed from the confounding of the two species of Logical Quantity — Comprehensive and Extensive. They are no less serious than what might be supposed to follow from confounding lines with surfaces in geometry, as has been done by some who through this fallacy have fancied they have solved the great problem of the Quadrature of the Circle.

It will not be amiss to recapitulate the principles which, as we have seen, cover the relations of Thought to its matter.

1. The object-matter of Thought is a duality of cognitions.

2. These cognitions are viewed in Thought only in the relation of Same and Different, or derivatively, as Wholes or Parts.

3. Such cognitions as Wholes or Parts are of different kinds which, in order to perfect knowledge, Thought must distinguish. There are two generic divisions of Wholes — (1.) Those of Thought itself. (2.) Those external to Thought.

4. The Wholes of Thought are either — (1.) Conditions of Thought, as the Affirmative and the Negative, which, as Complementary Parts, make up what may be called *The Dianoetic Whole;* or, (2.) Products of Thought, the Wholes of Comprehension and Extension, called Logical Wholes.

5. The Wholes external to Thought are — (1.) Those of Forms of Being, called Integrate, comprising the two species of Spacial and Numerical. (2.) Those of Being itself, subdivided, in reference to the two modes of Being, into (*a.*) Substantial, and (*b.*) Causal.

§ 83. The Material Perfection of Science involves in its largest import the reality of the matter, as well as the correctness of the thought. We distinguish in all Science, in all Thought, three elements: the object known, the knowing subject, and the act of knowledge itself. Now although a science can

Two virtues in Material Perfection of Science, — Adequateness and Accuracy.

be regarded as perfect only when these three elements are in their respective perfection, only when there is a true matter, a true intelligence, and a true knowledge, Logic — Discursive Logic, as the Science of the Laws of Knowledge as Knowledge — dismisses the two related extremes, the perfection of the Matter and the perfection of the Intelligence, and limits itself to the consideration of the third element — that of the relation between them. It leaves to the proper Nomology of the Presentative Faculties — the Nomology of Perception, the Nomology of the Regulative or Intuitive Faculty — to prescribe the conditions of a perfect cognition of the matter which it appertains to them to apprehend. Such a cognition might be denominated the Material Perfection of Knowledge, as importing only that the matter as presented by these faculties to the Discursive Faculty is correctly apprehended by them; that is, in correspondence with its true being. But the Material Perfection of Science which falls within the domain of Logic is widely different from this. As Thought is the relation between the Thinking Subject and the Object Thought, which, it should be remembered, is not the original object of the Presentative Faculties, but ever a cognition, it has a double aspect, looking both inward to the subject and outward to the object. Now, Thought, to be perfect in this outward relation — in relation to the cognition presented to it — must be conformed to its object. It must both be conformed to the outer limitations of the matter, be conterminous with it, be *adequate*, filling out the entire field of the matter without transcending it; and it must also, in like manner, be conformed to all parts or contents of the object — must be *accurate*. These two, then, are the two virtues comprised in the Material Perfection of Science, so far as it falls within the domain of Logic: — Adequateness and Accuracy.

§ 84. The Formal Perfection of Science comprises three virtues: — one common to it with other cognitions, as those of Perception and Intuition, founded in the very nature of the Intelligence, viz: *Clearness;* the second, founded on the general characteristic of Thought itself, its relativeness, viz: *Congruence,* otherwise called *Harmony or Agreement;* the third, on the specific characteristic of this relativeness in Thought, as being that of Whole and Parts, viz: *Distinctness.*

<small>Three virtues of Formal Perfection of Science:— Clearness, Congruence, and Distinctness.</small>

The one Essential Perfection of all Intelligence, viewed irrespectively of its relations to its objects, is *Clearness.* A perfect cognition and a clear cognition are convertible expressions, if we regard cognition only on its purely formal side — cognition simply as cognition. This perfection of Thought is determined to it, then, by the very nature of the Intelligence of which it is one product.

But Thought is a relative cognition, being by this attribute of relativeness distinguished from other products of the Intelligence. That there should be this relation apprehended in all Thought is thus indispensable to its perfection. The terms, which constitute the factors in this relation, must be in correlative or logical harmony — must be congruent. This is, indeed, but the principle of Identity in its special application to Method.

Once more, Thought takes cognizance of its objects only in the relations of Identity or Quantity. It deals with Wholes and Parts. Now a clear cognition of the parts of a whole as parts, is denominated a *distinct* cognition.

Clearness thus respects the outward relations of an object of thought — its relations to other objects. Distinctness respects its internal relations — its relations to the parts of which it is composed.

§ 85. All human science, moreover, stands in a relation of dependence, more or less entire, upon Language. If Language must be admitted to be the product of Thought, it is yet equally undeniable that Language is the necessary instrument of its progress. Thought not only works through Language; it also exhibits the results

<small>Verbal Perfection of Science.</small>

of its operations, step by step in its endless working, in language. And, still further, it contemplates, criticises, verifies its work, as thus exhibited in language. Its relationship to language appears, thus, to be most intimate and vital. It becomes important, therefore, to determine, somewhat more precisely than we have yet done, this inter-dependence between Thought and Language, in order to ascertain the conditions of perfect science.

The object of Thought as an activity, we have found to be ever a cognition. Thought begins with a cognition as the necessary prerequisite of its movement. Leaving out of view, now, those cognitions which are the products of Thought itself, and which are presented to it by itself as the objects of its activity, the primitive original objects of Thought are the simple, individual, or irrelative objects of the Presentative and Intuitive Faculties. With these objects given as cognitions by one or the other of these Faculties, Thought originally begins. But simultaneously with these cognitions arising in the consciousness, the process of naming, of speech-making, begins. It begins, too, there can be no reason to question, under the superintendence of the principle of all Thought, the principle of Identity; at least, we must believe, in harmony with it. Let us suppose, now, a cognition presented through the Perceptive Faculty, through the sense of sight, for example, the sun. A name would, under the native tendencies of the human soul, at once be given it; and the name as sound, would be one bearing some analogy, identical in some respect, with some other accidental modification of the consciousness at the time. We may imagine it to be possibly an ejaculation prompted by the joy which the first perception of the sun would naturally produce. That ejaculatory sound would naturally furnish the materials in sound for a name of the sun, because identified with its first experience of that object. It is now the name of an individual, simple, in other words, irrelative cognition. But we will suppose the moon subsequently to come into the experience, producing the identical effect of joy in kind through its common attribute of brightness. It would be named like the first — be designated by the same sound in speech. But now the name no longer denotes a single object; it denotes a plurality of objects identified in having a common attribute — brightness. It is now the name of a concept, formed upon the predicate Base — brightness. We will suppose, further, a third object producing the same effect, a star, to enter the experience. The name is as naturally extended to that. The star is, in other words, gathered into the class on the same Base; and the concept is enlarged in its extension. Thus the process goes on indefinitely in this direction.

But we will now suppose another attribute to be given in the experience. The sun is perceived to be *round*. *Bright* and *round* are now apprehended as belonging to the same subject — *sun*. The predicates are combined, and a concept in comprehension is the result. The name before given to the concept in extension is now found to denote more than one attribute; and the name is used now in both senses, denoting Comprehension as well as Extension. Other attributes may be added, and thus the concept may grow in both quantities — the limit being always, that in the synthesis of subjects there be predicates common to all; and in the synthesis of predicates, there be subjects to which they all in common belong. The original name first applied to denote the irrelative object, *sun*, thus comes to denote a concept embracing an indefinite number of objects having the same complement of predicates, and also embracing an indefinite number of predicates all concurring in each of the subjects — in other words, a Concept with exactly correlative quantities of Comprehension and Extension.

But in the progress of Experience and Thought, another parallel process begins. A body enters the experience which is bright, and which, therefore, at first might have been united with the sun into a concept under that attribute as common to both objects, but it is not round. It cannot, therefore, be gathered into the class of *bright round* bodies. A concept is now formed of bodies that are merely bright, with no reference to figure; and a name to signalize the union is given to it — say, *luminaries.* The first object, *sun,* now belongs to two classes, is embraced in two concepts. To indicate it, a name is made up by combining so many of the predicates as will suffice to distinguish it from other objects embraced under the concept. Thus arise modifying words or adjectives; and by the use of them we are enabled to indicate in language the primitive individual object with which the process began, by calling it *the sun,* or *the great heavenly luminary.* We thus clearly separate it from all other objects embraced in *sun,* regarded as a subject-concept — that is, in its Extension — in other words, *define* it by the use of certain adjectives, called, hence, *Definitives.* In a precisely analogous way, we indicate the primitive individual attribute or predicate. We say *the bright sun,* meaning that one property of the complement of characters that have been gathered into the word regarded as a predicate concept, that is, in its comprehension, employing here certain adjectives called in this case *Epithets.* Or convenience or occasions of use may bring in, during the progress of speech, a new word derived from some other language, as *Phœbus,* or suggested by some other accident in experience. And from this word may start a new process in word-formation.

Precisely in the same way the concept-word may be narrowed to a species only; that is, to a part of the comprehension, instead of being carried through to the individual attribute. Here, too, new series of word-formations may originate.

Such is the genesis of language, so far as concept-words, whether concretes, that is, subject-concepts, or abstracts, that is, predicate-concepts, and the thought-element in them are concerned. The consideration of the genesis of the sound-element in words is foreign to Logical Science.[1] It appears

[1] See Appendix B.

from this that it is a gross error to suppose that Language originates with general ideas. Such ideas are the product of thought alone, and, therefore, presuppose the individual cognition. Nothing can be conceived more preposterous than that the process of generalization, from which alone general ideas can arise, precedes the cognition of individual objects and attributes. Generalization presupposes, also, the naming of these individual objects and attributes. Moreover, the instinctive generalization that has gone on in the genesis of language, has been step by step, by the addition of one object and one attribute at a time. It may be, indeed, that that object or attribute may have been a group or an aggregate that subsequently has been found to embrace a plurality of separable objects or attributes, but when first apprehended in thought it must have been viewed as one — as individual. To trace back the history of a concept word, whether concrete or abstract, in the expectation of finding a generic or comprehensive cognition at the origin, is to proceed in contradiction of the first principles of thought. *Bright*, for example, is now a generic appellation; but it could have become so only by being found, in the progress of Experience, to belong to a plurality of objects. It was, if we may assume it here to be a primitive word, originally given as a property of an individual. It is, also, now, a composite abstract, embracing such involved characters as *radiant, undulating, sense-impressing;* but it must have been originally simple, and could only in the progress of experience come to be regarded as a composite.

Now it is apparent from this summary view, that only the few words which are first applied to designate individual objects and simple characters or attributes, come from any other faculty than that of thought; that Thought, as the principle of Identity in all acts of the Intelligence, presides over the first naming of these; that these names of individual objects and simple attributes, begin at once to pass into concepts, which are the pure products of Thought, and even individual objects and simple attributes come to be designated by concept words used to modify one another. Thus Language comes finally to be made up, to a large extent, of words which have been determined as to their meaning and use by Thought.

But the view we have taken shows, also, that Language is not less the instrument than the product of Thought. The results of previous processes of Thought are taken as materials and conditions of new processes. Thought takes concepts already formed, and combines them with other concepts, thus forming new concepts, and still new combinations onward indefinitely. Now it is obvious that as the concept must always maintain the exact correspondence between the two quantities of Comprehension and of Extension, and as Thought does not bring up in review all the individual objects and simple characters which have in successive combinations entered into the concept, there must be great liability to error. Moreover, there is a constant tendency for the very sake of precision in Thought, to narrow the import of words. Thus, for example, the word *Thought*, itself, formerly included in its meaning all acts of the mind, emotions and volitions, as well as acts of Intelligence, but now is limited to the acts of one of the Faculties of the Intelligence. Still further, when we say Thought has shaped Language, we use metaphorical diction. Men, thinkers, individual thinkers, acting indeed together in their intercourse with each other, and under common regulative principles, have produced all words, created all language. Hence the extreme necessity that Thought, as it presses its products into verbal forms, should be aware of the many liabilities to error, and protect itself against them as far as may be, in order to arrive ·at its goal of truth or perfect science. Only when it has verified its incorporation of its products into language expressing certain truth, can it be assured of having reached this its goal. In this, is attained the Verbal Perfection of Science, when Knowledge, conformed to the realities of things as apprehended by the Presentative Faculties, and ·shaped into its own essential form by Thought, appears at last in its proper embodiment of language.

To recapitulate these views of the relations of Thought to Language:—

Relations of Language to Thought; as Product, as Instrument, and as Embodiment.

1. The cognitions, attained by the Perceptive and Intuitive Faculties, of individual objects and of simple attributes, are named under the guidance and prompting of the proper principle of Thought — that of Identity.

2. The concepts, elaborated by Thought out of these primitive cognitions, which make up the great body of notion-words in a language, are expressed in language in words derived from the names of those primitive cognitions, and are equally under the guidance of Thought.

3. On the other hand, all the movements of Thought are through words; and all its products attain to permanent life only as embodied in words. Language is the Instrument as well as the Embodiment of Thought.

§ 86. The Verbal Perfection of Science, implying its perfect embodiment in Language, involves two characters or virtues:—1. Correctness; 2. Perspicuousness.

Verbal Perfection of Science; its two virtues — Correctness and Perspicuousness.

CORRECTNESS is founded upon the relations of Thought to its outward body, language. It requires that the thought be truly rendered in the words that express it. More specifically, correctness requires —

1. That the naming of the primitive cognitions given by the Presentative Faculties to Thought, be founded on some identity cognizable in proper Thought.

2. That the naming of concepts be founded on the recognized identity in respect to their Base, of the subjects or of the predicates which are respectively combined to form the concept.

3. That the relations of the Terms in Judgments be expressed in such wise as truly to represent the specific character of the Judgment, and, also, the specific nature of the kind of whole in which the Judgment moves.

PERSPICUOUSNESS is founded upon the essential quality of Thought as Intelligence, viz., Clearness, and requires that the Thought appear clearly through the verbal expression.

Subordinate qualities of Perspicuousness are Significance; Perspicuousness Proper, requiring use of unambiguous words and right arrangement of relative words; and Brevity.

§ 87. It is evident that inasmuch as there are various products of Thought, whose perfection must respectively be determined by their bearing these several virtues of Thought in their modified applications, Logic must accommodate its Method to the consideration of these virtues in detail, as they pertain to these several products of Thought. *Divisions of Methodology.*

The products of Thought, although alike the products of the same Faculty, — the Discursive Faculty or Faculty of Comparison, whose essential and characteristic function it is to identify what is common to a plurality of objects, — vary, as we have seen, as different gradations from one another. The simplest and most fundamental of these gradations is the Judgment. Now, inasmuch as a Judgment is the identification of an attribute or character as belonging to an object, the Logical Perfection of a Judgment is attained by securing the conditions of an identification of the attribute or character with its object. The determination of these conditions will accordingly form the matter of a Methodology of the Judgment.

A Concept, being produced by an act of synthesis, — by combining into a unity the several subjects identified with a common predicate, or the several characters or attributes identified with a common subject, — will attain perfection by securing the conditions of such synthesis or combination. And Methodology, as applied to this element of thought, will determine and indicate these conditions.

A Reasoning, being derived from a Judgment, either by an act of Transformation or of Analysis, will attain its logical perfection by securing the conditions of this transformation and analysis. The Methodology of Reasoning will accordingly investigate and point out the conditions of these two modes of derivation.

Logical Methodology will thus consist of three departments corresponding with the three Elements of Thought: 1. The Methodology of Judgments. 2. The Methodology of Concepts. 3. The Methodology of Reasonings.

CHAPTER II.

METHOD IN SPECIAL. — METHODOLOGY OF JUDGMENTS.

§ 88. THE full Perfection of a Judgment involves the several conditions of Material, Formal, and Verbal Perfection, as these virtues may characterize an identification of an attribute with its subject. *The Three Conditions of Perfection in Judgments.*

These three conditions, accordingly, — 1. That in respect of its matter, the predicate be recognized as agreeing with the subject; 2. That in the thought this identity be determined or declared in the judgment; and, 3. That the verbal statement correspond with the identity as thought, — are the self-evident, as they are the most fundamental, conditions of a perfect proposition.

In regard to the first condition lying in the matter, it may be remarked that it is not incumbent on Logic to verify the matter that is originally given it as the object of thought. But when matter is thus given and the Discursive Faculty applies its energy to it, what is given must be treated in conformity with its own nature. Thought must not deal with Being as if it were only Mathematical Form. Accepting the formula $I = I$ as mere formula expressive of the identity of every object of Thought with itself, it must not then convert this form without content into form with content; in other words, surreptitiously foist in Being into this empty form, and flatter itself it has proved the reality of Existence. In like manner, if its given matter be Substance, it must not in the handling of it treat it as if Cause. Thought must comprehend its own matter, and must be held responsible for the maintenance of its purity throughout all its processes.

Hence the rule that the Judgment be so framed that in the matter as given by the Presentative or the Representative Faculties, that which is taken as subject or as predicate be clearly recognized in accordance with the kinds of whole in which the matter is viewed. No rule in Method is more fundamental than this, or more wide-sweeping. It would be impossible to exclude error from a Judgment, incongruence from a Concept, or fallacy from a Reasoning, except on this condition: that the Judgment admit of a ready reference of its terms to its matter as given, so far as the kind of Quantity is concerned, for a verification of its truth. While in strictness Logic takes only what is given, and is concerned purely with the form, not with the matter, it must never ignore the relationship of form to matter, and must order its procedures in harmony with this relationship. The principle of this relationship is that of Quantity. That we can think any object implies that the object contains the principle of Whole and Parts and thus answers to Thought, which moves only according to this principle. The two virtues of Thought to be secured by this Law are those of Adequateness and Accuracy. It is the Objective Law of a Judgment, and aims at the Material Perfection of Science.

The next rule is that the identity between the Terms affirmed in the Judgment be clearly recognized. This is the Subjective Law of a Judgment, and aims at the Formal Perfection of Science.

The third rule is that the Language in which the Judgment is embodied be recognized as truly representing the thought. This is the Verbal Law of a Judgment, and aims at the Verbal Perfection of Science.

The distinct enumeration of these fundamental Rules of a Judgment is important both to correct thinking, and also to correction of error in the results of thinking. Only as the mind has become habituated to discriminate these three several kinds or degrees of truth in a proposition — correspondence of the notions to the terms, agreement between the terms, and correspondence of the words to the notions — can it proceed safely in the exposition of its thoughts. And only as it is enabled readily to distinguish the several ways in which error can creep into its thoughts, can it verify them or purge them from the error that vitiates them.

§ 89. The foregoing are the general conditions or rules of a perfect Judgment. We proceed to those that are special. These will vary according to the special nature of the several kinds of Judgments. *Rules of Negative and Disjunctive Judgments.* The most general distinction of Judgments is in respect of their essential Quality, as Affirmative, Negative, or Disjunctive. The Rules for the Affirmative Judgment are obviously the same as those that have been given for Judgments as such. The Rule for the Negative Judgment is, that the terms of the Proposition be recognized as opposed or different — as non-identical. Nothing need be said in explication of this rule, as it is only the negative phase of the rule for affirmative Judgments.

The Disjunctive Judgment presents peculiar difficulties, and requires more extended consideration. This Judgment, it must be borne in mind, is founded on the third and fourth Laws of Thought, the Law of Disjunction and of Exclusion or Excluded Middle, which obliges us to think that of two contradictory attributes one must, and only one can, belong to the subject. The obvious condition of a perfect Disjunctive Judgment, then, is that the disjunction affirmed be a true contradictory disjunction.

The liability to error in forming Judgments of this class arises from the inadequacy of Language to furnish terms for all the contradictory oppositions that may arise in Thought, and the resulting necessity of a recourse to the so-called opposition of Contrariety, which gives only a mediate disjunction. In this case, to secure that the Judgment be a perfect Judgment, the disjunction will need to be carried up into one of contradictory opposition. For illustration, in the Disjunctive Judgment, *Angles are right, acute, or obtuse*, we test the perfection of the Judgment by applying the principle of Contradiction successively to the several pairs of disjunct members. We say, first, *Angles are right or are not right;* then we say, *Angles that are not right are acute or obtuse*, that is, *less or greater than right;* and in this way attain a proper logical or contradictory disjunction. Only so far as we can carry through this contradictory disjunction between the members, can we have the logical basis of a perfect Disjunctive Judgment.

The two Rules, then, which are involved in the conditions of a perfect Disjunctive Judgment, are, —

First, if the disjunction be one of two members, they must be recognized as contradictories to each other.

Secondly, if it be one of more than two members, the members must, by being properly paired with each other, or with others to be supplied, be reducible to the form of a series of Disjunctive Judgments of Contradictory Opposition.

As disjunction in thought and disjunction in the verbal expression are expressed in language by the same particles, *or, nor; either, or; neither, nor;* it becomes necessary to apprehend which is intended. The following proposition is equivocal: *Consequently space is divided from itself by space, or is not divided at all.* The disjunction may be interpreted to apply to the Judgment, when the meaning will be, *Space either is divided from itself by space, or is not divided at all;* or to the mode of expression, when the meaning will be, *Space is divided from itself by space*, in other words, *is not divided at all.*

It should be remembered that a perfectly pure disjunction can only be in the copula. *A either is B or is not B*, is not always convertible into *A is either B or non-B*, in which the disjunction is in the terms, the *datum* of the Judgment.

§ 90. The second distinction of Judgments we found to be grounded on their Modality. The conditions of a perfect Judgment imposed by this distinction are that its character as Pure, that is, assertory, or as Modal, and if Modal, as Problematic or Apodictic, be clearly recognized. *Rules of Modal Judgments.* The special liability to error here originates in the fact that through the imperfections in language the modality of the judgment which lies in the copula alone, may be covertly slipped over to the predicate. Thus the judgment, *Alexander may have conquered Darius*, is easily converted into the proposition, *Alexander was a possible conqueror of Darius*,[1] which is a very different proposition; and although in certain uses the two are equivalent, in other uses they would have a very different import. The one is a purely concessive proposition, which, from its nature, may require no proof; the other is an assertory proposition, and proof may reasonably be required of him who puts it forward.

The several species of Judgments given by this distinction differ from one another in strength. The Apodictic is the strongest, and involves the Problematic and the Assertory; and the Assertory involves the Problematic. The danger, therefore, is that what has been problematically enounced should be mistaken for an assertory or a necessary judgment; or that a mere assertory judgment or enunciation should be mistaken for an apodictic or necessary judgment.

Further, as no sensible symbol, no sight or sound, can adequately express a purely mental act, and language from its felt impotency even forbears often any expression of the act of judging, it is to be expected that the distinctions of judg-

---

[1] It is remarkable, to illustrate this liability, that Sir William Hamilton calls the proposition, *Alexander conquered Darius honorably*, a Modal Proposition; and as he readily converts it into the form, *Alexander was the honorable conqueror of Darius*, when the modification is unquestionably one of the predicate, not of the copula, he concludes that the distinction of propositions on this ground of modality is futile. — See *Lectures on Logic*, xiv, page 181. Boston edition.

ments in themselves would be left subject to imperfect and equivocal means of expression. The forms of language used to denote these distinctions are, in fact, borrowed from those appropriated to other uses. It becomes necessary, therefore, in order to secure correct thought, to weigh carefully the language in which it is conveyed; — to apprehend whether the forms used do, indeed, express modality at all, and if so, whether that modality is adequately determined in them. The distinctions of modality are denoted in the English Language by the auxiliaries *may or can* with their respective tense inflections for the Problematic, and *must* for the Apodictic Judgment; and also by Adverbials, as *possibly, probably, necessarily*, and the like. Now all these modal forms may attach to the matter thought, or to the Thought itself, and hence arises the equivocality in expressing modal distinctions. Thus in the Judgment, *John may recover in a month*, the meaning may be that his disease is such as to admit of his recovery, and the Judgment itself be strictly assertory. Or, on the other hand, the contingency may lie in the Judgment itself. Although in ordinary, loose discourse, it may answer equally well to connect the contingency with the predicate or with the copula, yet correct thinking may often require that the distinction be clearly noted.

§ 91. The third distinction of Judgments is founded on the degree which is regarded in the determined agreement between Subject and Predicate.

Rules of Partial Judgments.

The conditions of a Perfect Judgment imposed by this distinction, are: —

1. That the Identity affirmed be distinctly recognized as Total or as Partial, both in respect of Thought and of Verbal Expression.

2. That if the Identity be Partial, the precise part of the containing whole, whether it be in the Subject or in the Predicate which the affirmation respects, be distinctly recognized.

§ 92. The fourth distinction of Propositions is into the two species of *Categorical* and *Hypothetical*, according as the whole regarded in them is an object or truth. *Rules of Hypothetical Judgments.*

The first condition, then, prescribed by this distinction, is that the Judgment be recognized as belonging to the one or to the other of these species.

The difficulty here will be found chiefly with the Hypothetical Judgment, in discriminating accurately wherein the identity affirmed in the Judgment between the terms lies, as the real nature of the Judgment is obscured by the form in which it is expressed, as well as by the name which has inaptly been given to it. It should be fully understood that there is nothing more conditional or hypothetical in the nature of a Hypothetical Judgment than in any other. The simple import of every such Judgment is that the truth expressed in the subject, or, as it is called, the first or antecedent member, involves or conditions the truth of the predicate or consequent member. Now, inasmuch as for the most part Propositions in discourse are only expressions of a partial identity between the subject and the predicate — only affirm that some one part of the subject is identical with the predicate, or some one part of the predicate is identical with the subject, or, it may be, some one part of the subject is identical with some one part of the predicate, — the liability to error in the so-called Hypothetical Judgment is far greater than in the case of a Categorical Proposition, inasmuch as it is more difficult to identify the parts of a truth than the parts of an object. The hypothetical form of the Proposition, moreover, disguises the true nature of the Judgment, and so increases the liability to error.

This dissection of the Hypothetical Proposition, accordingly, prescribes the following conditions of a Perfect Hypothetical Judgment : —

1. It must be clearly apprehended in its true nature as a Judgment, the terms of which are Truths or Judgments, not simple objects — not Concepts nor Integrate Wholes.

2. The specific parts in the terms — in the Antecedent and the Consequent Members — between which the identity affirmed lies, must be distinctly recognized, as also the truth of these members as themselves judgments.

3. It is further necessary to recognize whether the Judgment is in the relation of Whole and Part, or in that of Part and Complementary Part.

To illustrate the application of these conditions, we will take the Hypothetical, proceeding in the relation of Whole and Part: *If there be a God, the world is governed by Providence.* The first condition requires that we distinctly recognize the proposition as one in which the terms, here called the Antecedent and Consequent Members, are Truths or Represented Judgments, assumed *pro hac vice* to be true; as meaning, in other words, that the truth *that a God is*, contains in it the truth *that the world is governed by Providence.* The second condition requires that we recognize the parts of these several truths which are asserted in the proposition to be identical. We do this by analyzing the terms of the first member, *that God is*, and discovering that one part of the notion *God*, is *providential ruler.*

To illustrate these Rules in a Hypothetical proceeding in the relation of Part and Complementary Part: *If virtue is voluntary, vice is voluntary.* First, we recognize the proposition as meaning that *The truth that virtue is voluntary, involves in it the truth that vice is voluntary.* Next, we recognize those parts in the members which are identical. The attribute of morality belongs alike to *virtue* and *vice*, as parts complementary of each other. In that respect they are the same — they are both *moral.*

It will have been observed that the Hypothetical Judgment occurs often in discourse as a true reasoning, as a kind of Enthymeme, one of the premises being suppressed. The terms of the Judgment, in fact, stand in the relation to each other of a conclusion to a premise; and they are hence appropriately called respectively the Antecedent and Consequent members of the Judgment.

METHODOLOGY OF JUDGMENTS.

§ 93. The Fifth distinction of Judgments is into Extensive and Comprehensive or Intensive Judgments, being founded on the Logical Quantity of their terms. The conditions of a perfect Judgment given by this distinction is that its Logical Quantity be distinctly apprehended, so that it be recognized whether the subject or the predicate is the containing whole. This can always be effected by changing the form of the Judgment so as to put it into the phraseology distinctive of the two Quantities. Thus the proposition, *Man is rational*, expressed in Comprehensive Quantity, would read: The whole, *man*, contains in its complement of attributes the part or attribute *rational*. In Extensive Quantity: The part or species, *man*, is contained under the whole or genus, *rational*. Rules of Judgments in different Logical Wholes.

§ 94. The sixth distinction of Judgments is founded on the kind of Whole that is thought in the matter of the Judgment, whether an Integrate, a Substantial, or a Causal Whole. Rules of Judgments in different Wholes of Matter.

This distinction imposes this condition of a perfect Judgment: that the kind of Whole expressed by the terms be clearly recognized, whether an Integrate Whole, the parts of which lie out of each other; or a Substantial Whole, the parts of which permeate each other as simply congruent; or a Causal Whole, the parts of which permeate each other, not only as congruent, but also as determined through the same Causal Whole. Thus Parts in a Mathematical Whole are Parts *of* that Whole; Parts in a Substantial Whole are Parts *in* or *under* that Whole, according as the Whole is a Comprehensive or Extensive Whole; Parts of a Causal Whole are Parts *through* that Whole. In the Mathematical or Integrate Whole, the *nexus* is simply aggregation; in a Substantial Whole, the *nexus* is substance; in a Causal Whole, it is cause.

§ 95. To recapitulate the conditions of a Perfect Proposition, that is, of a true Judgment truly expressed, it is necessary to recognize it —

1°. As to its Verbal Form, as having perfect correspondence between the Thought and the words.

2°. As to its Quality, whether Identifying, or Differencing, or Disjoining in contradictory or in contrary opposition.

3°. As to its Modality, whether simply Assertory, or Problematic, or Necessary.

4°. As to degree of its Identification, whether Total or Partial, and if Partial, in respect of what part.

5°. As to the logical Gradation of its terms, whether Judgments, Concepts, or Integrate Wholes; in other words, whether Hypothetical or Categorical.

6°. As to the logical Quantity of its Terms, whether if Logical, an Extensive or an Intensive Whole; or, if Material, whether an Integrate, a Substantial, or a Causal Whole.

CHAPTER III.

METHODOLOGY OF CONCEPTS.

§ 96. THE Perfection of a Concept as a Synthesis of the homologous terms of two or more Judgments identified through the sameness of the other term, involves three conditions, corresponding respectively with the three fundamental virtues of perfect science. *The three conditions of Perfection in Concepts.*

The first condition is, that the terms, which being combined form the concept, be the homologous terms of Judgments having their other terms the same. This is the Objective Law of the Concept, giving it its Material Perfection.

The second condition is, that the concept itself be thought in its perfectness as a Whole in its relations both to other Concepts and to its Parts. This is the Subjective Law of a Concept, giving it its Formal Perfection.

The third condition is, that the verbal body of the Concept truly represent the matter as thought in it. This is the Verbal Law of a Concept, giving it its Verbal Perfection.

§ 97. The Objective Law of the Concept enjoins two things:

1°. That the terms combined to form the Concept be recognized as homologous terms. *The Objective Law of a Concept.*

2°. That these terms be recognized as from Judgments having the other terms the same — that is, that the Base be recognized.

The validity and binding force of these two rules will be recognized at once, as they are seen to be but the application of the principle of Identity, or, as it is in this relation denominated, the Law of Congruence, to Concepts.

The terms united to form the Concept must be homologous;

— that is, must be either all subjects or all predicates. To attempt the union of subjects with predicates in the same notion, would be to attempt the union of things unlike in respect of the same relation in which they are to stand in the union — to identify non-identities, or opposites.

Further, it is plain that not all homologous terms can be synthesized into a concept. The principle of Identity that governs all thought requires that the terms be related to one another by having a common element for each of the other terms of the primitive Judgments, which common element we have called the Base of the Concept. Thus if the Concept be in Extensive Quantity, the subjects must be all identified in the Judgments with the same predicate, as its Base. If, on the other hand, the concept be one in Comprehensive Quantity, the predicates which compose it must be all identified in previous Judgments with the same subject, as its proper Base.

It is to be observed, moreover, that in Thought a term is not the same unless it be thought in the same kind of Whole. We may suppose terms which can be identified in Judgments with the same subject or the same predicate, but in different kinds of whole; they cannot be synthesized into a Concept any more than solids and surfaces. Thus we have as true Judgments: *Man is biped; Man is soul and body; Man thinks;* but the incongruence in the kinds of Wholes in which the thought moves, forbids the synthesis of the predicates into a Concept.

In order, therefore, to the more thorough-going determination of the question whether two given terms are congruent or not, the kind of whole to which the concept belongs should be carefully distinguished. In a Mathematical or Integrate Whole, the parts of which lie out of each other, incongruent parts are, of course, only such as overlap each other. Circles and rectilineal figures cannot thus be united in thought as making up any polygon, for they must overlap each other. They are incongruent parts. *Head* and *Bones* are incongruent parts of *Body;* *Fiber* and *Leaf,* of *Plant;* *Thought* and *Predicate,* of *a Sentence;* *Sanction* and *Promulgation,* of *Law.* These several Wholes, conceived as Integrate Wholes, are not made up of such kinds of Parts as appear in each of these pairs. The parts in each couplet overlap each other. Thus a circle may be contained in a polygon; but its complement, the part or parts which with the circle make up the polygon, cannot be rectilinear. *Head* is a part of *Body* regarded as an Integrate Whole; but *Bones* are not the complement of *Head,* nor do they with any other part make up such complement. And a similar view must be taken of the other examples. The parts are not complementary of each other. They are, in reference to the same Whole, incongruent, inasmuch as in any attempt to fill out the given whole, some part must overlap some other.

In a Substantial Whole, in which the Parts permeate each other, the incongruence will lie in the opposite nature of the Qualities that are ascribed to the Subject; or, inasmuch as a Relative Whole may be represented in Thought under the analogies of a Substantial Whole, in the opposite nature of the Relations ascribed to the Subject. Thus, *Blue* and *Red; Round* and *Angular; Rough* and *Smooth; Stiff* and *Flexible; Thick* and *Thin; Skillful* and *Indolent; Moral* and *Deceitful,* are respectively pairs of Opposite Incongruent Parts. So far as they creep into the same Thought, the union is fatal to the Thought.

In a Causal Whole, the incongruence will lie in the union of parts which are not determined by the same cause. The distinctive relationship of the parts in these several wholes as before observed, is, to some extent, indicated in the prepositions that are commonly used to express it. In an Integrate Whole, the parts are parts *of* the whole; in a Substantial Whole, they are *in* or *under* the whole; in a Causal Whole, they are *through* the whole. Thus Integrant Parts of the notion *Man,* are *Body* and *Limbs;* Substantial Parts are *Rational* and *Animal;* Causal Parts are *Virtue* and *Vice.*

All the effects which may be through the cause are proper parts of a Causal Whole, as all the properties which are contained in an object conceived as Substance, are proper parts of that substance. *Man*, thus, as Free cause, that is, Moral, contains *virtue* and *vice* through this freedom. These are Congruent Parts of the Causal Whole, *Man* as Moral; Incongruent Parts would be *Virtue, Vice, Suffering*. So of the notion *Sculptor* as cause, Incongruent Parts would be *Statuary, Relief, Carving, Mosaic*, the last being not through a Sculptor as such.

It might be thought that the Objective Law of the Concept, as thus interpreted, would not be adequate to secure in full the Material Perfection which it proposes. But in strict logical consideration, the matter of a Concept is given in the Judgments from which it is derived; and consequently, the law of its formation cannot be expected to go back of the Judgments which are its proper matter. The question whether our concepts, which make up, as we have seen, the great body of our notion-words in discourse, do actually answer to the external realities to which we unconsciously in speaking and thinking refer them, is one indeed of momentous concernment to us. Are these notions which we fabricate so freely in our thought, all unreal, having no correspondences in the world of being around us; are our references of them to this objective world all illusory and deceptive; or, on the other hand, is the outer world constituted on the same principle of Identity which underlies and governs all Thought, having its likes and its unlikes, its samenesses and its differences in infinite variety and extent, exactly answering to the infinite variety and extent of our Thought-products — is the universe around us resolvable into the self-same species and classes which appear in our concepts, so that, if our thinking be legitimate, we may rest assured that there are corresponding species and classes of things about us? — these are questions, indeed, of most vital interest to us; but they lie properly out of the domain of Pure Logic.

Yet two observations may without impropriety be introduced here.

First, the forming of Concepts, as, for instance, the gathering into classes is determined by the special occasion or object of our thinking. Logic does not prescribe that, any more than does Arithmetic prescribe to what object we shall apply its processes — to the calculation of Interest, or the computation of Magnitudes. Logic only prescribes the proper movements of Thought, when Thought is required for any work to which it is fitted. We must not then expect that the outer world of realities should be broken up into precisely such parts as the occasions of our thought may happen to require. In other words, we must not expect that the lines of separation in the various objects of the actual world are distinctly drawn just where the uses of our thought may lead it to draw them, — that there are so many classes of animals or vegetables or minerals in the universe as we may in legitimate Thought choose to enumerate. Classifications, Concepts, vary with the occasions of our thinking, with the advancement of Science; the world around is constant in the relationships of its multiform contents. Generalizations in Science, thus, will sometimes be founded on essential attributes, sometimes on extrinsic attributes or relations; sometimes on one of these essential attributes, or of these relations, sometimes on another. Even systems of natural science will vary, in respect of the principle of classification and consequently in respect of the entire method of the particular system, with the advancements of the science. Accepting the doctrine that classification in the science of nature must be, "so far as it is accurate, the literal interpreter of the creative plan of God,"[1] and must rest, therefore, on intrinsic or essential attributes, — as those of proper Quality as in plan of structure for higher classifications, and of those of Quantity as in complicity of plan for lower, — we yet see that even here there is room for much diversity among naturalists

[1] L. Agassiz, *Methods of Study in Natural History*, chap. iv.

in their perfectly logical systems of generic arrangement, until science reaches its ultimate limit. "The plan of God in creation as expressed in organic forms" has remained the same unchanged through the successive systems of Aristotle, Linnæus, Cuvier, Baer, and their co-workers in this great field of science, and will abide the same through all the changing systems of classification as they go on in the ever-advancing progress to a perfect science which shall be founded on an accurate apprehension of all the facts, and a congruent representation of them in forms of classified knowledge, convenient for the uses of man in his perfected nature and condition.

Secondly, that there is a true correspondence between legitimate Thought and the universe of Being with which it is conversant, it is most irrational to question. Even if there be not, it is to us just as if there were; and therefore it is unreasonable to call the correspondence in question. Further, it can never be proved that there is no correspondence; for thought is impossible where there are no relations — no correspondences. To presume such want of correspondence so as to throw the burden of proof upon the party that affirms the correspondence, is but most unjustifiable arrogation — the presumption, whatever there may be, being all on the other side, so that the skeptic must be held to make good his doubt, that is, must invalidate his own skepticism. Still further, reason and revelation agree in teaching that legitimate thought has its counterpart in the realities of its objects. Reason postulates one universe, one Creator, one principle of creation — unity in the wondrous diversity, harmony in the infinity of parts, sameness in endless difference; and so we are taught every created thing is created "after his kind." This principle of *kind*, of identity in creation, stamped upon it at its origin, and maintained ever by the same Divine agency, never contradicting itself, that first brought it into being, is the fundamental principle in the universe of things, exactly answering to Thought. There is a true *kind*, a species in things, that never perishes, forbidding transformation into other kinds, and commingling of kinds, so that if such appear, we instinctively and truly recognize them as monstrosities, prodigies, which we forbear to account for till we attain a higher point of view from which to look out on the orderly arrangement of things that appear around us — a higher, purer light in which to study the well-ordered universe of God. Language, in its various forms, as shaped by the most cultivated portions of the human race, attests the general acquiescence of men in the correlativeness of thought and specific identity in nature. The words *genus, kind, kin, can, know,* and numerous others, all of one stock, and similar in the different dialects of the great Indo-European family, connect causative power, intelligence, and specific identity in clearest and closest relationship. Things are alike because the creatures of the same causative power; things correspond to our thoughts, because we and they are products of the same power and all are akin to it. In this are grounded alike the necessary outward condition of all science and the universal instinct of science in man. Without this correspondence between Thought and Being, science is an empty form; and the innate aspiration for science is a cheat and a lie. Accepting this correspondence with a natural and overpowering faith, man through the identities cognizable and validated in thought rises surely and successfully along the identities of creation, upward into the unity of the single creative power in the universe, and attains perfect science.

§ 98. The Subjective Law of a concept respects the thought side, as the objective law respects the object side, of this product of the Identifying Faculty. It prescribes the conditions of a perfect cognition in a concept so far as they respect the thinking subject.

The Subjective Law of a Concept.

The two virtues of a cognition lying in the nature of Thought itself, are *Clearness* and *Distinctness* — Clearness constituting the perfection of a concept regarded as one whole in relation to other wholes; Distinctness being its perfection regarded in relation to its own parts. Inasmuch as these are exhaustive complementary views in thought of a thought-cognition — as we can take no third view of it beyond the view of it as a part in relation to other complementary parts, and the view of it as a whole in relation to its own parts — these are the only two virtues which constitute its perfection as a Thought.

The Subjective Law of a Concept, accordingly, enjoins —

1. Clearness, or that the concept be recognized as distinguished from all other concepts.

2. Distinctness, or that the concept be recognized as to the several parts of which it is composed.

The process by which Clearness is attained is called *Definition*.

That by which Distinctness is attained is called *Analysis*.

"To Leibnitz we owe the precise distinction of concepts into clear and distinct, and from him is borrowed the following illustration. In darkness, the complete obscurity of night, we see nothing — there is no perception, no discrimination of objects. As the light dawns, the obscurity diminishes; the deep and uniform sensation of darkness is modified; we are conscious of a change; we see something, but are still unable to distinguish its features; we know not what it is. As the light increases, the outlines of wholes begin to appear, but still not with a distinctness sufficient to allow us to perceive them completely; but when this is rendered possible, by the rising intensity of the light, we are then said to see clearly. We then recognize mountains, plains, houses, trees, animals, etc., that is, we discriminate these objects as wholes, as unities, from each other. But their parts — the manifold of which these unities are the sum — their parts still lose themselves in each other, they are still but indistinctly visible. At length, when the daylight has fully sprung, we are enabled likewise to discriminate their parts; we now see distinctly what lies around us. But still we see as yet only the wholes which lie proximately around us, and of these only the parts which possess a certain size. The more distant wholes, and the smaller parts of nearer wholes, are still seen by us only in their conjoint result, only as they concur in making up that whole which is for us a visible minimum. Thus it is, that in the distant forest, or on the distant hill, we perceive a green surface; but we see not the several leaves, which in the one, nor the several blades of grass, which in the other, each contributes its effect to produce that amount of impression which our consciousness requires. Thus it is, that all which we do perceive is made up of parts which we do not perceive, and consciousness is itself, a complement of impressions, which lie beyond its apprehension. Clearness and distinctness are thus only relative. For between the extreme of obscurity and the extreme of distinctness, there are in vision an infinity of intermediate degrees. Now, the same thing occurs in thought. For we may either be conscious only of the concept in general, or we may also be conscious of its various constituent subjects or attributes, or both the concept and its parts may be lost in themselves to consciousness, and only recognized to exist by effects or relations which indirectly evidence their existence.

"The perfection of a notion is contained in two degrees or in two virtues, viz: in its clearness and in its distinctness; and, of course, the opposite vices of obscurity and indistinctness afford two degrees or two vices, constituting its imperfection. A concept is said to be *clear*, when the degree of consciousness by which it is accompanied is sufficient to discriminate what we think in and through it, from what we think in and through other notions; whereas if the degree of consciousness be so remiss that this and other concepts run into each other, in that case the notion is said to be *obscure*. It is evident that clearness and obscurity admit of various degrees, each being capable of almost infinite gradations, according as the object of the notion is discriminated with greater or less vivacity or precision from the objects of other notions. A concept is *ab-* [Clearness and Obscurity as in Concepts.]

solutely clear, when its object is distinguished from all other objects; a concept is *absolutely obscure,* when its object can be distinguished from no other object. But it is only the absolutely clear and absolutely obscure which stand opposed as contradictory extremes; for the same notion can at once be relatively or comparatively clear, and relatively or comparatively obscure. Absolutely obscure notions, that is, concepts whose objects can be distinguished from nothing else, exist only in theory; an absolutely obscure notion being, in fact, no notion at all. For it is of the very essence of a concept, that its object should, to a certain degree at least, be comprehended in its peculiar, consequently in its distinguishing, characteristics. But on the other hand, of notions absolutely clear, that is, notions whose objects cannot possibly be confounded with aught else, whether known or unknown — of such notions a limited intelligence is possessed of very few, and, consequently, our human concepts are, properly, only a mixture of the opposite qualities — *clear* or *obscure* as applied to them, meaning only that the one quality or the other is the preponderant. In a logical relation, the illustration of notions consists in the raising them from a preponderant obscurity to a preponderant clearness, or from a lower degree to a higher. So much for the quality of clearness or obscurity considered in itself.

" But a Clear concept may either be Distinct or Indistinct; the distinctness and indistinctness of concepts are therefore to be considered apart from their clearness and obscurity.

The Distinctness and Indistinctness of Concepts.

" We have seen that a concept is clear, when we are able to recognize it as different from other concepts. But we may discriminate a whole from other wholes, we may discriminate a concept from other concepts, though we have only a confused knowledge of the parts of which that whole or of the characters of which that concept is made up. This may be illustrated by the analogy of our Perceptive and Representative Faculties. We are all acquainted with many, say a thousand individuals; that is, we recognize such and such a countenance as the countenance of John, and as not the countenance of James, Thomas, Richard, or any of the other nine hundred and ninety-nine. This we do with a clear and certain knowledge. But the countenances, which we thus distinguish from each other, are, each of them, a complement made up of a great number of separate traits or features; and it might, at first view, be supposed that, as a whole is only the sum of its parts, a clear cognition of a whole countenance can only be realized through a distinct knowledge of each of its constituent features. But the slightest consideration will prove that this is not the case. For how few of us are able to say of any, the most familiar face, what are the particular traits which go to form the general result; and yet, on that account, we hesitate neither in regard to our own knowledge of an individual, nor in regard to the knowledge possessed by others.

"Continuing our illustrations from the human countenance: we all have a clear knowledge of any face which we have seen, but few of us have distinct knowledge even of those with which we are familiar; but the painter who, having looked upon a countenance, can retire and reproduce its likeness in detail, has necessarily both a clear and distinct knowledge of it. Now, what is thus the case with perceptions and representations, is equally the case with notions. We may be able clearly to discriminate one concept from another, although the degree of consciousness does not enable us distinctly to discriminate the various component characters of either concept from each other. The Clearness and Distinctness of a notion are thus not the same; the former involves merely the power of distinguishing the total objects of our notions from each other; the latter involves the power of distinguishing the several subjects, the several attributes, of which that notion is the sum. In the former the unity, in the latter the multiplicity, of the notion is called into relief."

§ 99. The term Definition is used in a wider and looser, or

in a narrower and stricter sense. The general process itself which it denotes, as applied to various objects, is also variously modified.

Definition; its kinds.

As the object of all definition is clearness, which is a quality variable in degree, the term *definition* is naturally employed to denote processes that imply more or less clearness, from its lowest degree in mere indication, when by any peculiarity whatever, even of the most accidental kind, we separate one object from another in our view of it, up to complete logical definition, which entirely bounds out the object. The process, again, may be applied to words, to concepts, or to any cognition of the Presentative Faculties, viewed in the relation of Whole and Part. As applied to words, the process is called Verbal or Nominal Definition. This is effected either by synonymous words or expressions, or by indicating the etymology of the term to be defined. The term *concept*, thus is defined synonymously as a *notion*, and etymologically as *that in thought which is taken with something else; breakfast* as *morning-meal*, or as *that by which we break fast; definition* as *dilucidation*, or as *the act of bounding or limiting off.*

As applied to concepts and carried out to completeness in order to perfect science, it is called Logical Definition.

As applied to cognitions other than concepts, it is called variously Dilucidation, Description, or Definition, with or without modifying words.

In its application to an Integrate Whole, we have exemplifications of its use in Mathematical Definitions; as a Sector is mathematically defined to be *a portion of a circle bounded by two radii and the arc interrupted between them.* Such definitions have the completeness of a proper logical definition. They completely separate the object from its complementary part. An approximation to this logical completeness is attained in the definition of the Fore-arm, thought as part of an Integrate Whole, as *that part of the human body bounded by the wrist and the elbow.* More vaguely and incompletely is Head defined as *the upper portion of the body.*

In its application to Substantial Wholes, when the differencing element must be found in an attribute by which it is distinguished from other substances, it may be exemplified by the definition of *man* as substance, that is, *rational animal* — a definition, as will be seen, that corresponds with the process in a proper logical whole. The only difference is, that here the defining members, *rational -animal*, are viewed as *real*, not as *thought, attributes*. Parts of a Substantial Whole, that is, attributes, may be defined by differencing them from complementary attributes of the same substance.

In its application to a primitive cognition, viewed as a Causal Whole, definition is the separation of one cause from other causes by a differencing effect, or of one effect from the complementary effect of the same cause. Thus, heating is defined as *the effect of the Sun in expanding bodies; expanding* being the effect which differences *heat* from other causal agencies of the sun.

Logicians, it may be observed here, have vaguely distinguished three kinds of Definition — *Verbal* or *Nominal, Real*, and *Genetic*. A Verbal Definition is the elucidation, the rendering clear of the term or object through its name. Thus, a Verbal or Nominal Definition of *Concept* would be, *That in thought which is taken with something else.* A Real Definition of *Concept* would be, *A synthesis of the homologous terms of two or more judgments with the same base.* A Genetic Definition would be, *A product of Thought arising from the synthesis of homologous terms*, &c. A Verbal Definition thus elucidates — renders clear — through the Word; a Real Definition through the Substance; a Genetic Definition, through the Cause producing.

§ 100. The process of proper Logical Definition consists essentially in recognizing the object defined as a part in distinction from other like parts of a larger logical whole; that is, in distinction from its complementary part. *Logical Definition; its nature.*

It is Extensive or Comprehensive according as the concept is viewed in the one or the other of these kinds of Logical Quantity. *Definition either Extensive or Comprehensive.*

The nature and validity of this distinction require no illustration. It is important to enounce it articulately, that in undertaking the process of definition the mind may move intelligently and freely. As the same name is ordinarily applied in Language to a Concept made up in either Quantity, it becomes the more necessary to determine at once in defining in which the concept is to be viewed, whether as a subject-concept or a predicate-concept. Definition in Extension respects the subjects of which the concept is composed; Definition in Comprehension, the predicates or attributes.

It will be sufficient to exemplify the process in each kind of Quantity. In Extension, then, to define will be to discriminate the concept from all coördinate concepts; as the whole here is evidently the genus made up of the concept to be defined, and the coördinate species. We attain extensive clearness, then, in a concept of a right-angled triangle when we discriminate it from all coördinate triangles. We attain clearness in the concept *man*, regarded as part of the Extensive whole, *animal*, when we discriminate it from all *non-rational animals;* in the concept *hope*, when we recognize it as complementary of *fear*, in the class of emotions called *desires*.

In a Comprehensive Whole, clearness is attained by a recognition of that character or that complement of characters in the concept which it has as peculiar to itself, and not in common with other concepts. Thus we attain clearness in the concept of a *right-angled triangle* in comprehension, when we view it as possessing the peculiar property of *having one of its angles right;* of *man*, when viewed as *rational*, and thus making up with the generic property of a brute, the total comprehension of *rational animal*. We fasten attention here on the attribute; while in attaining extensive clearness we look at the subjects of which the attribute is predicated. As for the most part terms may be construed in either quantity, the results attained by the definition will so far be expressed in similar terms.

The examples given have been indiscriminately in contradictory and in contrary opposition, and also in positive and in negative characters. The strictest logical definition will proceed in contradictory opposition — accordingly will be *dichotomous*, or through the two sections of Part and Complementary Part, expressed logically as *A* and *non-A*, these two contradictories making up the proper whole of Thought. Plato's definitions are characterized as of `this form — dichotomous or bi-sectional, proceeding in contradictory opposition. We evidently attain strict logical clearness when we thus discriminate a concept from its complementary part. Now, as in the case of any concept there may be recognized many kinds of parts standing in this relation of being complementary to it, that is, as making up with it so many kinds of wholes, it is obvious there may be as many perfect definitions of the same concept as there are different kinds of wholes in which it is a part. Plato's definition of *man* as *bird without feathers*, is beyond criticism, if the whole be taken as *biped*, so long as only feathered and unfeathered beings are known to belong to this class; for it discriminates perfectly *man* as part of this whole from its complementary part. The so-called Aristotelian definition of *man* as an *animal walking on two feet*, is just as obnoxious to criticism as Plato's, and no more so. How this should be is sufficiently shown in the mode of forming concepts, if, at least, we take into view, also, in connection with this, the inadequacy of language to signalize by a distinct word every possible synthesis of subjects more or less, or of predicates more or less, on any Base more or less composite. What shall be the particular whole in which the concept to be defined shall be viewed, and consequently, what shall be the definition, depends then on the occasions of use. A moral philosopher would define *man* in one way; a physiologist in another; a political economist in a still different way; and so on, and each variously on the varying occasions of his discourse. The process as a movement of Thought remains ever the same — discrimination as part from the complementary part.

But as such movement it is properly in its first step only dichotomous, or by discrimination of one part as complementary. As, however, in contrary opposition generally, so here the thought may move on by successive definitions in the strict Platonic method, till we attain the degree of clearness required. Or we may abridge the process by leaping at once to the results of such continued dichotomous definition, just as the arithmetician, when the two factors of *seven* and *nine* are given, leaps to the product *sixty-three*, without going through the entire process, step by step, of adding seven units to other seven, and seven more to those, and so on.

Further, we may define indifferently by positive or by negative characters, as we may discriminate *man* from its complementary part, *brute*, either by the positive character *rational*, or the negative character *not-brute* or *not-irrational*. Evidently what is positive in respect of one part is negative in respect of the other part. The movement of Thought is indifferent from the one or the other, and the same in both. The occasions of discourse, however, generally, and of preference, demand the positive. It is hence, from the occasions of discourse, that the rule springs which prohibits definition by negative characters.

The convenient and logically sound rule which directs us to define by *naming the next higher genus and the specific difference*, has the recommendation of being dichotomous, and, by an easy process of conversion, of being explicable in either Quantity. Thus the definition of *man*, as *rational animal*, may be interpreted: *Man* is of the genus *animal*, and the species *rational*; or, *Man* has the generic attribute of *animal*, and the specific attribute of *rational*. Or as defined by the naturalist, as *bi-manous* or *two-handed mammal*, it may mean: of the genus *mammal*, and species *bi-manous;* or, having the generic character of *mammal*, and specific character of *bi-manous*. Obviously, however, the rule has relation only to proper concept wholes.

§ 101. The conditions of Distinctness in a concept are, 1. That the kind of parts to be distinguished be first recognized; and, 2. That each of these parts be clearly discriminated from the other parts. Distinctness; its Conditions.

If a still higher degree of distinctness is required than that which is given in the discrimination of the first set of parts, then each of these parts may be treated as new wholes, in which successively distinctness is to be attained. The process will be the same as in distinguishing the first set of parts.

Logical Analysis, then, will consist of the two processes, first, of recognizing the kind of parts to be attained in the Analysis; and, secondly, of separating into these parts. The first is the necessary antecedent condition of analysis; the second is the analysis itself.

§ 102. The first Law of Distinctness requires that the kind of parts, whether Material Parts, as Integrate, Substantial, or Causal, or proper Logical Parts, as Extensive or Comprehensive, which are to be distinguished, be recognized. For the fuller distinctness, indeed, the parts of each of these kinds may be discriminated. Thus, the concept *Man*, may be distinguished into the Integrant Parts of *Head*, *Body*, and *Limbs*; or into the Intensive Parts of *Rational* and *Animal*; or again into the Extensive Parts of *Black*, *Tawny*, and *White*; or the Causal Parts of *Loving* and *Hating*. But in any case the kind of Parts to be discriminated must be recognized. The necessity of this Law it is unnecessary further to illustrate.

§ 103. The particular kind of parts to be discriminated having been recognized, the next step is to effect the distinction. This is Proper Analysis. This part of the procedure will vary with the kind of parts, giving rise to so many subordinate kinds of processes. Analysis; its kinds.

That process by which Distinctness is attained in Integrant Parts may be called *Dissection*; also, *Formal Analysis*;

That by which Extensive Parts are obtained is called *Division;*

That by which Intensive Parts are obtained is called *Partition;*

That by which Causal Parts are obtained may be called *Resolution;* also, *Evolution,* or *Causal Analysis.*

It will not escape notice that one kind of wholes is omitted in this enumeration of the processes of analysis — that of Substantial Wholes. The reason is, that while the ground of distinction exists, yet language does not enable us to distinguish except by tedious circumlocution to which quick thought and speech will not submit, the *real* from the *thought* characters of an object of thought — actual properties from thought attributes. We should, accordingly, be forced to use the same terms, and lay out the same rules for analysis in Substantial Wholes as for analysis in Comprehensive Wholes. With this intimation of the reality of the distinction, and of the consequent necessity in the strictest thought of observing it on supposable, if rare, occasions, to avoid perplexity, analysis in Substantial Wholes is formally omitted, its nature and laws being readily gathered from the exposition of analysis in Comprehensive Wholes.

§ 104. There is one general Law of Analysis applicable to all the subordinate processes alike. It is the general Law of Adequacy appearing here in the specific form of the Law of Completeness requiring that all the Parts in the given Analysis be recognized. The necessity of this is obvious. So far as the Analysis is incomplete some one or more parts being omitted from the recognition, the cognition fails in distinctness. Besides this, it must of necessity be partial and one-sided, and positive error will be the result. For example, if in analyzing Faith as a Christian virtue, I recognize only the characters of Intellectual Belief, and Sentiment of the Heart, leaving out all Moral Disposition, Purpose, or Will, I make it a merely involuntary state, and, of course, exclude from the notion all freedom, all responsibility, all morality.

Law of Completeness.

The practical importance of a careful observance of this Law of Logical Analysis is to be seen in the fact that by far the greatest part of erroneous opinion in all departments of knowledge arises from the incomplete apprehension of the objects of knowledge. Most dissensions in science and in belief would be ended by a complete survey of all the constituent elements of the matter in dispute. It is mainly because the parties look, one at one element, the other at another, and each to the exclusion from his view of some element or character important to a correct opinion, that any dissension arises.

§ 105. Passing now to the subordinate processes of Logical Analysis, the first, FORMAL ANALYSIS or DISSECTION, is that which gives as its result Integrate Parts. These are of two kinds — Spacial and Numerical. The distinctive characteristic of each kind is that the parts lie out of each other. The fundamental condition of a correct analysis here, accordingly, being that no part overlap another, we have the comprehensive Law of Formal Analysis or Logical Dissection that it proceed from a single principle; that, for instance, but one point of departure in lineal, one line in superficial, one plane in solid dissection, be taken; and in numerical parts, one unit of separation. Thus in dissecting *tree* regarded in simply lineal extent, to take, as one part, that below the ground, and as another, that between the branching of the roots and the branching of the boughs, would vitiate the process, as giving parts that overlap each other. So to analyze the *United States of America* as a spacial extent by taking the *Atlantic States*, the *Pacific States*, the *Lake States*, the *Gulf States*, and the *Mississippi Valley States*, even if it were complete, would be incorrect, for the lines of dissection cross each other, giving overlapping parts. So to dissect *hope* into *expectation, desire,* and *pleasure,* is vicious, inasmuch as *pleasure* is not attained by the same line of dissection as the other parts. It overlaps both.

Dissection: its two kinds.

So in Numerical Parts, to dissect a *dollar* into *shillings* and *dimes* would necessarily give overlapping parts; or to separate *solar light* into *full splendor*, *cloudiness*, *moonlight*, and *twilight*, the unit of Degree of Intensity not being apprehended, the parts overlap one another; or to distinguish *merit* as *perfect*, *average*, *fair*, and *zero*, the third distinction of degree not corresponding with the other three.

§ 106. The second kind of Logical Analysis is that of DIVISION, which gives, as its proper result, the Extensive Parts of a Logical Whole; — in other words, the objects contained under the whole which must here ever be regarded as a *genus* or class, that is, a subject-whole.

Division.

The first step in Division is to recognize the specific kind of parts that are sought in the Analysis. From the very nature of a subject-concept, that may have as its Base a plurality of attributes, there may be as many modes of division, each giving its own set of parts, as there are different attributes synthesized in the Base. Thus, *man* is a subject-concept with a Base of the two intrinsic attributes, *rational* and *animal;* and the concept may be analyzed into rational parts, as *cultivated* and *barbarous;* *learned* and *unlearned; intellectual*, *sentimental*, and *practical;* or into animal parts, as *tall* and *short; white, tawny,* and *black; sanguine* and *bilious,* and the like. The concept has likewise a Base of manifold extrinsic attributes, or attributes of Relation, which will furnish so many other modes of division and sets of parts; as *European*, *Asiatic*, &c., in relation to country or place; *antediluvian* and *post-diluvian; governors* and *governed,* and the like. An analysis that should present parts of these various kinds, taken indiscriminately and confusedly, would obviously be of no worth, as it would be without logical method. We must then, as the first step in division, apprehend the attribute in the Base of the concept in reference to which the analysis is to be made. The attribute selected for this purpose is called the Principle of

Division. Thus the Division of *man* into *cultivated* and *barbarous* has for its principle of division the attribute *cultivated*, being comprehended in the more comprehensive attribute *rational;* that of *man* into *white, tawny,* and *black,* is *color,* being an attribute comprehended in *animal.* A Division, it is seen thus, is effected simply by adding an attribute to the Base of a Subject-concept, or Extensive Whole, as by adding to *rational animal* the attribute *cultivated,* or *black,* we obtain corresponding divisions of the concept *man.*

The first and the only proper logical division is *dichotomous;* giving the two parts, one having the attribute which forms the principle of division, the other not; as *man* is of the two species, *cultivated man* and *not cultivated,* that is, *barbarous man;* angles are *right angles,* and *angles that are not right.* But generally a farther division is required, and in the enumeration of the parts those that are negative are not specially mentioned, but are represented in the subordinate divisions. Thus instead of a division of *man* in respect of Color, first into *white* and *not white,* and then *not white* into the two colored species, *tawny* and *black,* the division is made at once into the three varieties; and *angles* are divided into *right, acute,* and *obtuse.* The three parts thus obtained are in looser language denominated coördinate, inasmuch as each is complementary of the other two. In such case the more comprehensive attribute is the principle of division; as color and magnitude respectively in the examples given. In the same way there may be any number of parts.

The first thing, then, to be done, in effecting division, is to recognize the principle of division, or the attribute in respect of which the division is made. This being done, the one law of division is —

That all the coördinate, that is, complementary parts, given by the principle of division, and none others, be distinguished.

This comprehensive Law comprehends the following particulars : —

1°. That none but parts — individuals or species — contained under the given Whole, be taken.

2°. That no objects or parts be taken which are not strictly coördinate with one another under the adopted principle of division.

3°. That subordinate objects or species be apprehended as contained under the super-ordinate.

4°. That all the coördinate species be distinguished.

§ 107. The third kind of Logical Analysis is that of PARTITION, which gives as its proper result the Comprehensive Parts of a Logical Whole ; in other words, the characters or properties, inherent or relative, that make up the whole. The parts in this species of whole permeate each other, and are comprehended in the whole.

Partition.

The first step in Partition is to recognize some one character or property as that which shall determine the kind or class of properties sought in the Analysis. What that character shall be it is not the province of Logic to prescribe; that is to be determined by the object proposed in the Analysis, the consideration of which belongs to Rhetoric or the Art of Discourse. Logical Science cannot discriminate between the characters or properties that make up a concept, as to their relative importance. It can only discriminate them as Intrinsic or Extrinsic ; as Conflicting or Congruent ; as Involving, or Involved, or Coördinate ; for it cannot transcend the relationship of Whole and Part.

Some one particular character or property having been thus selected which shall determine the set of characters to be taken as making up the concept, the Law of the Analysis itself will be derived from the indicated relations of the character to the Whole and to the other characters. This Law is —

That none but coördinate characters, and all of them, be distinguished.

This general Law contains the following particulars:—

1°. That none but actual characters be taken.

2°. That no conflictive characters be taken.

3°. That involved characters, if distinguished at all, be apprehended as contained in the involving character.

4°. That all the coördinate characters be distinguished.

§ 108. The Fourth kind of Logical Analysis is that of RESOLUTION, otherwise called *Evolution* and *Causal Analysis*, which gives as its proper results the Causal Parts; in other words, effects as parts of the concept viewed as Cause.

Resolution.

The first step here is to recognize the kind of effects into which the concept is to be resolved by apprehending some one effect, which with all the others shall make up the complement of effects through that Cause. Here it should be remembered that, from the imperfectness of Language, the same name may denote Causes of widely variant effects. Thus *Man* is a name of a Causal agency operating in many conceivable different spheres; as, for instance, materially, as counterpoising more or less weight; chemically, as forming by decomposition, nitrogen, carbon, and other chemical elements; organically, as breathing, digesting, &c.; spiritually, as thinking, desiring, willing, and the like. The cause in counterpoising, it is obvious, is not the same as in breathing, or in thinking. It becomes necessary in order to Distinctness in a Causal Whole to apprehend first the kind of effects which constitute it, which is done by taking some one effect as the determining one of the set of effects to be attained in the Analysis.

This being done, the Comprehensive Law of Causal Analysis for attaining Distinctness is —

That none but coördinate effects, and all of them, be distinguished.

This Comprehensive Law comprises the following particulars:—

1°. That none but actual effects of the given Cause be taken.

2°. That no effects be taken which are not strictly coördinate with one another.

3°. That derivative effects be apprehended as contained through the original effect from which they are derived.

4.° That all the coördinate effects be distinguished.

§ 109. The VERBAL LAW of a concept divides itself into two parts, one determined by its relation to the Thought expressed in it, the other by the nature of verbal expression.

I. The Verbal Law of a concept requires that the Expression be exactly conformed to the Thought to be expressed. This involves —

1°. That the Expression contain the exact Thought;

2°. That it contain all the Thought; and —

3°. That it contain no more than the Thought.

The necessity of a careful observance of these laws rests chiefly on the fact that Language is at best an inadequate expression of Thought. It furnishes but a single term for a great multiplicity of thoughts. Hence the necessity of choosing, in the first place, the fittest terms for expressing the Concept and the parts contained in the Analysis; and, in the second place, when the term is not exactly adequate to the Thought, of modifying it so as to make the thought and the expression exactly coincident.

One application of this part of the general Verbal Law of the Concept is of especial interest and importance. It respects the verbal expression of the quantity of the concept. The importance of a distinct recognition of this application of the law originates in the fact that Language ordinarily fails to distinguish in the form of the word the kind of quantity which is intended. The word *tree*, for example, may be used to denote an Extensive, an Intensive, or an Integrate Whole; — to denote a class of objects, a complement of attributes, or a certain individual object. When such words are used without modifying words to indicate the quantity, they may be taken in either one of these several meanings; and when they are repeated in the same general movement of thought in different relations, there is great liability to confusion and error, which can be detected, perhaps, only through a discrimination of these several kinds of quantity. Logicians even, for a single exemplification, have often failed to recognize the difference between the expression, *No man is immortal*, and the proper negative proposition, *Man is not immortal*. They class and treat them both as alike universal negative judgments. But there is a most material difference in the import of the two propositions. *Man*, in the first proposition, is necessarily to be construed as an Integrate Whole; while *man*, in the other proposition, is a Class Whole. How easily error may creep into a continuous movement of thought, through the loose employment of words of this kind, may be seen in an example of a fallacious reasoning. Thus: *Man is not philosopher; Newton was a man; therefore, Newton was not a philosopher.* The truth of the sumption, interpreting the term *man* as a class whole, is unquestionable. Equally so is the truth of the subsumption. Yet the reasoning is fallacious, being, in fact, an instance of that kind of fallacy to be explained in the sequel, called the *fallacy of four terms*. Palpable as the error is here, it is easy to see that in the progress of continuous discussion the fallacy might readily creep in. The familiar rule of formal logic requiring the distribution of one term in a reasoning is aimed, in part, against this sophistry in some of its forms.

II. The Verbal Law of a Concept requires, in the second place, that the verbal expression conform to the laws of expression. This involves —

1°. That the expression be significant.
2°. That it be perspicuous.
3°. That it be brief.

The first of these particulars prohibits all unmeaning terms, all needless repetitions, all tautological expressions. Significance should characterize the whole and every part of the expression.

The second prohibits the use of ambiguous, obscure, and figurative terms; and also requires such a structure as the settled principles of language impose in order to perspicuousness.

The third prohibits all unnecessary words, and also periphrastic expressions not necessary for accuracy and adequateness.

CHAPTER IV.

METHODOLOGY OF REASONINGS.

§ 110. THE triform perfection of Thought generally, Material, Formal, and Verbal, requisite to perfect science, imposes upon the Reasoning process as a derivation from one or more Judgments the three Laws which we have distinguished as the Objective, the Subjective, and the Verbal. We will consider the application of these Laws to the different forms of Reasoning under each Law in order.

Before entering upon this consideration, however, it is proper to recall a distinction of methods already stated, founded on the different ends for which thought is exerted. We have distinguished the two ends of attaining truth and of communicating truth — here appearing specifically as those of Investigation and Probation. The process of thought in the two methods is essentially the same; but the movement is generally and characteristically in opposite directions. Thus, in attaining truth, in investigating, we begin with the proper logical antecedent — with the premises; while in communicating truth, in probation, we ordinarily begin with the conclusion. This difference, however, is not one of strict logical concernment. The movement in investigation is that which is most proper for logical consideration; and to verify thought in probation, the doctrine of which belongs properly to Rhetoric, it becomes necessary, therefore, to reverse the movement, so that the conclusion, which in argumentation is ordinarily placed first, shall stand in its true logical position after the antecedent. As we shall see, many of the fallacies ordinarily

Probation and Investigation distinguished.

considered in systems of Logic, being purely fallacies of probation and not of investigation, belong to Rhetoric.

It may be added here, that in probation the thought is generally presented but in part, as in the Enthymeme, in which one premise is suppressed. To verify the thought, Logic requires that it be filled out in all its essential parts.

Objective Law of Reasonings. § 111. The OBJECTIVE LAW of a Reasoning requires that the Antecedent be distinctly recognized as to its form and import.

The Antecedent in a Reasoning, it will be recollected, is the Judgment, or the Judgments, which are given, from which the Consequent or Conclusion is to be thought out in the Reasoning. It is the proper matter or *datum* in the process, and must, consequently, in order to perfect science, be accurately and adequately apprehended.

This Law, then, presupposes the perfection of the Judgment or Judgments which form the Antecedent as the *datum* of the Reasoning. It prescribes as additional requisites to perfect science —

1°. That the Antecedent be recognized, whether as Simple or as Composite, that is, be recognized as to the number of Judgments of which it is made up.

2°. That the specific character of each Judgment in the Antecedent be recognized in its Quality, whether Affirmative, Negative, or Disjunctive; in its Modality, whether Assertory, Problematic, or Apodictic; in its Degree, whether Identical or Partial; in its Form, whether Categorical or Hypothetical; in its Logical Quantity, whether Extensive or Comprehensive; in its Material Quantity, whether Integrate, Substantial, or Causal.

3°. That the Verbal Expression be recognized as correctly and unequivocally rendering the Thought, and in a form appropriate to the Reasoning process, or at least reducible to such form.

The logical soundness of these rules it would be superfluous to vindicate at length and in form; but the importance of forming the habit of thus weighing in each integral part the *datum* of a reasoning, can hardly be overrated. It is only necessary to add that while it is not difficult to form the habit, so that instinctively and unconsciously as it were, the precise matter of the reasoning shall be so fully apprehended as to bring to light any defect or ground of fallacy, this can be only by a conscious separate attention at first to each essential part of the Antecedent.

The applications of this Law, so far as they are peculiar to any one kind of reasoning, will be considered under each one, and in connection with its Subjective Law.

§ 112. The SUBJECTIVE LAW of a Reasoning respects the movement of Thought itself in deriving the conclusion or consequent from the Antecedent. It will vary under its more general twofold form in the two different relations of Whole to Part, and of Part to Complementary Part, with the particular kind of Reasoning. We will accordingly consider the Law in its various forms of application to the different species of Reasoning in order, beginning with Immediate Reasonings in their several forms of Conversion, Quantitative Restriction, Modal Restriction, Transference, Disjunction, and Composition; and continuing with Mediate Reasonings in their several species of the Syllogism, Categorical and Conditional, and the Polysyllogism. *[Subjective Law of Reasonings.]*

Inasmuch, however, as fallacious thinking generally, if not always, is occasioned by the complication of divers simple processes in one, it becomes necessary to premise one general rule of high importance to correct thought.

§ 113. In every case of the intermingling of several processes of Thought in the same general movement, the attainment of assured Truth requires that each process in the complex thought be distinguished and verified through its entire progress. *[Law of Complex Thought.]*

No perfectly simple process of thought, perhaps, even with the dullest intelligence, can mislead or err. It is only when processes are blended together and the thought becomes intricate that error or fallacy is possible. The proper and the only certain and universal cure is the separate recognition and verification of each distinct process that enters into the complex movement.

The enunciation of this general Law will preclude the necessity of multiplying specific rules for all the different kinds of complex reasoning. It will be sufficient here to exemplify the Law in reference to these complications in a very general way.

Conversion is often combined with Restriction, whether in Quantity or in Modality, and also with Transference. Logicians have accordingly distinguished so many different kinds of Conversion with tabular forms, showing when inference is possible, when not, and on what conditions, with as much reason for any practical utility, as if a mathematician should tabulate all the possible combinations of addition, subtraction, multiplication, and division in any arithmetical process, for directing how to compute in each. We may, indeed, generalize the statement, by enouncing that Immediate Reasonings intermingle in all possible combinations, not only with one another, but also with Mediate Reasonings of all kinds, subject only to the general laws of Thought. Examples of the former kind are Conversion *per accidens*, as, Convertend, A *is* B; Converse, *some B is A*, where Conversion is combined with Quantitative Restriction: Conversion by Contraposition, as, Convertend, A *is* B; Converse, *no Non-B is A*, where Conversion is combined with Transference. Examples of the latter kind are in a kind of Epichirema, as, B *is* A; C *is* B, *for it is non-D*; *therefore*, C *is* A; or in concrete matter: *Vice is odious; Avarice is a vice, for it is unsympathizing; therefore, avarice is odious.*

In the same way, Mediate Reasonings are combined with one another. One form distinctly treated by logicians, and already noticed, is the Hypothetico-Disjunctive, or Dilemma. So in the Sorites manifold combinations of the several processes are possible within the limits of legitimate Thought.

To assure certainty in all such instances of complicated reasoning, the rule to verify each distinguishable process by its own conditions, is the one simple and universally efficient rule. At first, as in arithmetical computation, the procedure, being thus step by step, will necessarily be slow; but soon the mind acquires power to analyze and verify the most complicated processes as it were by instinct, precisely as after practice it reaches by one leap in multiplication the product from given simple factors, without going through the many additions involved, or attains the result of manifold simpler processes in higher applications of numerical principles.

§ 114. In Logical Conversion, which consists in the simple transposition of the terms of a Judgment, the one condition of a perfect derivation or reasoning is, that the quantity of the terms be not changed in the transposition. *Subjective Law of Conversion.*

In this reasoning the Quality of the Judgment is not affected; the derivation respecting simply the terms. Now every Judgment being essentially an identification of two objects of thought, it is a matter of indifference to Thought in which direction the movement takes place; whether we say $A = B$, or $B = A$. If we may say the one, the very nature of Thought authorizes us to say the other also. The problem in Conversion is this: Having one term given as subject and the other given as predicate, how with the maintenance of the integrity of the Thought we may transpose these terms. We could, evidently, do this as freely in Thought generally as we do in Algebraic equations, were it not that for the most part the language of Thought, its notation, is not as unequivocal as that of mathematical science. The Judgment *Man is mortal* cannot as securely be converted as we convert an Algebraic equation by transposing the terms, because it is but a partial Judgment, whereas all Algebraic equations are properly Identical Judgments. It means only that one of the characters that make up the notion *man,* is identical with *mortal;* or that *man* is identical with one of the parts that make up the class *mortal*. When thus interpreted, the conversion becomes as simple and as certain as in Algebra. This, then, is the one condition of Simple Conversion : that no more and no less be expressed by the terms after the transposition than was thought in them before.

<small>Subjective Law of Quantitative Restriction.</small> § 115. In Quantitative Restriction, the one condition of perfect Thought is, that the quantity thought be restricted in both terms in equal degree.

The only difficulty to be encountered in this kind of reasoning is one exactly analogous to that in Conversion. If from the Judgment *Man is rational animal*, we wish to derive a Judgment restricted in the subject only, as, *this man, American men*, &c., *are rational animal*, we do it without fear of fallacy, because we interpret the *datum* at once in Extensive Quantity, and derive the restricted Judgment as meaning that a part of the subject *man* is part of the class *rational animal*. But we should with equal legitimacy be able to restrict the predicate also. We can do this, however, under our ordinary use of language, only as we rather force the interpretation by viewing the proposition in its Comprehensive Quantity ; then the difficulty vanishes. Thus, if we explicate it, the notion *man* contains in it, as one of its component characters, that of *rational*, this being one of the complement of attributes *rational animal ;* we recognize the validity of the process. We then reason : The notion *man* contains the composite attribute *rational animal ;* therefore, it contains the attribute *rational.* In like manner : Man is *rational ;* therefore, he is *intelligent.*

It will be observed that if another judgment be required in order to show that the new predicate is a part of the predicate in the sumption, the mediate reasoning or the syllogism will be called forth.

<small>Subjective Law of Modal Restriction.</small> § 116. In Modal Restriction, the one condition of perfect thought is, that the restriction follow the order of logical descent from the Apodictic to the Assertory and Problematic ; from the Assertory to the Prob-

lematic. If the modal restriction be carried further into lower degrees of the Contingent, as may be done by means of the adverbs of modality, then the law requires that the restriction be from the higher to the lower, and never the reverse. Thus from *necessarily* true we may infer to the *actually* true, or to the *probably* true or *possibly* true, not conversely.

§ 117. In Immediate Reasonings by Transference, there are two distinct kinds — one consisting in the transference of Quality, the other in the transference of Modality from the copula of the Judgment to the terms. It was shown in the former Part, § 63, that in order to preserve the integrity and purity of the Thought, it is necessary to keep the transference within the strict lines of Thought; that is, since Thought can recognize only the relations of Whole and Part in its object-matter, all legitimate transference must be within the limits of those relations. In Transference of Quality, accordingly, the condition of perfect thought is, that the terms must be recognized as under the same Whole. Thus, in the proposition *A is not B*, in order to transfer the negation from the copula to the predicate, so as to infer *A is non-B*, *A* and *B* must be recognized as being in the same Whole. From the proposition: *The scorpion is not vertebrate*, we may legitimately infer the proposition, *The scorpion is invertebrate*, only as we can recognize the term *scorpion* as belonging to the Whole *animal* of which *vertebrate* and *invertebrate* are complementary parts.

In the other kind of Transference, that by transfer of Modality, as, *A is possibly B, therefore, A is a possible B*, there is need of the same caution not to slip a quality of the thought surreptitiously over to the matter. If in the derived proposition, *possible* be interpreted as pertaining still to the copula, as it may be, there is, of course, no proper logical, but only a verbal, transference. But if it be taken as limiting the term *B*, then it can be a legitimate process of thought only, as in the case of Transference of Quality, when the term as before transfer and the term as after transfer are complementary parts of a whole of which the other term must be a lower part. Thus we cannot from the proposition *Sponge may be animal,* that is, *Sponge is possibly animal,* infer *Sponge is possible animal,* that is, has all the characters which make up the concept *animal,* and only lacks the character *real.* But from the proposition *Sponge may be an animal,* we may infer *Sponge is a possible animal,* having recognized it as possessing the essential character of an animal — to wit: an alimentary cavity.

§ 118. Of derivations of Judgments by Disjunction and by Composition, it is unnecessary to add to what has been, in the First Part, §§ 64, 65, indicated as constituting the essential conditions of the two processes.

<small>Disjunction and Composition.</small>

§ 119. In the Categorical Deductive Syllogism, the subjective conditions of perfect thought are:

1°. That there be three and only three terms bearing the relation to each other of Major, Middle, and Minor; the Middle being contained in or under the Major, and containing the Minor.

2°. That the Sumption affirm or deny the Major to contain the Middle term, and the Subsumption affirm the Middle to contain the Minor term.

3°. That the Conclusion affirm or deny the Major to contain the Minor term, according as the Sumption affirms or denies.

4°. That the Thought in the Conclusion be not illegitimately changed to a higher modality than in the Antecedent.

.The first part of this Law requires that the Middle Term be recognized as standing in the relation of containing Whole, and contained part in the same kind of Whole, to the Major and Minor terms respectively. Violations of this Law involve the following fallacies: —

The fallacy of using the word expressing the middle term in two different senses in the two premises. This fallacy is called the *Logical Quadruped*, as it really introduces four terms instead of three into the Reasoning, and thus makes it go, as it were, on four feet. If the term is expressed by a single word, the fallacy is called simply an Equivocation; if in a phrase, it is called an Amphibology. The following are examples: *Mus est syllaba; mus caseum rodit; ergo, syllaba caseum rodit.*

Herod is a fox; a fox is a quadruped; therefore, Herod is a quadruped.

Air is ponderable; spirit is air; therefore, spirit is ponderable.

You should eat what is sold in the market; raw meat is sold in the market; therefore, you should eat raw meat.

Seven and two are odd and even numbers; nine is seven and two; therefore, nine is odd and even. This last is an example of what is called the Fallacy of Composition and Division, in which the middle term is used in one premise in its composite sense, in the other, in its distributive.

The king can do no wrong; Herod was king; therefore, he was innocent. This is an example of the Fallacy *a dicto secundum quid ad dictum simpliciter*, consisting in the use of a word employed in one relation in one premise, and in another relation or without relation in the other.

To this class belongs also the Fallacy of Unreal Universality, as, *The Cretans are liars; Epimenides is a Cretan; therefore, Epimenides is a liar.* The word expressing the middle term in the Subsumption denotes the whole class of *Cretans;* in the Sumption, it denotes only a large part of the class.

In these fallacies there is a term which stands in each of the premises expressed by the same word; but as this word is used in two different meanings, we have really two terms; consequently there is no mediation of the Judgment — no proper derivation, no true reasoning.

The fallacy in probation called *petitio principii*, Begging the Question, also, is to be detected by this Law. It consists in taking as one of the premises a proposition equally needing proof as the conclusion itself. It appears in divers forms. First, generally, when a premise is assumed which is as much denied by the party addressed as the proposition to be proved; as, when it is attempted to prove the Divinity of Christ to a Mohammedan from the authority of the Bible which he rejects; or the cause of the planetary motion to be an ethereal vortex. This is the *petitio principii* proper; but the name has been applied to fallacies generally which lie in an illicit premise.

A second form of this fallacy, the *petitio principii*, is the *Hysteron proteron*, in which the truth of the antecedent is dependent upon the conclusion; as, when Scriptural testimony is urged in favor of the Being of God; Scriptural testimony being valid only as it is the testimony of God, and therefore presupposing his existence.

A third form of the *petitio principii*, is the *Circle*, in which the conclusion is disguised in one of the premises; as, *Lead falls to the ground quicker than feathers, because it is heavier.*

This vice is just the reverse of that in the Logical Quadruped; as here the same meaning is conveyed in different language, so that there appear to be two distinct propositions, while really there is but one. In the Logical Quadruped, on the other hand, two different meanings are hidden under the same guise of words. Dr. Whately has well observed that the English language peculiarly favors this fallacy, as we may express the same thought in Saxon or in Norman words; thus: "To allow every man unbounded freedom of speech must be best for the State; for it is highly conducive to the interests of the community that each individual should possess unlimited liberty of expressing his sentiments."

Still another fallacy in probation is the *Saltus*, in which one of the premises is neither expressed nor necessarily implied. This fallacy is practicable only by reason of the circumstance that the Enthymeme is ordinarily admitted in place of the full reasoning. To verify an Enthymeme, it becomes necessary to supply the suppressed premise, when this vice in the thought at once shows itself.

Further, it is implied in the rule that the terms be significant, — contain veritable thought. If, therefore, in the course of the reasoning, a term become insignificant, be a zero in thought, the reasoning is fallacious. This is exemplified in the familiar Algebraic demonstration that $7 = 23$. For putting $x = 7$ and $y = 23$, then as $x + y = x + y$, and so $ax + ay = ax + ay$, and by transposition $ax - ax = ay - ay$, we have, by dividing by $a - a$, $x = y$ or $7 = 23$.

Fallacies under the second part of the Law are liable to occur when it is not clearly distinguished which is the sumption and which the subsumption, so that the middle and minor terms are really differenced, instead of the major and middle; in other words, the subsumption is of negative quality. Thus, *Men are mortal; angels are not men; therefore, angels are not mortal;* or, *Men are mortal; brutes are not men; therefore, brutes are not mortal.*

Fallacies under the third part of the Law are such as follows: *Wise and good men were condemned by the Athenian populace; Socrates was condemned by the Athenian populace; therefore, he was a wise and good man.* Here the conclusion has for its terms the minor and the middle. There is really no subsumption in this example, as the middle and the minor terms are compared only in the conclusion.

Here belongs also the famous Fallacy, called *Ignava Ratio*, or Lazy Reason; also the Reaper, the Controlling Reason, the *Argumentum de Fato*. Cicero thus states it: *If it be fated that you recover from your present disease, whether you call in a doctor or not, you will recover; again, If it be fated that you do not recover from your present disease, whether you call in a doctor or not, you will not recover: but one or other of the contradictories is fated; therefore, to call in a doctor is of no consequence.*

Although it appears here in the form of a Hypothetico-Disjunctive Syllogism, and thus appears more plausible and difficult to detect, it is easily reducible to a Categorical Deductive, thus: *What is fated is unavoidable by any exertion; the alternative of recovery from this sickness or death is fated; therefore, the issue alike whether recovery or death is unavoidable by any exertion.* The sophism thus reduced is a palpable amphibology; the conclusion has not the same term as minor that is contained in the subsumption; — in the latter proposition it is an alternative of which something is predicated, while in the conclusion it is of the two factors of the alternative taken separately of which the predication is made. The only valid conclusion is: *The alternative of recovery or death is unavoidable by any exertion;* which is a very different proposition from this: *This alternative, whether the one or the other — whether recovery or death — occur, is beyond the power of exertion to determine.*

By the application of this part of the Law, further, we may expose most of the diverse fallacies in probation classed under the generic name of *mutatio elenchi*, in the sense of change of the issue. The conclusion being the proposition which was originally in doubt and was to be proved, if the terms are not the same as in the original doubt a fallacy arises. Thus, if a person should undertake to prove the existence of ghosts, and should only prove some unusual noises and appearances during the night, he would exemplify this kind of fallacy.

The violation of the fourth part of the Law may occur in two different forms, the first when a necessary Judgment is derived from an assertory or problematic, or an assertory from a problematic; and the second, when the modality of the thought is covertly transferred to the matter.

The first form may be exemplified thus: *It rains when the moon changes; the moon changes to-morrow; therefore, it must rain to morrow.*

Of the second the following is an example: *For aught we*

know the deaf may be sensible of sounds within the ordinary hearing distance; the deaf mute, Laura Bridgman, was within that distance when her teacher spoke to her; therefore, Laura could have heard the direction of her teacher.

The common Fallacy of *Non causa pro causa*, or *Post hoc, ergo propter hoc*, in which only general antecedence is accepted as universal, or a causal connection is inferred from such general antecedence, belongs under this species. This variety of fallacy is extremely common; but like popular reasonings it is generally in the form of an Enthymeme, the sumption being suppressed. Thus: *The moon will change to-morrow; therefore, it must rain to-morrow.*

§ 120. In the Categorical Inductive Syllogism, the subjective conditions of perfect thought are:

1°. That there be three and only three terms, two of which bear the relation to each other of Part and Complementary Part, and the third bears the relation of Whole alike to each of these two.

2°. That the Sumption affirm or deny this third of one of the other two, and the Subsumption affirm these two to be Complementary of each other.

3°. That the Conclusion affirm or deny the third of that term of which it is not predicated in the Sumption.

4°. That the Modality be not illegitimately changed.

Of the application of this general Law of the Inductive Syllogism, it will be unnecessary to speak in detail, except in respect to the one feature in which it differs from the Deductive. This peculiar element in the Law is in the second part which requires that the Subsumption affirm two of the terms to be complementary of each other, and the main difficulty is in the objective bearings of the rule, in verifying this premise as a true judgment. As in Deductive Reasoning, so in Inductive and to a much greater extent, a part of the Antecedent is usually suppressed in discourse; and inasmuch as logical literature has confined itself mainly to the former, we are less familiarized with the process of supplying the suppressed part in Induction in order to verify the reasoning. There is still another difficulty arising from the fact that this reasoning more commonly proceeds in Causal Wholes with which logical systems have concerned themselves as little as with Induction, and with the movements of Thought generally in the relation of Part and Complementary Part.

As Logical Methodology aims to guide to true Science by unfolding the conditions of perfect thought, both material and formal, and as all proper thought is under the general relationship of Whole and Part, including, of course, that of Part and Complementary Part, we shall more intelligently and securely reach the conditions of a true Induction by illustrating the process in its application to the several kinds of quantity separately.

And, first, in proper logical wholes — the wholes of Extension and Comprehension. These wholes, we have seen, are the pure products of thought. We have seen how they are produced; how concepts are formed by a synthesis of the homologous terms of two or more judgments having the same analogous term, which we have called the Base of the concept. We have seen how concepts, thus springing into existence in the progress of human intelligence, at once embody themselves in words. We have seen how by two movements in opposite directions but perhaps synchronous, according as the subject or the predicate of the primitive judgments is taken as the Base, the concept and its embodiment — the word becomes narrowed or extended, whether by occasion of the more extended observation of its matter, and the consequent rectification of its objective import, or of the needs of thought for fuller or more discriminating symbols. Now these concepts so formed and modified, and these words, their verbal embodiments, may become matter of thought — matter of inductive thought. They are accepted as its *data*. If they have been perfectly formed, then the inductive process begins with objective truth. So in fact it ordinarily begins. It is obvious that just so much of contingency as attaches to the original *data* as thus furnished by the conspiring and restless energies of all who use the language and formed the concept, must attach to the results of the induction itself; and, so far as its material perfection is concerned, no more.

We will now look at the subjective element — the inductive process itself — to see how far necessary certainty may attach to it, and how far this process may be relied on to advance knowledge. It is apparent at once, from the very nature of a concept, then, that the Base of the concept, and any part of the Base, must belong to every part of the concept itself alike. If *horse, ox, dog*, are parts of the concept *quadruped*, then the Base on which the concept was formed, *four-footed*, and every part of *four-footed*, must belong to each part alike, to *horse, ox, dog*. Now in Induction as applied to concept wholes, the problem is simply this: Given *horse* as *four-footed* for one premise, and given, also, *ox, dog*, as complementary part of *horse*, as the other part of the antecedent, and we induce with absolute certainty that *ox, dog*, are four-footed. This is but retracing the steps by which the concept was formed — the analysis of the original synthesis; and if that was true, the result of the induction is also true.

While unhesitating assent must be yielded to this representation of the validity of the inductive process, yet it may remain in doubt whether there be any advance made in any real knowledge, as we seem to have no more than we had when we formed the concept. But a brief reflection will convince us that induction in mere concepts — the pure products of human thought, — gives to each of us a large share of all the knowledge we severally possess. Concepts, words, are not the product of one individual thought, but, so to speak, of the conspiring thought of the race. Each thinker has contributed to their formation and modification. How much, for instance, *quadruped* imports, has been determined by this conspiring thought. If all that forming, shaping thought could be imagined to be garnered up in one body of living activity, preserving the entire complicated movement that shaped the concept, then to such an activity no advance of knowledge could, perhaps, be supposed to be effected by the analysis of the forming movement in induction. But the fact is that no individual thinker contributes more than the minutest fraction to the whole formation. To the individual, therefore, the analysis may bring all the knowledge that was possessed by all the contributors to the formation. But, farther, the work of forming concepts and concept-words is a silent, unintentional, and so far unconscious work, even on the part of their very framers. They are the spontaneous, instinctive product of man as a social organism, as a thinking and speaking yet coöperative nature. The very creator of language can know his own product only as he can take to pieces again the wondrous complication. Induction, thus, is the condition and chief means not only of individual progress in intelligence, but of that of the community, the race. Accordingly, a great part of the advance of knowledge on the part of individual learners consists in the resolution of concepts by a proper induction — by inducing the Base or parts of the Base from any given part to any proper complementary part.

Not only this, but the sum of human knowledge is augmented more by Induction than by any other of the processes of thought, if it be possible to separate in such a comparison mutually dependent processes. This will appear at once from the consideration that while the enlargement of the Base of the concept may be effected by observation applied to any one part of it, every such enlargement enures to the spread of our knowledge over all the parts. Thus, in the concept *quadruped*, if an observer of nature discover in his inspection of an individual *horse* a previously unknown property or character belonging to it so far as quadruped, we will suppose some structure of a joint necessary to the motion of such an animal, before unnoticed, he not only induces from the individual horse observed to every other horse, but to every other quadruped. Nor does the increase of knowledge originating in this single discovery stop here. But from this property other properties may be induced indefinitely, as to mode of locomotion, position, and numberless other relations of other parts of the animal structure, habits of life even, and utilities without end.

Subjectively, then, Induction in concepts bears the character of absolute certainty. Objectively, it bears the character of contingency which attaches to the *datum* — the concept itself. This, however, as the legitimate product of mankind as speech-forming, is to be accepted as valid. Here more than anywhere else does the adage hold true — *Vox populi, vox Dei* ; — the conspiring thought of the race is the thought of truth. Even the skeptic accepts the concept as valid; he could not advance a step in his argumentation but as he is supported on the truth of concepts. Moreover, Induction is not only a *valid* instrument of knowledge, it is a *chief* instrument of knowledge to thinking, speaking man. And the simple condition of perfect thought which shall give us assured truth or perfect science is that we keep within the relationship of part to complementary part. This, however, is by no means difficult in case of concept wholes. The chief liability to fallacious reasoning lies in our not rightly apprehending the base of the concept.

Induction in the wholes proper to the object-matter of thought, bears the same character of subjective certainty. That the part necessitates its complementary part is a necessary truth.

Objectively, the validity of Induction in this kind of wholes depends on the truth of the *data*, first, that the given part is a part of the whole object thought; secondly, that the other part is truly complementary. In an Integrate Whole, thus, if *head* be given as part of *man*, and *body* be given as complementary part, then we may induce that whatever is true of *head* as part of *man* — for instance, *organic* — is true of *body* ; while we induce the different of it as complementary; thus, if *head* is higher, *body* is lower; if *head* is guiding, *body* is guided, and the like.

In a Substantial Whole, if *bi-manous* be given as part of *man* as physical, and *mammal* as complementary, then whatever of physically human may be true of *bi-manous* as part, *cellular*, for instance, may be induced of *mammal ;* while, on the other hand, we may induce of it as complementary, the different; as that, if *bi-manous* is *prehensile, mammal* is *non-prehensile*. In the same way if *rational spirit* be given to us as a substance having the attributes of *intelligent, emotional,* and *voluntary,* we may induce that whatever is true of *intelligent* simply as part of *rational spirit* is true of *emotional* and *voluntary,* as, for instance, that they are *active, capable of growth, dependent on conditions, limited,* and the like; and also as complementary, that they are *not cognitive, not reasoning,* and the like.

So in a Causal Whole, if the cause with one part of its effect be given, we may induce to the complementary effect the same and also the different. If, thus, *solar heat* be given as cause, and *this piece of expanded iron* be given as part effect, we may induce the same of every piece of iron within the sphere of the causal agency. So if there be given a causal agency in creating, which produces a flower with a definite number, order, figure, color of organs, and a definite fragrance, we induce the same of every other flower within the same causal sphere. The principle of Induction, that the part necessitates its complementary part, holds here as everywhere else. The peculiar difficulty here lies in observing the objective law of induction — in verifying the *data,* determining the causal whole and the complementary parts. All the numerous rules prescribed in material Induction so called, are comprehended in this one objective law of Induction — Verify the parts as complementary of each other in the same causal whole. This principle will determine whether one observation or more are necessary. One observation may in some cases be sufficient to ascertain the existence of the cause, its sphere, its liability to be overborne by other causal agencies, or to be hindered by failing conditions, — may, in short, verify the *data*. In other cases more may be required; and how many may be requisite must be determined by the occasions of the induction or by the specific peculiarities of its object-matter.

All this is, however, aside from the proper design of pure logic. It belongs to Applied Logic to prescribe the mode of ascertaining the causal sphere, to indicate the degree of contingency that attaches to the matter, the *datum* attained for the inductive process, and by what methods, if by any, that degree may be reduced to a minimum. It is impossible to eliminate all contingency; for, as has been shown, the necessary lies exclusively in the realms of thought, and all that is foreign to thought must bear the character of contingent. But this contingency may be, for any particular use in our thinking, an infinitesimal; and thought may accept the *datum* as not to be questioned. In fact, we do accept the reality of External Existence; we accept the reality of Being, both as Substance having attributes, and as Cause producing effects; we accept the diversity and the stability of things — that each thing, whether substance or cause, has its own permanent attributes, so that each substance will retain each essential property that it is now found to possess, for to-morrow and the next year, and each cause work its own proper effect here and elsewhere alike. The contingency that rises in all this we dismiss from our thought, and treat such matter as true beyond impeachment. But when we pass one step further, and endeavor to ascertain the real diversity of substances with their several properties and of causes with their several effects, we come upon a contingency that may invalidate our whole thought-process applied to it. We cannot induce that any one property which belongs to a given substance to-day will be found to belong to it to-morrow, or belongs to a substance having all the other properties elsewhere, until we have discriminated it as an essential property, not an accidental one; we cannot induce that any one effect which we find to-day proceeding from a given cause before us will be found proceeding from it to-morrow, or from a cause working all the other effects, but working elsewhere. How to discriminate the essential from the accidental, it is the province of Applied Logic in each department of knowledge to indicate — to determine by what methods, and to what extent these methods must be carried that the contingency may be reduced to the requisite degree, and to prescribe the tests, and checks also, as well as the methods of observation. Such a science, both in its general principles and also in its bearing on each of the departments of knowledge, is a great desideratum, as well for the more rapid advancement of science as for its verification. Not a little will be gained, however, in the interest of human knowledge, if the thought-process be carefully discriminated from the matter to which it is applied, and its nature and laws be well understood. And a further gain, by no means inconsiderable, will also be secured, if it is ascertained precisely what is to be done in constructing a methodology for any particular field of scientific induction, in so far as regards the several conditions of perfect science.

§ 121. In the Hypothetical Syllogism, the Law of perfect cognition requires —

1°. That the premises, the terms of which are here Judgments, be recognized and verified, and particularly the mode of relation which is affirmed between the terms of the Sumption, whether that of Whole to Part, or of Part to Complementary Part.

2°. That the Conclusion affirm the consequent member of the Sumption in the Affirmative or Ponent form, and deny the antecedent member in the Negative or Tollent form of the Syllogism.

The difficulty in respect to the first or objective condition of a valid Hypothetical Reasoning is twofold: that of supplying the part of the antecedent which is suppressed; and that of distinguishing, in order to verification, the character of the Sumption, whether it expresses the relation of Whole to Part, or of Part to Complementary Part. Either premise may be suppressed, and in either relation of the terms of the Sumption. Thus we may reason, either: *If the sun had arisen, it must have been light; therefore, the sun could not have arisen,* suppressing the subsumption; or, *The sun had arisen; therefore, it was light,* suppressing the sumption. We may also reason: *If virtue is voluntary, vice is voluntary; therefore, vice is voluntary,* suppressing the subsumption, *but virtue is voluntary;* or, *Virtue is voluntary; therefore, vice is voluntary,* suppressing the sumption.

One of the chief liabilities to error in the subjective element of the reasoning arises in the negative form, when the antecedent member of the sumption is also negative, from the doubling of negatives; as, *If vice be not voluntary, virtue must be necessitated; but virtue is not necessitated; therefore, vice is not voluntary.* Here the fallacy is obvious; but it may be covered up and especially in a chain of reasoning, in extended phrases, so as to escape ready detection.

§ 122. In the Disjunctive Syllogism, the Law of perfect thought requires —

1°. That the disjunction in the Sumption be verified, and if it be in the terms or in contrary opposition by reduction to strictly logical contradiction.

2°. That the Conclusion always be in quality opposed to the Subsumption, and have for its predicate the disjunct member not subsumed.

In application of this principle of method, the chief difficulty will lie in reducing the opposition to strict logical contradiction. The most fallacious form of this reasoning is, perhaps, where there is true opposition, but it lies in the terms, the matter, not in the thought; as, A *is* B *or non-B.* But it is unnecessary to add here to what has been already said of this distinction, which has been overlooked even by logicians generally.

§ 123. In the Hypothetico-Disjunctive Syllogism or the Dilemma, the Law of perfect thought requires —

1°. That the antecedent be verified, in respect both to the disjunction and the hypothetical judgment in the Sumption, and, also, in respect to the positing or the sublation in the Subsumption.

2°. That the Conclusion sublate the antecedent member of the Sumption, or posit the Consequent, and not conversely.

A fallacy in this process of reasoning has become quite famous. There are two accounts, the Greek and the Roman. "The Roman account is given us by Aulus Gellius, and is there told in relation to an action between Protagoras, the prince of the Sophists, and Euathlus, a young man, his disciple. The disciple had covenanted to give his master a large sum to accomplish him as a legal rhetorician; the one half of the sum was paid down, and the other was to be paid on the day when Euathlus should plead and gain his first cause. But when the scholar, after the due course of preparatory instruction, was not in the same hurry to commence pleader as the master to obtain the remainder of his fee, Protagoras brought Euathlus into court, and addressed his opponent in the following reasoning: 'Learn, most foolish of young men, that however matters may turn up — whether the decision to-day be in your favor or against you — pay me my demand you must. For if the judgment be against you, I shall obtain the fee by decree of the court; and if in your favor, I shall obtain it in terms of the compact, by which it became due on the very day you gained your first cause. You thus must fail, either by judgment or by stipulation.' To this Euathlus rejoined: 'Most sapient of masters, learn from your own argument, that whatever may be the finding of the court, absolved I must be from any claim by you. For if the decision be favorable, I pay nothing by the sentence of the judges; but if unfavorable, I pay nothing in virtue of the compact, because, though pleading, I shall not have gained my cause. The judges, says Gellius, unable to find a *ratio decidendi*, adjourned the case to an indefinite day, and ultimately left it undetermined. A parallel story is told, among the Greek writers, of the rhetorician Corax, *anglice* Crow, and his scholar Tisias. In this case, the judges got off by delivering a joke against both parties, instead of a decision in favor of either. We have here, they said, the plaguy egg of a plaguy crow; and from this circumstance is said to have originated the Greek proverb, κακοῦ κόρακος κακὸν ὠόν."

The fallacy in the reasoning of Protagoras lies in the ambiguity of the second member of his disjunction, that if Euathlus won the suit, the money would be due by the terms of the compact; it would *become* due only after the decision, and by virtue of it. The fallacy in the reply of Euathlus, lies also in a similar ambiguity in the second member of his disjunction, that the decision of the court reached to a claim that would arise only on the event of that decision. Before the decision Protagoras had no claim, and of course must lose his suit; on losing his suit, his claim emerged to full validity, and after that could be enforced. In both reasonings there is thus the fallacy of substituting in the conclusion a different claim from that which is presented equivocally in the antecedent: in the one, a claim before the decision of the case, in the other a claim coming to be only after the decision.

§ 124. In the Polysyllogism, whether Epichirema or Sorites, we have only to verify the several links of the chain, both objectively and subjectively, as in any case of composite reasoning, at the same time attending to the consecution of the thought that that be ever legitimate. In categorical reasonings the attention will be chiefly directed to the middle term, to see that there be a true middle in every separate link of the chain; and to the carrying forward of the same judgment from the place of conclusion in one link to that of antecedent in the next. In conditional reasonings, in like manner, the attention should be chiefly directed to the mediating judgments, and then to the carrying forward of the conclusions in the several links.

PURE LOGIC.

PART III.
LOGICAL PRAXIS.

CHAPTER I.

I. EXERCISES IN JUDGMENTS.

EXERCISE 1. *Judgments to be severally discriminated as to —*
1. Quality: whether Affirmative, Negative, or Disjunctive;
2. Modality: whether Assertory, Problematical, or Necessary;
3. Degree of Identity: whether Total or Partial;
4. Nature of Terms: whether Categorical or Hypothetical;
5. Logical Quantity: whether Comprehensive or Extensive;
6. Nature of Whole: whether Integrate, Substantial, or Causal; and the parts of the Sentence respectively containing the Terms and the Copula to be indicated.

MODELS. — The Judgment *Man is mortal*, is Affirmative, Assertory, Partial, Categorical, Comprehensive, Substantial; the Judgment, *Alexander may not have practiced what he had learned of his teacher*, is Negative, Problematical, Partial, Categorical, Comprehensive, Causal. The Judgment, *If Alexander had been a consistent disciple of Aristotle, he would have ruled his appetites,* is an Affirmative, Assertory, Partial, Hypothetical, Comprehensive, Causal Judgment. *If Alexander had ruled his ambition, he would either have made no conquests or have maintained them*, is a Disjunctive, Assertory, Partial, Hypothetical, Comprehensive, Causal Judgment.

1. Iron is magnetic.
2. Iron is not soluble in water.
3. Iron either is magnetic or is not magnetic.
4. Iron must be magnetic.
5. If iron be magnetic, it has polarity.
6. Iron is a metal.
7. Iron nourishes plants.
8. Steel is carbonized iron.
9. Thought is a cognition.
10. Thought is a relative cognition.
11. Thought either is a mediate cognition or is an immediate cognition.
12. If thought is a mediate cognition, it is beyond its province to account for its object.
13. Logic is the science of necessary thought.
14. Logic methodizes knowledge.
15. Logic contains the doctrine of elements and the doctrine of method.
16. If logic is the doctrine of thought, it is the necessary guide to all intelligent and certain thinking.
17. Thought does not amplify the matter of knowledge.
18. Thought either creates all truth or creates no truth.
19. Truth is knowledge of things as existing.
20. The knowledge of things as existing is relative cognition.
21. The elements of thought are judgments, concepts, and reasonings.
22. A cognition is either relative or irrelative.

EXERCISE 2. *Disjunctives in Contrary Opposition to be reduced to Contradictory Opposition.*

MODEL. — Angles are right or not right; as not right they are acute or not acute, that is, obtuse.

1. Angles are right, acute, or obtuse.

2. Triangles are equilateral, isosceles, or scalene.

3. A quadrilateral figure is either a square, an oblong, a rhombus, a rhomboid, or a trapezium.

4. Bodies are in stable, in unstable, or in indifferent equilibrium.

5. A body will be supported if the point of support be applied at, below, or above the center of gravity.

6. A body is at rest, in relative motion, or in absolute motion.

7. Motion is either horizontal, perpendicular, inclined, or rotary.

8. Winds are constant, periodical, or variable.

9. Mirrors are plane, convex, or concave.

10. The kingdoms of nature are the mineral, the vegetable, and the animal kingdom.

11. A carnivorous animal either walks on the sole as man, on the toes as the dog, or is amphibious as the seal.

12. A ruminant animal is either horned like the ox, or a camel or a llama.

13. The thick-skinned order of animals either have trunks like the elephant, or have no trunks like the swine, or are single-hoofed like the horse.

14. He is either standing, or sitting, or lying.

15. The color is blue, or yellow, or red.

16. Attention is either purely spontaneous, prompted by desire, or voluntary.

17. Space is finite, infinite, or ideal.

18. A judgment is either affirmative, or negative, or disjunctive.

19. The world is either eternal, or the result of chance, or the work of an intelligent Creator.

20. The virtues are either passions, faculties, or habits.

21. The languages are either monosyllabic, agglutinative, or inflectional.

EXERCISE 3. (1.) *Judgments, the Modality of which is to*

be changed; as from *Problematic* to *Assertory* and *Apodictic*, and the reverse.

1. It may rain to-morrow.
2. It is possible that Encke's comet will appear again in three and a third years.
3. There may have been such a character as the Wandering Jew.
4. Such a rain must have been accompanied by atmospheric movements of great violence.
5. Judicious exercise must invigorate.
6. No man can know that he reasons soundly who does not know something of the laws of thought.
7. No possible benefit can result.
8. Alexander possibly conquered Darius.
9. Integrity will certainly reap its reward.
10. Two wrongs cannot make one right.

(2.) *Propositions, the Modality in which is to be discriminated, whether in the Copula or the Terms; or if equivocal, the ambiguity to be removed.*

1. He is a possible witness.
2. No merely probable issue will justify the adventure.
3. A relapse is possible.
4. The relation between cause and effect is a necessary relation.
5. He must go; the command is peremptory.
6. No possible good can result.
7. Perhaps he will succeed.
8. It necessarily comes about that we are here to-day.
9. Altogether unnecessary is all this display.
10. Life must end soon.

EXERCISE 4. *Partial Judgments to be explicated so as to show the Parts of the Terms which are identified.*

MODEL. — One of the characters that make up the concept, *man*, is identical with *mortal; man* is one of the parts that make up the class *biped*.

1. Man is mortal.
2. Man is a mortal.
3. Man is two-footed.
4. Man is a biped.
5. Bucephalus is one-hoofed.
6. Bucephalus is a quadruped.
7. A judgment is a product of thought.
8. A judgment is an act of thought.
9. A judgment is thought.
10. The judgment is correct.
11. The judgment is partial.
12. The proposition is complex.
13. The proposition is true.
14. Virtue is voluntary.
15. Veracity is a virtue.
16. Veracity is voluntary.
17. Whatever is moral is voluntary.
18. Every voluntary act is moral.

EXERCISE 5. *Hypothetical Judgments to be explicated.*

MODELS. — In the Hypothetical, *If I think I am*, the Judgment that *I think* involves the Judgment that *I am*, as action is part of being as cause. In the Hypothetical, *If virtue is voluntary, vice is voluntary*, the Judgment that *virtue is voluntary* involves the Judgment that *vice is voluntary*, as *virtue* is the complementary part of *vice*.

1. If one dozen dozen are twelve dozen, half a dozen dozen are six dozen.
2. If one acre contains one hundred and sixty square rods, one fourth of an acre contains forty rods.
3. If the world were eternal, there would be records prior to the Mosaic.
4. If the English are Anglo-Saxons, they are Caucasians.
5. If I think, I am.
6. If the universe exhibit design, it is the work of intelligence.
7. If a digestive cavity marks an animal, the polyp is an animal.

8. If matter is entirely inert, there is a higher moving power.
9. If we cannot help an evil, we should not fret about it.
10. If we can help an evil, we should not fret about it.

EXERCISE 6. *Judgments to be explicated in Comprehensive and also in Extensive Quantity.*
1. Man is rational.
2. Glass is brittle.
3. Gold is ductile.
4. Thought is spiritual.
5. Passion is catching. ..
6. Ignorance is degrading.
7. To lie is cowardly.
8. To be ungrateful is base.
9. To die is to sleep.
10. To be an Athenian is to dare.
11. That we still breathe is of mercy.
12. That God reigns is truth of richest comfort.
13. Wisdom is no inheritance.

EXERCISE 7. *Judgments in Integrate, Substantial, and Causal Wholes to be discriminated, explicated, and, when necessary, corrected.*
1. The surface of a square is double that of a triangle on the same base and of the same height.
2. A whole is equal to the sum of its parts.
3. A square is equal to the sum of the squares of any two parts into which it may be divided, together with double the rectangle of its parts.
4. A whole contains each of its parts.
5. The solar system contains the sun, planets, and their satellites.
6. The body consists of solids and fluids.
7. Atmospheric air is composed of oxygen and nitrogen.
8. Water consists of oxygen and hydrogen.

9. Percussion is a combination of friction and compression.
10. A square is rectangular.
11. The sun is luminous.
12. The atmosphere has weight.
13. Europe is temperate.
14. Fire burns.
15. The wood burns.
16. The bellman rings.
17. The bell rings.
18. The sun illuminates the earth.
19. The earth reflects the light of the sun.
20. Vulgar eyes judge rather by the event than by the intention.
21. Fortunate is better than wise.
22. The mind's excellency can solve the real blemishes of the body.

EXERCISE 8. *Propositions to be corrected, with indication of the particular imperfection, whether in respect of Matter, of Judgment, or of Expression.*
1. Triangles are either equilateral or equi-angular.
2. Triangles are right-angled, isosceles, or scalene.
3. All that glitters is not gold.
4. The gods of the heathen are no gods.
5. No God is worshiped there.
6. Not all the ills of earth can mar my joy.
7. Some prudence is commendable.
8. We do not admit a possible failure into our plans.
9. A bold front must win for us.
10. Animal body is composed of flesh, bones, and muscles.
11. The atmospheric air is made up of oxygen, nitrogen, carbonic acid, and electricity.
12. Root, trunk, bark, and branches form the tree.
13. Embryos in pines are radicles or stemlets.
14. Every chemical substance has combining or equivalent members.

214 PURE LOGIC.

15. Simple bodies are divided into two classes, metals and metalloids, or non-metallic elements.

16. Leaves are opposite or alternate.

17. The eastern winds here are winds that blow from the tropics or trades.

18. Oxygen forms with silicon silica or silicic acid.

19. Of spiry or spire-shaped trees, the firs or spruces are the best illustrations.

II. EXERCISES IN CONCEPTS.

EXERCISE 9. *Concepts to be defined; to be analyzed, also, both by Division and Partition.*

1. Animal. 2. The Lynx. 3. The Beaver. 4. The Armadillo. 5. The Zebra. 6. The Dromedary. 7. The Reindeer. 8. The Antelope. 9. The Dolphin. 10. The Eagle. 11. The Thrush. 12. The Linnet. 13. The Sparrow. 14. The Jay. 15. The Hoopoe. 16. The Lapwing. 17. The Flamingo. 18. The Pelican. 19. The Teal. 20. The Basilisk. 21. The Chameleon. 22. The Cobra Capello. 23. The Salamander. 24. The Flying-Fish. 25. The Torpedo. 26. The Argonaut. 27. The Lobster. 28. The Tarantula. 29. The Cochineal. 30. The Thistle Bird. 31. The Violet. 32. The Pomegranate. 33. The Cypress. 34. The Amethyst. 35. The Emerald. 36. Topaz. 37. Heat. 38. Crystal. 39. Carbon. 40. Mercury. 41. Oxyd. 42. Monsoon. 43. Botany. 44. Grammar. 45. Psychology. 46. Intellect. 47. Virtue. 48. Hope. 49. Purpose. 50. Habit. 51. State. 52. Church. 53. Government. 54. Money. 55. Art.* 56. Industry. 57. Agriculture. 58. Ship. 59. Navy. 60. Judiciary.

III. EXERCISES IN REASONINGS.

OBSERVATION.—As the movements of Thought in ordinary discourse are abbreviated and complicated, it is necessary, in order to verify them, to reduce them to their full logical form in their several distinct elements. In order to this, it will be found convenient to separate the Terms, and mark them by familiar signs, as W, P, and

M, for Major, Minor, and Middle Terms, respectively, and to place the Judgments in a fixed order, the antecedent with its Sumption and Subsumption, if it be a Mediate Reasoning, above, and the consequent below. Begin with the conclusion; mark the Terms as W and P respectively; then find the Middle Term or Terms, and construct the Sumption and the Subsumption. The reasoning will then be readily recognized as valid or not by the application of the Rules of Reasoning.

EXERCISE 10. *Complex Reasonings to be resolved.*

1. All poets are men of genius; therefore, some men of genius are poets.

2. He who is content with what he has, is truly rich; a covetous man is not content with what he has; therefore, no covetous man is truly rich.

3. All the righteous are happy; therefore, all who are unhappy are unrighteous.

4. All insincere men are dishonest; therefore, all honest men are sincere.

EXERCISE 11. *Reasonings with suppressed Premises to be supplied.*

1. All tyrants deserve death; therefore, Cæsar deserved death.

2. Whatever comes from God is entitled to reverence; therefore, the Scriptures are entitled to reverence.

3. Of two evils, the less is to be preferred; occasional turbulence, therefore, is to be preferred to rigid despotism.

4. Wine is hurtful; for all stimulants are hurtful.

5. An infant has no moral power; therefore, it has no responsibility.

6. Kings have no friends; for they have no equals.

7. The lion is a predaceous animal; therefore, it is not ruminant.

8. Innate ideas cannot be enumerated; therefore, they do not exist.

9. Solon was a wise legislator; for he suited his laws to the genius of his nation.

10. The Epicureans cannot be regarded as true philosophers; for they did not reckon virtue a good in itself.

11. Shame is not a virtue; for it is more a passion than a habit.

12. Gambling implies a desire to gain by another's loss; therefore, it is a violation of the tenth commandment.

13. Onesimus was a servant of Philemon; Philemon was a hearer of Archippus; Archippus was a minister at Colosse; therefore, Onesimus was a resident at Colosse.

14. The nervous fluid is not electricity; for electricity may be transmitted along a nervous trunk which has been compressed by a string tied tightly round it, whilst the passage of ordinary nervous power is as completely checked by this process as if the nerve had been divided.

EXERCISE 12. *Reasonings to be discriminated as to their nature, as Immediate, Categorical, or Conditional, with indication of Mediating Judgments in the latter, and Middle Terms in Categorical Syllogisms.*

1. Equilateral triangles are equi-angular; therefore, equiangular triangles are equilateral.

2. Government is either a property or a trust; it is not a property; it must, therefore, be a trust.

3. If there were no divine Providence, no human government could long subsist; various human governments have subsisted long; therefore, there must be a divine Providence.

4. The early and general assignment of the Epistle to the Hebrews to the Apostle Paul as its author, must have been either from its professing to be his, or from its really being his; but it does not profess to be his; therefore, it is really his.

5. No person can serve God and mammon; the covetous man serves mammon; he cannot, therefore, serve God.

6. If the prophecies of the Old Testament had been written without knowledge of the events of the time of Christ, they

could not have corresponded with them exactly; and if they had been forged by Christians, they would not be preserved and acknowledged by the Jews: but they did correspond with those events, and they are preserved and acknowledged by the Jews; therefore, they were neither written without knowledge of those events, nor were they forged by Christians.

7. The favor of God must be bestowed either with respect to men's persons or with respect to their conduct; but "God is no respecter of persons;" therefore, his favor must be bestowed with respect to men's conduct.

8. If any complete theory could be framed to explain the establishment of Christianity by human causes, such a theory would have been proposed before now; but no such theory ever has been prepared; therefore, none can be framed.

9. If the system of the universe is not the best possible, we must suppose either that the Creator did not prefer a better one, or that he knew no better one, or that he could not create a better; but we can entertain neither of these suppositions, for we should thereby limit his goodness, his intelligence, or his power; therefore, the system of the universe is the best.

EXERCISE 13. *Fallacies to be detected.*

"By discourse," says Chillingworth, meaning by the word the operation of the discursive faculty, or Thought, "no man can possibly be led into error; but if he err in his conclusions, he must of necessity either err in his principles or commit some error in his discourse; that is, indeed, not discourse but seem to do so."

1. All men are mortal; therefore, all mortals are men.

2. No man is infallible; therefore, every fallible being is human.

3. All men are not virtuous; therefore, all men are vicious.

4. All unjust acts should be punished; therefore, all acts not punished should be just.

5. No evil should be allowed that good may come of it; all punishment is an evil; therefore, no punishment should be allowed that good may come of it.

6. A problem is neither affirmative nor negative; every proposition is either affirmative or negative; therefore, a problem is not a proposition.

7. An enslaved people are not happy; the English people are not enslaved; therefore, the English are happy.

8. None but whites are civilized; the ancient Germans were whites; therefore, they were civilized.

9. If it is our duty now to love our neighbor, it was our duty to love him before he was born; for the law of duty is unchangeable.

10. Change is agreeable; death is a change; therefore, death is agreeable.

11. Those who work hard deserve reward; those who work on the treadmill work hard; therefore, they deserve reward.

12. "No nation," says Earl Russell, in his speech in Parliament, March 23d, 1865, "has a right to blockade one of its own ports when seized by insurgents, without recognizing such insurgents as belligerents;" therefore, Irish insurgents seizing any port in Ireland have a right to open commerce or to be recognized as belligerents.

13. No one who lives on terms of confidence with another has a right in any circumstances to take his life; Brutus lived on terms of confidence with Cæsar; therefore, he had no right to take his life.

14. He that destroys an usurper, does right; Brutus destroyed an usurper; therefore, he did right.

15. None can perform impossibilities; miracles are impossibilities; therefore, none can perform miracles.

16. A story is not to be believed, the reporters of which give contradictory accounts; the story of Bonaparte is contradictorily reported; therefore, it ought not to be believed.

17. That which requires self-denial is not habitual; all

virtue requires self-denial; therefore, no virtue can be habitual.

18. Have you the ten marbles I gave you? No; I have not ten, for I have lost three. Have you lost all that you have not got? Yes. Then you must have lost ten.

19. Do you know what I am to ask? No. Then you do not know whether fish is fowl; for that is what I was to ask.

20. Do you know who that is in the street yonder? No. Then you do not know your own father.

21. Does one grain of corn make a heap? No. Do two? No. Three? No. Nine hundred and ninety-nine? No. One thousand? Yes. Then one grain makes the difference between a heap and no heap.

22. Have you cast your horns? No. Then you must have them still.

23. Can a body move where it is not? No. Can a body move if it continue where it is? No. Then a body cannot move at all, for it must move where it is or where it is not.

24. Can a cause act except where it is? No. Then how can the sun cause heat on the earth?

25. Every man is an animal; a swan is not a man; therefore, no swan is an animal.

26. No man is inanimate; snow is not man; therefore, snow is not inanimate.

27. A horse may be white; snow is not a horse; therefore, snow is not white.

28. Honey is yellow; gall is yellow; therefore, gall is honey.

29. He who is silent cannot speak; John is silent; therefore, John cannot speak.

30. The wise are good; some ignorant people are good; therefore, some ignorant people are wise.

31. Animal food may be entirely dispensed with, for the Brahmins live without it; and vegetable food may be dispensed with, for the Esquimaux live without it: but all food consists of animal food and vegetable food; therefore, all food may be dispensed with.

32. In a perfect vacuum, nothing can be supposed to be; therefore, in a perfect vacuum there can be no motion.

33. No one desires evil, knowing it to be so; to do wrong is evil; therefore, no one desires to do wrong except in ignorance.

34. The action of living organism is vital action; a fever is action of living organism; therefore, a fever is vital action.

35. No trifling business will enrich those engaged in it; a mining speculation is no trifling business; therefore, it will enrich whoever engages in it.

36. He who is most hungry eats most; he who eats least is most hungry; therefore, he who eats least eats most.

37. He who calls you a man speaks truly; he who calls you a poet calls you a man; therefore, he who calls you a poet speaks truly.

38. Nothing is heavier than platina; feathers are heavier than nothing; therefore, feathers are heavier than platina.

39. All cold is to be expelled by heat; this man's disorder is a cold; therefore, it is to be expelled by heat.

40. What we eat grew in the fields; loaves of bread are what we eat; therefore, loaves of bread grew in the field.

41. We eat what we buy in the market; we buy in the market raw meat; therefore, we eat raw meat.

42. Jupiter is next to Mars; Saturn is next to Jupiter; therefore, Saturn is next to Mars.

43. If Aristotle was infallible, Logic is worthy of being cultivated; but Aristotle was not infallible; therefore, Logic is unworthy of being cultivated.

44. If the Mosaic Law was designed only for Hebrews, the worship of images is not forbidden to Christians; but it was not designed only for Hebrews; therefore, the worship of images is forbidden to Christians.

45. Every thing that exists, exists in space; but space does not exist in space; therefore, space does not exist.

46. All rules have exceptions; this very rule, itself, then,

that all rules have exceptions, has exceptions. It is not true then that all rules have exceptions.

47. Let 9 be represented by x and 30 by y. Then if we take the self-evident equations $ax = ax$ and $ay = ay$, add them together, and transpose the terms, we shall have $ax - ax = ay - ay$. Dividing by $a - a$, we have $x = y$; or $9 = 30$.

EXERCISE 14. *Topics for discussion or investigation.*

1. History of the changes in meaning of the term *Thought*.
2. What are the faculties of the intelligence?
3. Which are faculties of original cognition?
4. Diversity of opinion as to the proper sphere of Logic.
5. The relationship of the true, the beautiful, and the good.
6. How much of truth is there in the Hudibrastic couplet —

   "That all a Rhetorician's rules
   Serve only but to name his tools"?

7. Enumerate the intuitions of the mind.
8. Classify the possible predicates in thought.
9. The forms in which the subject of a sentence may be expressed in language.
10. Enumerate the modals or modal adverbs in current use in the English language.
11. Enumerate the general classes of concrete nouns in language.
12. Enumerate the general classes of abstract nouns.
13. What constitutes a species in the natural world?
14. What is the difference between *reason* and *reasoning*?
15. The meaning of the word *Idea*; its etymological import, and the significance given it by Grecian, Roman, and modern philosophers.
16. The meaning of the word *Intuition*, as determined by its etymology and use.
17. The Nominalist controversy.
18. The difference in meaning between *substance* and *subject*.

19. The difference in meaning between *truth* and *reality*.
20. The fundamental postulate in human belief.
21. Belief and knowledge.
22. Can a concept be imagined?
23. Example and induction.
24. What is form?
25. Classification of the sciences.
26. The application of induction to moral matter.
27. History of Logic.
28. Indian Logic.
29. Law and general fact.
30. Law and idea.
31. Identity and resemblance.
32. Is all inference from particulars to particulars?
33. Is all deduction from a previous induction?

34. Comparison of the two methods of advancing science by observation: 1. By adding to the number of individuals or of species in the class; 2. By adding to the attributes that belong to the class.

35. Importance to success of consciously distinguishing the two methods of observation, stated above.

36. Advancement of science by multiplication of classes, whether (1) by higher generalizations, or (2) by lower subdivisions.

37. Advancement of science by observation of attributes, whether (1) by discovery of new attributes, or (2) by analysis of known attributes that are composite.

38. Advancement of science by observation of attributes, whether (1) of properties, or (2) of relations.

APPENDIX.

A.

INDUCTION.

The proper nature and function of Induction as a process of Thought have been involved in much confusion and dispute, and, of course, in obscurity and error. To such extent is this true that Sir William Hamilton does not hesitate to declare in unqualified terms that all to be found in logical treatises on this subject " is utterly erroneous." Yet it is noticeable that with this disagreement there is still a harmony of view in regard to the leading characteristics of Induction, when they are regarded separately from the special theories held by the differing logicians; which characteristics, thus separately admitted by all, or at least by the great majority, when brought together and wrought into system, make up a complete and altogether consistent and trustworthy doctrine of Induction.

All agree in admitting Induction to be a *process of Thought*, and in regarding all Thought, as Thought, as properly within the purview of logical science. This admission at once disposes of the marvelous error of Hamilton in rejecting common, material Induction, from the sphere of the Science of Thought. If this Induction is not a process of Thought, what is it indeed? As well might he claim that engineering calculations do not come within the province of Arithmetical or of Geometrical Science. We can as well calculate in engineering without conforming to arithmetical and geometrical principles, as induce in Natural Science without conforming to logical principles.

Again, all agree in regarding Induction as a *reasoning process*. As a reasoning, it differs from a concept, inasmuch as the one terminates in a new judgment, while the other results in an object of thought which may be used as either subject or predicate in a new judgment; but agrees with it in being a derivative process which gives a result not contained in the several given judgments from which the process starts as a *datum*, if they are taken separately. But it is a logical illusion to throw the result into the form of a Categorical Judgment instead of a Concept, in order to make it appear as an Induction. This disposes of the theory of those who confound Inductions with Concepts, and who exemplify this process thus: *Socrates is rational, Plato is rational, Xenophon is rational; Socrates, Plato, Xenophon are men; therefore, men are rational.* We have here a true method of forming a concept; but we have no reasoning, only a fantasy; for we have only substituted a single word for several expressing precisely the same object of thought. For evidently if we have attached any other meaning to *men* than what we mean by *Socrates, Plato, Xenophon*, either as to their Sphere or Extension, or as to their Comprehension, the whole process is a fallacy. It is equally illusive as it would be to say, *Horse is four-footed; equus is horse; therefore, equus is four-footed*, and suppose we have attained a new judgment respecting *equus* as an object of thought. This theory has soundness in it so far as it exemplifies a process of forming and naming concepts, but so far as designed to exemplify a reasoning, is merely a play upon words.

Further, all agree in admitting a real distinction between Inductive and Deductive Reasoning. This distinction they recognize as lying in the direction of the movement of the Thought — the one moving from the Whole as its starting-point, the other from the Part. They all accept the following as an example of true Inductive Reasoning: *This, that, and the other magnet attract iron; therefore, so do all.* Now this admission should preclude the attempt to bring it under a deductive reasoning with a suppressed universal Major Premise or Sumption, as do Whately and others, or under a deductive reasoning with a suppressed Minor Premise or Subsumption, as does Aldrich. This is just to contradict their admission as well as to run counter to the teaching of their great authority, Aristotle, who expressly teaches that Induction is from the particular or individual, having apparently confounded the inductive process of Aristotle with what he calls the syllogism from induction. Aristotle's extant writings nowhere indicate that he viewed induction itself as syllogistic, and so analytic; on the other hand, he ever opposes the one process to the other.[1] To suppose Induction to be an Enthymeme with Major Premise or Sumption suppressed, is entirely irreconcilable with such doctrine. This admission should preclude, also, any such fallacious attempt as that of Hamilton to make Induction a process from all the parts to the whole. This procedure is to be rejected equally with that which we have already exposed as confounding the mere substitution of one verbal expression for another with a new Judgment, and on the same ground. This will be seen at once from Hamilton's illustration: " *This, that, and the other magnet attract iron; but this, that, and the other magnet, etc., are conceived to constitute the genus magnet; therefore, the genus magnet attracts iron.*" To say nothing of the irregularity in introducing in the Subsumption the very significant *etc.* into the middle term, it is clear that the Subsumption is a merely tautological proposition, and forms no part of the reasoning process. All the reasoning process has terminated when we have added the *etc.* There is the same fallacious substitution of a concept-forming process for a proper reasoning that has been already exposed.

All agree in making the goal of the movement of Thought in Induction a conclusion which embraces in its subject the part complementary of that which formed the starting-point, as illustrated in the example already given. *This, that, and the other magnet attract iron; therefore, all magnets attract iron.* Of the class-whole *magnet, this, that, and the other*, forming the starting-point, are one part; the conclusion evidently embraces with this the complement of the genus. But with this harmonious teaching so far, we find a great divergence of views in the further exposition of the result attained in an Induction. Hamilton and others, as has been shown, represent that the result is a simple gathering of the part given in the Major Premise with the complementary part into a concept; thus, *The part observed of magnets attracts iron; therefore, this part and the part unobserved make up the genus magnet.* There is no proper reasoning in this; it is simply a naming process disguised under the garb of a reasoning. Others, as Whately, shun this error of Hamilton, but represent the subject of the conclusion to be a genus, including, of course, both the *datum* and the complement. Others, as Thompson, in his " Laws of Thought," make the result of Induction " a

---

[1] See his *Topics*, I. 10; *Prior Analytics*, II. 25; *Rhetoric*, I. 2.

Law." But his Law is but the convertible term of General Fact, in the two different forms in which we apprehend Being. When, thus, we conceive of material bodies under the form of Substance, we say it is a General Fact that they are gravitating, — have this attribute; when, on the other hand, we conceive of them under the form of Cause, we say it is the law of material bodies that they gravitate. Still another view is that which, through misinterpretation of Aristotle, distinguishes Induction from Example as different processes of Thought — making one result in a genus, the other in a part as subject of the conclusion. But there is no essential difference in the movements of Thought; they differ only in mere accidents of form and occasion. When from a given part we have induced to the complementary part, we have, in fact, comprehended the whole; as, if P and C are the two parts which compose the whole W, then if what we know of P we have induced to be true of C, we have attained what is true of P and C, and accordingly of W, for W is but P and C taken together.

Gathering up, now, the several teachings of logicians so far as they agree, we attain the following results as the accepted characteristics of Induction : —

1. It is a process of Thought that is identical in essential character in all those movements of Intelligence which induce, which infer mediately otherwise than by deduction. There is but one Induction, as there is but one Deduction in all Thought.

2. It is a reasoning, being a derivative Judgment, not a Concept; an inference from a *datum*, implying a new proper Judgment-Cognition, not a mere synthesis of subjects or of predicates — that is, not a Concept.

3. It is a mediate reasoning, being derived not from a single Judgment, but from a plurality of Judgments, related to each other under the relationship of part to complementary part in two of their terms which are alike related to the third or middle term as parts to a whole.

Of the validity, independent character, and extensive use of this process of thought, the following extract from Mr. John Stuart Mill's " Treatise on Logic " gives a very satisfactory illustration : —

" If, from our experience of John, Thomas, &c., who once were living, but are now dead, we are entitled to conclude that all human beings are mortal, we might, surely, without any logical inconsequence, have concluded at once from those instances that the Duke of Wellington is mortal. The mortality of John, Thomas, and company, is, after all, the whole evidence we have for the mortality of the Duke of Wellington. Not one iota is added to the proof by interpolating a general proposition. . . . Not only *may* we reason from particulars to particulars without passing through generals, but we perpetually do so reason. All our earliest inferences are of this nature. From the first dawn of intelligence we draw inferences, but years elapse before we learn the use of general language. The child, who, having burnt his fingers, avoids to thrust them again into the fire, has reasoned or inferred, though he has never thought of the general maxim — 'Fire burns.' He knows from memory that he has been burnt, and on this evidence believes, when he sees a candle, that if he puts his finger into the flame of it, he will be burnt again. He believes this in every case which happens to arise; but without looking, in each instance, beyond the present case. He is not generalizing; he is inferring a particular from particulars." Page 125, New York Edition, 1860.

B.

ORIGIN OF LANGUAGE.

In all speculations upon the Origin of Language, the two elements in words, the thought-element — its significance, and the sound-element, should most obviously be kept entirely distinct. The thought-element must, further, be regarded as logically the antecedent, the occasioning, or prompting, and, so far at least, the determining element; however true it may be that chronologically the two emerge simultaneously into conscious experience. How the thought-element originates and changes in the progress of thought and language, has been sufficiently indicated in the text, § 85. The theory of Max Müller, as presented in the ninth of his First Series of Lectures on Language, that language originates with general ideas, " that names," to use his own language, " are all, without exception, derived from general ideas," is there characterized as gross error. But in addition to the considerations there presented in justification of this unqualified rejection of the theory, we may here present an exposition of the fallacy which vitiates his whole reasoning. The fallacy lies in assuming that a predicate is essentially, and, of course, primitively a general idea. All nouns he teaches " express originally one out of the many attributes of a thing, and that attribute, whether it be a quality or an action, is necessarily a general idea." "All naming," he says, " is classification, bringing the individual under the general." "Analyze," he says again, " any word you like, and you will find that it expresses a general idea peculiar to the individual to which the name belongs. What is the meaning of moon ? The measurer. What is the meaning of sun ? The begetter. What is the meaning of earth ? The ploughed." And still again, " The fact that every word is originally a predicate, that names, though signs of individual conceptions, (?) are all, without exception, derived from general ideas, is one of the most important discoveries in the science of language." Now this assumption, so quietly and yet so confidently employed in this reasoning, is utterly baseless. A primitive predicate must have been an individual property. A generic notion is a purely artificial notion — a mere product of thought — a creation of thinking man. It could not exist before man thought; and as his first thought was a judgment, a recognition of an attribute as belonging to an object, that attribute could not have been a genus, that is, a thought-product. The learned lecturer has undoubtedly confounded the actual with the potential, the simple germinant with the complicated mature. Because *moon* means *measurer*, which is assumed in the argument to be a primitive predicate, he assumes that it was so named because *measurer* at that primitive time of naming, was generic — included a class of objects as then known in human speech, for he is emphatic in his teaching that thought and speech originate together — " language and thought are inseparable." But all this is error. *Measurer* was not actually generic, but only potentially so; that is, the simple attribute of *measurer*, assuming it still to be a primitive word, originally applied to an individual object — say the moon, and to that only, was only afterwards, in the progress of thought and speech, applied to other objects, as one after another they came into human consciousness. Only in this way did it come to be generic. It could not have been generic, at first, in the possibilities of human experience; it became so. In other words, it was not actually, but only potentially generic. This fundamental fallacy vitiates his whole reasoning, and involves it in absurdities all along his path. His illustrations to prove the origin of words never go back to a first, but only to a prior, which must itself have had a prior. *Cave* was named from the idea *to cover*. But whence did *cover* originate ? Was it primitive ? Then it must have existed before its class, and, of course, could not have been at that time generic. Yet it is the origin of words, the rise of the first words, that the theory attempts to explain. So "all naming," he says, "is classification, bringing the individual under the general." How then could the first naming have been effected ? Was the general before the individual which it includes ? As "language and thought are inseparable," this general that is antecedent to all naming, that is, to all language, must have been before all thought. When and what was it?

The question as to the origin of the sound-element in the word, how a particular sound comes to embody a notion, what determines this and that sound to this and that idea, is a totally distinct question. M. Müller in his lectures mentions three theories. One is, that the roots of words are imitations of sounds; a second, that they are involuntary interjections. These two theories he rejects, and styles them respectively the Bow-wow theory, and the Pooh-pooh theory. The third is his own. These original phonetic roots in language are "*phonetic types* produced by a power inherent in human nature." "There is a law which runs through nearly the whole of nature, that every thing which is struck rings. Each substance has its peculiar ring." Man in his primitive state possessed a faculty that has now become extinct, since its object is fulfilled, "by which every impression from without received its vocal expression from within." By this faculty man created these phonetic types to an almost infinite extent at the beginning, but by a process of elimination reduced them ere long to some four or five hundred. This theory assumes this strange fact of a primitive faculty now extinct, without a shadow of warrant, except the necessities of the theory. It is, moreover, as unintelligible as it is baseless.

We must take the fact that man is capable of embodying his cognitions in vocal sounds, and is pressed by an irrepressible instinct to give such vocal expression to his thoughts, as an ultimate fact. Why he selects this and not that out of the multiplicity of vocal sounds to embody a given thought, is a question that can only be answered generally, that the selection is determined by some accidental association at the time of forming the word, that is, by some identification of the thought with the particular sound in its nature, its condition, or relation. The object named may be a sound, and the name may resemble that. It may be one that utters or makes a sound, and the name may be taken from resemblance to that. It may make an impression that shall occasion an exclamation, or that shall be similar in some respect to that made by another object already named, and be named accordingly. It may be associated with some sound from other objects at the time, or it may be associated with some other words already formed; or still other associations may exist, and so the particular name be determined as to its sound.

As language may reasonably be supposed to have originated in the desire to communicate, and not in the mere impulse to embody a mental state in sound, we may suppose that the first words were sounds which would be regarded by the first speaker as associated in some way with the mental state to be communicated as well by the person addressed as by himself. This mental state may have been a sight of some object visible to both, or of some sound audible to both, and the sound adopted to express it may have been either determined by some common experience of a sound-sensation, or arbitrarily connected with it by some demonstrative act on the part of the speaker. Or this mental state, to be communicated in the primitive word, may have been that of a sensation through some other sense, or through the general sensual organism. What more natural than to suppose that a sensation of cold may have prompted such primitive word, the sounds in which may have been such as would naturally express shuddering, as the Hebrew root *Kar* — cold? What may be thus supposed in regard to the first word actually spoken by man, may be supposed with like reason in regard to all proper primitives, or root-words. Thus we may imagine to ourselves how words in the progress of speech came successively into being in the instinctive desire in man to communicate his own experiences to his fellow, which desire he could gratify only through sensations common to both speaker and hearer, these sensations being identified by some determination of place or time, and being as various as the possible sensations of which man is susceptible, that can thus be identified by different persons. It is idle to argue in favor of any one sense or any one sensation, as furnishing the occasion for the production of the primitive word. It is worse to found a theory of language, as some able grammarians have done, upon the groundless assumption that the primitive thought, the first experienced or communicated, was a sight — as a motion, an activity, predicated of some object.

INDEX.

A.

Abstraction, 33.
Æsthetic whole, 28.
Affirmative judgment, 48.
Amplification of concepts, 73.
Analysis, 33; as a process of attaining distinctness, 173.
Antecedent of a reasoning, 93.
Apodictic judgment, 51.
Argumentation, 92.
Assertory judgment, 51.
Attention, 34.
Attributes, their various denominations, 19, 20.
Axioms, 61.

B.

Base of a concept, 63.
Begging the question, fallacy of, 191.

C.

Categorical judgment, 53.
Categorical syllogism, 103; two kinds, deductive and inductive, 105; its subjective law, 190.
Causal analysis, 174; how performed, 179; its law, 179.
Causal judgment, 58; rules of, 155.
Causal whole, 27, 28.
Chain of reasoning, 128.
Characters, a designation of attributes, 20.
Circle, fallacy of, 192.
Classification, 80.
Clearness a virtue in the formal perfection of science, 136; attained by definition, 104.
Coëxtension in concepts, 78.
Collective whole, 27.
Comparison, 34.
Completeness, law of, 174.
Composition, a variety of immediate reasonings, 102.
Composition and Division, fallacy of, 191.
Comprehensive judgment, 56; rules of, 155.
Comprehensive quantity of a concept, 73.
Comprehensive whole, 28.
Concept, formation, 62; definition, 63; under law of Identity, 63; a relative and one-sided cognition, 64; not a reality, 65; how to be realized, 66; a quantity, 72; amplification, 73; relations of in exclusion, coëxtension, subordination, coördination, intersection, 78; identical and different, 86; opposition, congruent and conflictive, 87; intrinsic and extrinsic, 89; methodology, 157; threefold perfection, 157; objective law, 157; correspondence with realities, 160–162; subjective law, 163; verbal law, 181.
Concept words, their genesis, 139–144.
Concretion, 75.
Conditional syllogism, 118; two modes, ponent and tollent, 119; distinguished in respect to quantity into hypothetical and disjunctive, 120.
Congruence, a virtue in the formal perfection of science, 138.
Consequent, a part of a reasoning, 93.

INDEX.

Consequents, a designation of attributes, 20.
Conspecies, 85.
Contradiction, law of, 24.
Conversion, 96; its subjective law, 187.
Coördination of notions extensive, 78; intensive, 89.
Copula of a judgment, 38.
Corporate whole, 29.
Correctness, a virtue in the verbal perfection of science, 144.
Correspondence between thought and reality, 162.

D.

Deductive syllogism, 105; two kinds, extensive and comprehensive, 109; its subjective law, 190.
Definition, the process for attaining clearness, 164; import of, 161; its kinds, 168; verbal, real, and genetic, 169.
Definitives, 141.
Demonstrable propositions, 60.
Determination of concepts, 74.
Determinations, a designation of attributes, 20.
Dianoetic whole, 27.
Differences, a designation of attributes, 20.
Dilemma, a kind of judgment, 55; a kind of syllogism, 122; its subjective law, 204.
Discourse, 92.
Discrete, or disjunct notions, 85.
Disjunction, law of, 24; a variety of immediate reasonings, 102.
Disjunctive judgment, 43; its three forms, 48; rules of, 149, 150.
Disjunctive syllogism, 125; ponent and tollent modes, 126; its subjective law, 203.
Dissection, a process of logical analysis, 173; its two kinds, special and numerical, 175.
Distinctness, a virtue in the verbal perfection of science, 138; attained by analysis, 164; its conditions, 173; its law, 173.
Division, a process of logical analysis, 174; how performed, 176; its law, 177, 178.

E.

Elements of thought, laws and products, 17.

Enthymeme, 94.
Epichirema, 129.
Epithets, 141.
Essential whole, 27.
Evolution, or causal analysis, 174; how performed, 179; its law, 179.
Exclusion, law of, 25; relation of in concepts, 78.
Exercises in judgments, 207; in concepts, 214; in reasonings, 214.
Experimental propositions, 61.
Extensive deductive syllogism, 109–111.
Extensive judgment, 56; rules of, 155.
Extensive quantity of a concept, 73.
Extensive whole, 28.

F.

Fallacies to be detected, 217.
Fallacy of composition and division, 191; of unreal universality, 191; *petitio principii*, 191; *hysteron proteron*, 192; of the circle, 192; *saltus*, 192; *ignava ratio*, 193; *non causa pro causa*, or *post hoc ergo propter hoc*, 195.
Formal perfection of science, 137; its three virtues — clearness, congruence, distinctness, 138.
Formal whole, 29.

G.

Generalization, 74, 80.
Generic difference, 84.
Genus, 82; of two degrees, 83.
Geometrical whole, 27.

H.

Heterogeneity, law of, 86.
Hindoo system of reasoning, 107.
Homogeneity, law of, 86.
Hypothesis, 61.
Hypothetical judgment, 54; rules of, 153.
Hypothetical syllogism, 120; two modes, ponent and tollent, 120; two varieties — proper hypothetical and dilemma, 122; its subjective law, 202.
Hypothetico-disjunctive judgment, 55.
Hypothetico-disjunctive syllogism, 122; subjective law, 204.
Hysteron proteron, fallacy of, 192.

I.

Identical judgment, 53.
Identical notions, 86.
Identity, law of, 24.
Ignava ratio, fallacy of, 193.
Illation, 92.
Immediate reasoning, 93, 94.
Indemonstrable propositions, 60.
Individual difference, 84.
Induction, its nature, 223.
Inductive syllogism, 112-118; its subjective law, 195.
Inference, 92.
Integrate judgment, 57; rules of, 155.
Integrate whole, 27.
Intensive deductive syllogism, 109-111.
Intensive judgment, 56; rules of, 155.
Intensive quantity of a concept, 73.
Intensive whole, 28.
Investigation and probation distinguished, 183.
Involution of concepts, 89.

J.

Judgment defined, 31; parts, 35; division, 39-47; judgments in relation to one another, 58; methodology, 147; three conditions of perfection in judgments, material, formal, and verbal, 147; rules of a perfect judgment, 148, 155, 156.

L.

Language, its relation to thought, 69, 138-144; its origin, 227.
Laws of thought, four in number, 21; how evolved, 21-24; of identity, 24; of contradiction, 24; of disjunction, 24; of exclusion, 25; subjective and objective laws, 25.
Lemmata, 61.
Logic defined, 1; whether an art or a science, 1; its object matter, thought, 2; its objective utility as science of thought, 3; as pure science, 4; its subjective utility as aid to discovery, 6; as builder of science, 6; as corrective of error, 9; as assuring truth, 9; as invigorating the understanding, 10; as affording a nomenclature, 10; its divisions, objective and subjective, 12; abstract and concrete, 12; pure and modified, 15; parts of pure logic — doctrine of elements and doctrine of method, 16.
Logical definition, 169.
Logical quadruped, fallacy of, 190, 191.
Logical whole, its two species, extensive and intensive or comprehensive, 28.

M.

Major premise, 107.
Major term in a syllogism, 106.
Marks, a designation of attributes, 20.
Mass whole, 27.
Material perfection of science, 136; its two virtues, adequateness and accuracy, 137.
Mathematical whole — numerical and spacial, 27.
Mediate reasoning, 94; of two classes, 102.
Method what, 132; its different ends, 132.
Methodology, 132; its divisions, 145; of judgments, 147; of concepts, 157; of reasonings, 183.
Middle term in a syllogism, 106.
Minor premise, 107.
Minor term in a syllogism, 106.
Modal judgments, rules of, 51.
Modal restriction, a variety of immediate reasonings, 98; its subjective law, 188.
Modality of a judgment, 40.
Modes of cogitable matter denoted by various terms, 19.
Monosyllogism, 128.

N.

Necessary judgment, 51.
Negative judgment, 48; rules of, 149.
Non causa pro causa, fallacy of, 195.
Notes, a designation of attributes, 20.
Numerical difference, 84.
Numerical whole, 27.

O.

Objective law of a judgment, 148; of a concept, 157; of a reasoning, 184.
Opposition in logic, 48; contradictory, 49, 88; contrary, 49, 88.

P.

Partial judgment, 53; rules of, 152.
Particular notions, 80.
Partition, a process of logical analysis, 174; how performed, 178; its law, 178, 179.
Perspicuousness, a virtue in the verbal perfection of science, 144; its subordinate qualities, 145.
Petitio principii, fallacy of, 191.
Polylemma, 123.
Polysyllogism, 94, 123; two kinds, Epichirema and Sorites, 129; mode of verifying, 205.
Ponent mode of the conditional syllogism, 119.
Post hoc ergo propter hoc, fallacy of, 195.
Postulate of logic, 29.
Postulates, 61.
Practical propositions, 60.
Praxis, 207.
Predicables, predicates, predicaments, designations of attributes, or modes of being, 20.
Predicate of a proposition, 35.
Principle of division, 176.
Probation and investigation distinguished, 183.
Problematic judgment, 51.
Problems, 60.
Products of thought, 31.
Progressive syllogism, 129.
Properties, designations of attributes, 20.
Proposition, 31.
Pure logic, its divisions, 16.

Q.

Qualities, their various denominations, 19.
Quantitative restriction, 97; its subjective law, 188.
Quantity, relation of, in all thought, 25; of concepts, extensive and intensive, 72; these quantities how opposed to each other, 77.

R.

Ratiocination, 92.
Reasoning, defined, 91; how denominated, 92; its parts, 93; immediate reasonings, 93; mediate, 94; methodology of reasonings, 183; objective law, 184; subjective law, 185; complex reasonings to be resolved for separate verification of parts, 185-187.
Regressive syllogism, 129.
Representative whole, 29.
Resolution, a process of logical analysis, 194; how performed, 179; its law, 179.

S.

Saltus, fallacy of, 192.
Scholia, 61.
Science, its threefold perfection — material, formal, and verbal, 133.
Sentence, 31.
Signs, a designation of attributes, 20.
Sorites, 94, 130.
Spacial whole, 27.
Species, 80; of two degrees, 83.
Specific difference, 84.
Specification, 80, 82.
Subject of a proposition, 35.
Subjective law of a judgment, 148; of a concept, 164; of a reasoning, 185.
Subordination of notions, 78, 79.
Substantial judgment, 57; rules of, 155.
Substantial whole, 27.
Subsumption, 108.
Sumption, 107.
Syllogism, 92, 93; single, 94; polysyllogism, 94; categorical and conditional, 94.
Synthesis, 34.

T.

Tautological judgment, 53.
Terms of a judgment, 35-38; three gradations, 37; in a syllogism, 106.

Theorems, 61.
Theoretical propositions, 60.
Thought, the object matter of logic, 2; its narrower import as product of the discursive faculty, 2; its essential nature, 17; a relative cognition, or a cognition of a duality of cognitions, 17; its four fundamental laws, 21; its products, 31; its relations to its matter, 136.
Tollent mode of the conditional syllogism, 119.
Topics for discussion or investigation, 221.
Transference, a variety of immediate reasoning, 98; its two kinds, as qualitative and modal, 101; its law, 189.
Trilemma, 123.

U.

Universal notions, 80.
Unreal universality, fallacy of, 191.
Utility of logic, 2.

V.

Verbal law of a judgment, 148; of a concept, 181.
Verbal perfection of science, 138; its two virtues, correctness and perspicuousness, 144.

W.

Wholes in thought enumerated, 27; *per se*, 27; *per accidens*, 29.

THE END.

RETURN TO the circulation desk of any
University of California Library
or to the
NORTHERN REGIONAL LIBRARY FACILITY
Bldg. 400, Richmond Field Station
University of California
Richmond, CA 94804-4698

ALL BOOKS MAY BE RECALLED AFTER 7 DAYS
- 2-month loans may be renewed by calling (510) 642-6753
- 1-year loans may be recharged by bringing books to NRLF
- Renewals and recharges may be made 4 days prior to due date.

DUE AS STAMPED BELOW

DEC 1 8 2002

UNIVERSITY OF CALIFORNIA LIBRARY

www.ingramcontent.com/pod-product-compliance
Lightning Source LLC
Chambersburg PA
CBHW021406230426
43666CB00006B/648